Freedom's Cry

The Popular Dimension in the Pakistan Movement and Partition Experience in North-West India

Freedom's Cry

The Popular Dimension in the Pakistan Movement and Partition Experience in North-West India

Ian Talbot

Karachi

Oxford University Press

Oxford   New York   Delhi

1996

Oxford University Press, Walton Street, Oxford OX2 6DP

Oxford   New York
Athens   Auckland   Bangkok   Bombay
Calcutta   Cape Town   Dar es Salaam   Delhi
Florence   Hong Kong   Istanbul   Karachi
Kuala Lumpur   Madras   Madrid   Melbourne
Mexico City   Nairobi   Paris   Singapore
Taipei   Tokyo   Toronto
and associated companies in
Berlin   Ibadan

Oxford is a trade mark of Oxford University Press

ISBN   0 19 577657 7

Printed in Pakistan at
Mueid Packages, Karachi.
Published by
Oxford University Press
5-Bangalore Town, Sharae Faisal
P.O. Box 13033, Karachi-75350, Pakistan.

To Martin

Contents

Section One
Popular Participation in the Pakistan Struggle

Section Two
The Human Face of Partition

List of Illustrations

Between pages 90 and 91.

1. Muslim League Working Committee Meeting, Bombay, November 1941.

2. Mohammad Ali Jinnah in procession, Allahabad, 1942.

3. Mohammad Ali Jinnah and Miss Fatima Jinnah, Quetta, 1943.

4. Balochistan Muslim National Guards.

5. Ahmedabad Muslim National Guards.

6. Muslim League procession, Delhi, 6 April 1947.

7. Mohammad Ali Jinnah, Miss Fatima Jinnah, Liaquat Ali Khan and Islamia College Students.

8. Mohammad Ali Jinnah in procession, Peshawar, 1945.

9. The crowd at Lahore Railway Station awaiting Jinnah's arrival, 13 January 1946.

10. Independence Day, 14 August 1947.

Foreword

In 1997 Pakistan will celebrate its golden jubilee. A whole generation has risen without any personal experience of the long freedom struggle. During the difficult days from 1940-7, hundreds of thousands of ordinary men and women stood solidly behind the leadership of Quaid-i-Azam Mohammad Ali Jinnah demanding a homeland where Muslims would be free to conduct their affairs according to their own 'traditions and genius.' The common people risked their livelihoods and freedom in the struggle against the opponents of Pakistan. Many died in the riots which raged across the whole of northern India during 1947.

It is a matter of pride and inspiration for us that the freedom we enjoy today is based on the immense sacrifices and idealism of the Pakistan struggle. People from all regions, sects and occupations were united in the freedom movement. As the Quaid-i-Azam himself declared in a speech at the Karachi Club in August 1947, the masses came instinctively to help him. Their support in the arduous struggle ensured the unparalleled achievement of the new Muslim sovereign state of Pakistan.

Dr Talbot has made a notable contribution to the literature on Pakistan's emergence. He has provided us with a vivid picture of the solidarity and discipline of the Muslim National Guards and the contributions of workers, students and women in the campaign against the Unionist Ministry in the Punjab. The great processions which enthusiastically greeted the Quaid wherever he travelled in India have once again been brought to life.

The task before us as we enter the next half century of Pakistan's existence is to draw strength from the tremendous sacrifice of the freedom struggle. We must ensure that we live up to the ideals of democracy and Islamic social justice which inspired countless men and women to work in full co-operation and complete harmony under the leadership of the Quaid-i-Azam.

(BENAZIR BHUTTO)
Prime Minister of Islamic Republic of Pakistan

Preface

This book approaches the emergence of Pakistan from 'beneath.' It examines the role of popular participation in the Muslim League movement and the social and psychological impact of Partition. The overall aim is to inject a human perspective into a historical discourse which has been dominated by events and issues at the elite levels of politics. In order to open up fresh perspectives, new sources have been utilized, including the extended use of fictional 'representation' which has been largely neglected by standard historical accounts. It is anticipated that this pioneering approach will provide a stimulus for further studies in this area.

This treatise has emerged out of a longstanding interest in the history of the Muslim League movement and the creation of Pakistan. I am grateful to many friends and colleagues for their encouragement and advice. It is impossible to list everyone by name. But I especially thank Professor Francis Robinson, Professor Anthony Low, Dr Partha Mitter and Dr Iftikhar Malik for reading and commenting on earlier drafts of the manuscript. I would also like to thank Professor Dietmar Rothermund for his hospitality at the Centre of South Asian Studies at the University of Heidelburg which enabled this manuscript to be completed. Professor Rothermund also kindly commented on an earlier version of Chapter One which was subsequently published by *The Journal of Imperial and Commonwealth History*, Vol. 21, No. 2 (May 1993).

Acknowledgement is also due to Agha Ata of Karachi, Imam Abduljalil Sajid of the Brighton Islamic Centre and Mr. J.M. Shah of Coventry who assisted me with translation. Iftikhar Malik kindly corrected the transliteration for me. I am especially indebted, however, to The late Khalid Shamsul Hasan. He was a great source of encouragement, providing me with regular shipments of the leading Urdu novels and short stories on the theme of Partition.

I am also grateful to Waheed Ahmad of the Quaid-i-Azam Academy in Karachi, the Director and Staff of the National Archives of Pakistan in Islamabad and to the staff of the India Office Library in London for their courteous assistance. Any errors of fact or omissions are my responsibility alone.

Ian Talbot
Coventry, September 1995

Introduction

The Popular Dimension in Perceptions of the Pakistan Movement and the Partition of India

This book introduces two new angles to the debate on the partition of India: the role of popular participation in the movement for Pakistan and what the experience of partition and migration actually meant to those who were caught up in its processes. In a century which has seen both the resurgence of political Islam[1] and immense displacements of people arising from the formation of new states,[2] the emergence of Pakistan and its accompanying large-scale migration remains an historical event of the greatest magnitude.

Despite the multitudes of Muslims who supported the Pakistan demand and who endured the processes of Partition, the historical debate about partition has concentrated on the activities of Muslim and British elites. Ordinary Muslims count for little in all this except for the occasional 'riots' with Hindus. This book is determined to restore the popular dimension to our perceptions of the Pakistan movement. It is necessary to begin by locating this argument both in the context of events themselves and the extensive literature which surrounds them.

I

The freedom struggle which culminated in the emergence of Pakistan can be traced to the reformist trend in Muslim thought formulated by Saiyid Ahmed Khan (1817-98). This in turn was just one of a number of intellectual movements which emerged in India from the late eighteenth century onwards in response to the decline of the Mughal empire.[3] It is important to realize, however, that subaltern sections of Muslim society also reacted to the emergence of the Christian Company Raj. Poor Muslim cultivators and landless labourers formed the core of support for what Peter Hardy has called the Bengali Muslim 'Lollard' movements of the 1830s.[4] The *fara'izis* in East Bengal combined a message of religious purification with campaigns against the new landlordism brought by the Permanent Settlement. Military force was eventually required to suppress Titu Mir's jacquerie in West Bengal.[5] Simultaneously, in northern India, thousands of Muslims were engaged in the militant 'Wahabi'movement of Saiyid Ahmed Bareilly. These activities reveal that whilst the *ashraf* dominated the later emergence of Muslim separatism, ordinary Muslims were not passive bystanders in the interaction between community and state.

Saiyid Ahmed Khan sought to reconcile the Muslim elite to British rule in the wake of the 1857 uprising. The Muhammadan Anglo-Oriental College which was established at Aligarh in 1877 was designed to produce Muslims who would be able to make their way in the new world brought by the colonial state.

Saiyid Ahmed Khan, in a celebrated letter to the 'nationalist' Muslim, Badruddin Tyabji, in January 1888, counselled against Muslim support for the Indian National Congress because of its political stance concerning political representation.[6] He was not alone in this concern[7], but his campaign, which climaxed in December 1896 with the drawing up of a memorial to the Viceroy calling for separate electorates, was the most influential. It was no coincidence that Aligarh educated men played a leading role in the development of the Muslim League. It was of course during the December 1906 Session of Saiyid Ahmed Khan's Muhammadan Educational Conference[8] that the All-India Muslim League was formally established.

The closing years of the nineteenth century had been a period of increasing insecurity for the *ashraf* (Muslim elite) of North

India. The Hindi-Urdu controversy[9] threatened both its opportunities for government service and its attachment to Urdu as a symbol of the community's cultural distinctiveness. The activities of the militant Hindu revivalist organization the Arya Samaj[10] brought violence to the towns of the Punjab. Its sponsorship of Cow Protection Societies led to a wave of riots across North India in 1893 which claimed a hundred lives. The participation of individual Congressmen in the activities of the Arya Samaj convinced many Muslims that despite the organization's claims, it was in reality a Hindu body. This view was reinforced by the rise of the extremist wing of the Congress. Tilak[11] reintroduced the Ganesh festival and encouraged the Shivaji historical tradition in order to give a populist appeal to the Congress in Maharashtra. In Bengal appeals were made to the Mother to mobilize support for both extremism and revolutionary activity. The use of such Hindu symbolism during the campaign against the Partition of Bengal in 1905, formed the final catalyst for the establishment of a separate Muslim political platform.

The Muslim League from the outset demanded separate electorates and 'weightage' to secure a fair representation. It followed the earlier example of the Congress in establishing a branch in London to forward its views to the Secretary of State.[12] Ameer Ali, the founder of the National Muhammadan Association of Calcutta, became its President. His behind the scenes activity was a contributory factor in the British acceptance of separate electorates in the 1909 Indian Councils Act.

The achievement of separate electorates ushered in a new era in the history of the Muslim League. Its headquarters were transferred from Aligarh to Lucknow. The Muslim League committed itself to the objective of self-government in 1913. This reflected the emergence of a new leadership which questioned the value of its traditional 'loyalism' following the reunification of Bengal and the official decision to forbid the League sessions which were scheduled for Delhi in 1911.[13] The rise of the so-called 'Young Party' was further encouraged by the outbreak of the Balkan Wars in 1912. One of its leaders,

Mahomed Ali, popularized pan-islamic ideals through the columns of his new weekly journal *Comrade*.

Concern for the future of Turkey and the security of the holy places of Islam intensified during the First World War. Energy was drained away from the Muslim League to the Khilafat Committee.[14] But not before the ascendant 'Young Party' had moved closer to the Congress in the 1916 Lucknow Pact. In return for its recognition of separate electorates, support was promised for the Congress's campaign for political reform. Muslim-Hindu co-operation during the Gandhian *satyegrahas* and Khilafat movement ended in the disillusionment of the Moplah rebellion'[15] (August to December 1921) and communal rioting in the Punjab, North West Frontier Province and Bengal. But the Khilafat movement is historically important for it represents as did the earlier *fara'izi* and 'Wahhabi' movement, the mobilization of vast numbers of ordinary Muslims.

Politics moved out of the drawing room into the steets and bazaars. Public places were used to acclaim Khilafat leaders who were taken in procession through decorated streets. There was a regular round of demonstrations, protests and strikes at the time of the Prince of Wales' visit in November 1921. Khaki clad Khilafat volunteers who numbered 75,000 in UP alone picketed buildings and organized demonstrations. Women and lower class Muslims were involved in public political activity for the first time along with the ulema.[16] There are many parallels here with the later mass participation in the Pakistan movement, but few historians have chosen to develop this theme. They have concentrated instead on the breakdown of communal relations which followed the Khilafat movement's collapse and the difficulties which faced the Muslim League. After years of political inactivity, it re-emerged only to divide itself into the Jinnah and Shafi factions over the issue of whether or not to co-operate with the Simon Commission[17] in 1928. The mixed Muslim reaction to the Nehru Report revealed the growing disarray.[18]

The emergence of competing claims to represent Muslim opinion in All-India politics was accompanied by a growing challenge to the Muslim League in the provinces. The Punjab Unionist Party was the most powerful of the League's local rivals. Indeed, under Mian Fazl-i-Husain's adroit leadership it extended its influence to the national level of politics.[19] In fact Jinnah's famous 'fourteen points'[20] largely reflected the interests of the Punjabi dominated All-India Muslim Conference. A strong provincial powerbase was essential for political influence under the conditions introduced by the 1919 Constitutional Reforms. The Muslim League found itself increasingly marginalized. It was to this background that Jinnah set sail from Bombay in October 1930 to begin his self imposed exile in London.

The Muslim League slumbered in his absence. The significance which hindsight has given to the December 1930 Session ignores the fact that it was poorly attended. Iqbal in his 1930 Presidential address called for a Muslim State in north-west India encompassing the North West Frontier Province, Punjab, Sindh and Balochistan. This 'final destiny' of the Muslim community was, however, to be achieved within the context of an Indian federation.

Three years later, however, Chaudhuri Rahmat Ali, a Punjabi law student at Cambridge, extended this vision still further. In a pamphlet entitled *Now or Never* he drew up a scheme for an independent Muslim state. 'The land of the pure' was to consist of the Punjab, the North West Frontier Province, Sindh, Balochistan and the Princely State of Kashmir. The pamphlet was, however, largely ignored at the time. The scheme was dismissed as, 'chimerical and impracticable' by a Muslim delegation to the Parliamentary Committee on Indian Constitutional Reforms in August 1933. Meanwhile outside of the world of 'student schemes', the Muslim League had split once more, this time into Aziz and Hidayat groups.[21]

This further division encouraged efforts to persuade Jinnah to return from his Hampstead exile. His forensic skills were sought to represent Muslim opinion regarding the new constitutional reforms which were eventually to pass into law as the Government of India Act on 2 August 1935. During the course of 1934, Jinnah shuttled back and forth between London and India. In October he was elected as the Bombay representative to the central assembly. Almost a year later, he returned from London for the final time to reorganize the Muslim League so that it could fight the first provincial elections to be held under the new constitutional reforms.[22]

Jinnah set up a Central Parliamentary Board to nominate Muslim candidates. But he faced an unpromising situation in the Muslim majority provinces, where well established local parties refused to co-operate. In Sindh all he could achieve was a loose and uneasy arrangement between the Muslim League Parliamentary Board and the Sindh Azad Party. Both the Sindh United Party of Abdullah Haroon and its splinter party, the Sindh Muslim Party of Ghulam Hussain Hidayatullah refused to come under the Muslim League umbrella.[23] He received an even frostier response in Lahore, than in his home town of Karachi. The ailing Unionist Party leader, Mian Fazl-i-Husain, sent him away empty-handed and embittered. The support of Iqbal and a handful of Lahore based politicians could not compensate for the Unionists' hostility in the crucial rural constituencies. The League was therefore doomed to defeat in the key Punjab province even before the votes had been cast. The old guard of provincial politics was, however, slightly more obliging in Calcutta. The United Muslim Party mainly because of its rivalry with Fazlul Haq's Krishak Praja Party agreed to take on the Muslim League's mantle.[24]

The results of the 1937 elections revealed the full extent of the League's weakness in the Muslim majority areas. It failed to elect a single candidate in both Sindh and the Frontier. This dismal record continued in the Punjab where it managed just two seats in the Unionist stronghold. Bengal provided the one bright spot in the gloom. There the League captured thirty nine seats, three more than the Praja Party, although it polled less votes. The Muslim minority provinces restored a little electoral respectability. The best performance of all was reserved for the UP where the League won 29 out of 64 Muslim seats. The raising aloft of the Muslim League flag there seemed a forlorn gesture, however, in the face of the Congress juggernaut. Congressmen had won 716 out of 1585 seats in the provincial legislative assemblies. Congress emerged from the elections clutching the fruits of power in 7 out of 11 Indian provinces.[25]

The 1937 debacle surprisingly formed the prelude to the Muslim League's dramatic advance which climaxed in the creation of Pakistan. One key to understanding this dramatic reversal in fortune lies in the fact that things were not so bad as they seemed. Whilst it was undeniable that the League's credibility had been undermined, the Congress's claim to represent Muslim opinion had also been tarnished. It had fought only 58 out of 482 Muslim seats in the provincial elections, winning just 26 of these contests.[26] Most of these successes had been achieved in the unique political circumstances of the Frontier. The Congress failed to secure a Muslim seat in the main majority areas of the Punjab or Bengal.

Regional parties held sway in these areas. Studies which focus on the drawn out negotiations between the League, the Congress and the British tend to obscure this fact. The Congress's resounding mandate in the General Constituencies has also tended to overshadow its decidedly disappointing performance in the Muslim seats. The Muslim League's task in overcoming powerful provincial Muslim parties should not, however, be underestimated. The struggle was particularly severe in the Punjab and was a close run thing until almost the eve of the British departure.[27] Nor of course was it a mere side-show to the main battle with the Congress. For it had to obtain a mandate from the Muslim majority provinces in order to cut any ice in constitutional negotiations at the Centre. If the League had not carried the Punjab, there would have been no Pakistan. The powerful Unionist leader, Sikander Hayat Khan, threw Jinnah a crumb of comfort at the 1937 Lucknow League Session, when he agreed to support the League in All-India politics, in return for a free hand at the provincial level. But this was a high cost for the Muslim League leadership to pay.

It is now commonplace that the period of Congress rule in the provinces marked a major turning point in Indian politics.

The 'mistakes' which the Congress made during the years 1937-9 are held to have reinvigorated the Muslim League. Moreover, the raising of the Pakistan demand itself is linked with the experiences of the Muslim minority communities at this crucial time.

The Congress leaders ignored their weak showing in the Muslim constituencies and continued to insist that only their organization counted in British eyes. In the politically sensitive minority province of the UP the Congress offered a poisoned chalice to such Muslim Leaguers as Choudhry Khaliquzzaman. They offered to admit them to the Cabinet, only if the League ceased to function as a separate group.[28] While there were good parliamentary and ideological reasons[29] for the stance which the Congress had taken, it was a grave blunder. This was compounded by the injudicious Muslim mass contact movement of 1938 and by the insensitivity of provincial ministries.

The mass contact movement arose from Nehru's desire to demonstrate that minority interests were safe with the Congress and that it alone could deliver India's pressing social and economic reforms. This new policy, however, merely acted as a goad to the Muslim League to establish its own base of popular support. The claims relating to the excesses of a Congress Raj in the provinces need not be related here.[30] Whilst the Shareef and Pirpur[31] Reports into Congress oppression were exaggerated, they were sufficiently credible to gain credence. The safeguard of separate electorates now appeared inadequate to many Muslim politicians. The Congress ministries had put Chaudhuri Rahmat Ali's calls for a separate Muslim homeland firmly on the political agenda. The ground was laid for the Pakistan demand by the deliberations of the October 1938 Sindh Provincial Muslim League Conference. The following March, Jinnah chaired a Muslim League Subcommittee which included Sikander, Fazlul Huq and Liaqat, to consider schemes for India's political future. This formed the background to the historic 1940 Lahore Muslim League Session.

Muslims from all over India gathered in the huge tent set up in Minto Park, in sight of Lahore's imposing Badshahi Mosque on 22 March 1940. Jinnah's two hour Presidential address given in English surveyed the developments which had occurred since the League's last Session in Patna. Most importantly, however, it spelled out the Two Nation Theory justification for the demand for a separate State.[32] This passed into history the following day as the Lahore Resolution. Pakistan was by no means inevitable from 1940 onwards. The Muslim League still had to demonstrate its credibility by overcoming its traditional weakness in the Muslim majority areas.

Historical explanations of the Muslim League breakthrough have focused on its post-1937 reorganization and on Jinnah's inspirational leadership. The growth of Muslim mass support for the Pakistan movement is of course linked with both these developments, but it is only touched upon obliquely, if at all in most accounts. The reduction of membership fees to the nominal 4 annas level set by the Congress in 1934 was followed by the establishment of many new branches by touring committees in such provinces as UP and Madras. The League was also given a more unifying appeal by the unfurling of its own flag at the Session. Greater involvement of members was ensured by the establishment of a 450-member Muslim League Council to be elected by the provincial branches.

The League's local organization was not of course uniformly strong. It was particularly weak in the Frontier and the Sindh. The Muslim League was in fact a latecomer throughout the majority areas. Its greatest advance in both the Punjab and Bengal occurred only from the Spring of 1944 onwards. In all, over half a million new members were enrolled in Bengal in 1944.[33] The Committee which toured the Punjab during June and July 1944 achieved less spectacular results. But large audiences were attracted in Multan and Montgomery.[34] For the first time ever, primary League branches were established in such rural areas as Sargodha and Mianwali. The growing groundswell of support for the League pressurized its Muslim landlord opponents to desert the Unionist Party.

So much has been written about Jinnah's role in the creation of Pakistan[35] that it is unnecessary to rehearse the well known details here. Two important aspects need to be stressed, however, to increase our understanding. First, we need to take note of his inspirational authority. From 1937 onwards, Jinnah came to symbolize both the unity and the aspirations of the Indian Muslim community. Jinnah accepted the adulation of the crowds, the title Quaid-i-Azam and donned the Punjabi *sherwani* long coat and the Persian lamb cap in order to strengthen the Muslim cause.

Second, we need to take note of Jinnah's ability to make the most of the bad hand dealt him in 1937-9 and then later to turn to his full advantage the changes in All-India politics brought by the outbreak of War. His lengthy and successful legal career suited him for this task, as did his dogged determination which so exasperated British officials from Lord Mountbatten downwards. Another key to his dealings at the Centre was the ability to sit tight and wait for his opponents to make a mistake. Gandhi, for example, could be deemed to have done this in his celebrated correspondence between July and October 1944. His action raised the Pakistan demand's status and confirmed Jinnah as the sole spokesman of the Muslim community.

Jinnah's greatest triumph was displayed at the June 1945 Simla Conference. The Conference was designed by Wavell to break the communal deadlock for the new post-war era. It collapsed over Jinnah's demand that all members of the Indian Executive Council should belong to the Muslim League. This outcome was a bitter blow for the Unionists who had sought a seat and for the Viceroy Wavell himself. A less determined negotiator than Jinnah would not have achieved this end.

Jinnah did not, however, singlehandedly create Pakistan. His negotiating skills would have counted for nothing, if ordinary Muslims had not been roused in their hundreds of thousands by his call for a homeland in which they could throw off the Hindu yoke. Their votes for the League in the 1946 Indian elections represented a crucial landmark in the emergence of Pakistan. The Muslim League captured all the reserved Central

Assembly seats and with the exception of the Frontier reversed the setback it had received in 1937 in the Muslim majority provinces.[36]

The best performance was in Bengal where the Muslim League won 115 out of 123 Muslim constituencies. Its decisive breakthrough, however, came in the Punjab where it stormed the Unionist citadel, recording victories in 75 out of 86 Muslim seats. This opened the way for Pakistan, although the remaining Unionists soldiered on in a Coalition with the Panthic Sikhs (21 seats) and the Congress (51 seats) in the 175 Member Assembly. The crucial fact was that the election results 'registered in terms the British allowed, legitimate'[37] the strength of Muslim support for the Pakistan demand.

Despite the difficult months of negotiations which lay ahead, the claim of independent Muslim nationhood was no longer questioned. The 3 June Partition Plan and the Boundary Commission's subsequent findings, particularly regarding the award of the strategic Muslim majority Gurdaspur district of the Punjab to India, was of course a very bitter pill for the Muslim League to swallow. But the freedom struggle had nevertheless achieved a goal which had seemed impossible even a decade earlier.

The large-scale movement of population which accompanied Pakistan's birth was equally unforseen. Jinnah never seriously suspected that massive demographic adjustments would accompany partition. No plans were made to cope with the permanent migration of Muslims to Pakistan or the reverse migrations of Hindus and Sikhs to India. Refugeeism is of course a tragically normal way of life in large areas of the contemporary world, whether it be Afghanistan, Somalia or the former Yugoslavia. In the 1940s it was a far more unusual phenomenon linked with such exceptional circumstances as the ending of the Nazi tyranny in Europe. Jinnah's unpreparedness was therefore shared by the British and the Congress leaderships, although they did not adhere to his hostage theory. This held that the safety of Indian Muslim minority communities would be ensured by the presence of Hindus and Sikhs in Pakistan.

There had been a number of warning signals before the tragedy of August 1947 unfolded. Communal violence in Bengal and Bihar in October 1946 and in the West Punjab the following March had led to the evacuation of large numbers of people drawn from the minority communities. The boundaries between the communal quarters of many large North Indian cities were barricaded from the autumn of 1946 onwards and had become 'no-go' areas. Most disquieting of all were the rumours circulating in the Punjab in July 1947 of a plan by Sikhs to 'ethnically cleanse' its central districts of their Muslim population.

Much of the violence which sparked off the migrations was, however, the result of emotional outbursts in a highly charged communal atmosphere. There were seemingly unending cycles of revenge killings. These took place in the vacuum created by Lord Mountbatten's hasty transfer of power. The debate still rages whether chaos would have been averted if the British departure had not been brought forward from June 1948 to August the preceding year. The flow of migrants might have been better supervised even in 1947, if the publication of the boundary award had not been delayed until two days after the emergence of Pakistan.

It is impossible to know for certain how many died and how many were made homeless during the disturbed months which followed partition. Estimates vary from a quarter of a million to a million fatalities. Around twelve million people moved each way across the Indo-Pakistan border. Beneath these bald statistics there are innumerable human tragedies which as yet remain untold.

The upheaval of partition continues to exert a profound impact in contemporary India and Pakistan. Each year, short stories and novels flood off the printing presses with this as their theme. Residence and voting patterns in such refugee cities as Delhi and Karachi reflect the partition related migration.[38] There has been bitter debate in Pakistan, especially in Sindh, that refugees ultimately benefited more from partition than did the indigenous population. Despite the popular interest in the human dimension of partition, the focal point of the bulk of the academic literature, however, lies elsewhere.

II

Pakistan's birth has produced a vast literature. It contains the recollections of officials and politicians on both sides of 'the great divide', the work of journalists and biographers, besides that of historians.[39] Much of this writing has generated more heat than light. Indian nationalist 'divide and rule' analysis,[40] Pakistani 'two-nation theory' history[41] and Cambridge School[42] approaches, all jostle to tell their 'truth' to the reader. To this might be added the 'Brass-Robinson' controversy over Muslim separatism[43] and the 'great man of history' approach with its focus on the role of the two key protaganists, Jinnah and Nehru in the end-game of Empire.[44] More recently, Farzana Shaikh has attempted to restore the view that Muslim separatism was encouraged and sustained by ideas rooted in the Islamic tradition.[45]

The opening of Government and private archives in the 1970s fuelled rather than resolved the controversies. The entire Cambridge School enterprise, for example, was built on the availability of material which shifted the locus of attention from All-India politics to the locality and province. The understanding of Muslim political mobilization in terms, not of Islamic symbols, beliefs and ideology, but of the framework provided by the Colonial State and the working out, within this, of elite factional rivalries soon became the new orthodoxy. Indeed it is now part of the received wisdom that the Muslim League movement expanded by tying itself into the extensive networks of landlord factions.

Standard accounts of Pakistan's emergence have neglected the concerns of the 'new' history. These have centred around the actions and consciousness of the previously 'historically disenfranchised'. The 'new' history was pioneered in Europe, but has recently found its South Asian exponents in the subaltern studies group.[46] It is also represented in the burgeoning literature on dowry, family relationships, gender, and politics.[47] Work on the genesis of Pakistan, however, remains steadfastly 'elitist', viewing political developments from the 'top down'.

Some scholars would argue that this is no bad thing, given the criticism of the 'new' history for its alleged 'subjectivity', 'polemicism', 'weak data base', and tendency to play down the importance of power politics.[48] Indeed, there has been a call for a return to 'traditional' narrative history by disillusioned American and British academics. The subaltern project has itself aroused controversy.[49] Not least because, despite its proclaimed agenda, official records provide much of the basis for its findings. Nevertheless, drawbacks still remain with a 'top down' approach. As Sumit Sarkar has perceptively remarked, an analysis which equates politics with factionalism is less useful when examining major conflicts involving large masses, such as the closing period of the Pakistan movement, than for periods of 'oligarchical' politics, 'bereft of fundamental tensions'.[50]

A 'top down' approach inevitably overlooks the nature and significance of popular participation in the Pakistan struggle. It conflicts with the historical reality in which large numbers of Muslims took part in processions, strikes, election campaigns and riots. This raises the question whether pressures from beneath influenced elite factional realignment behind the Muslim League. Equally importantly, did the Muslim masses set their own agendas during the Pakistan struggle, despite the efforts of Muslim elites to control them?

This understanding also ignores popular attitudes to Pakistan. What did its demand mean for ordinary Muslims? Why did they respond to the Muslim League message during the freedom struggle? How did they cope with the traumas of migration in 1947? Were there redeeming features in the experience of flight from India which helped make sense of the uprootedness?

These are important questions if the overall story of Pakistan's emergence is to be told. They also need to be asked because of the light they may shed on the new state's post-independence circumstances. Traditional accounts of the Partition, however, are so concerned with its causes that they ignore its impact on the individual. In this great human event, human voices have been strangely silent.

The first section of the book wrestles with the theme of popular participation during the Pakistan movement. Chapter 1 approaches it through the methodology of the crowd in history. An analysis is made of the varieties of crowd behaviour, the methods of crowd mobilization, and their significance in the freedom struggle. The second chapter focuses on the Muslim National Guards. It places their formation in the context of other volunteer movements in late colonial India. The various activities of the Muslim National Guards during the Pakistan movement are set alongside the symbolic significance of their ceremonial role. This area has been entirely neglected by historians. The final chapter in this section switches attention from urban popular participation to the rural Punjab. It looks afresh at the struggle between the Muslim League and the Unionist Party during the crucial years 1944-7. The analysis sets out to ascertain whether pressures from 'beneath' influenced either the political choices of faction leaders or the methods by which they transmitted the Pakistan demand.

Section 2 attempts to understand the emotional and psychological impact of Partition. This is explored through literary 'representation' and autobiographical accounts. The extensive use of such sources in itself marks a fresh scholarly departure. Particular attention is devoted to the novels and short stories of such writers as Saadat Hassan Manto, Qasmi, Krishan Chander and Bhisham Sahni. The verse of Faiz is also examined. From the seam of rich autobiographical material, the works of Khwaja Ahmed Abbas and Shahid Ahmed are mined. The autobiographical collections, *Jab Amritsar jal raha tha* and *Azadi key Mujahid*, are extensively utilized, as they contain valuable transcriptions of interviews with ordinary Muslims who were caught up in the disruptions of August 1947.

Chapter 4 breaks new ground in examining in detail Urdu, Hindi, Punjabi, and English literature on the theme of Partition. The methodological problems posed by such material are initially addressed. This is followed by a discussion of major works. From it, there emerge important insights which shed fresh light on the partition experience. These are further explored in the two succeeding chapters which rely on autobiographical material. This provides a much needed human dimension to the Partition experience.

It is impossible to examine the human impact of Pakistan's birth without reference to its effects on the Hindus and Sikhs who poured across the international boundary which separated the two parts of the Punjab in August 1947. It is beyond the scope of this study to consider in detail either the emotions of these refugees or the responses of the Indian authorities to their plight. But care has been taken to include sources which reflect their point of view and experiences as well as that of the Muslims who are the main concern of this work. All communities had their victims, survivors and aggressors.

The arguments in this book are suggestive rather than exhaustive. The aim is not to foreclose the historical discourse, but conversely to open up previously unemphasized and unexplored aspects. The study is timely as there is a growing realization that the discourse centred solely on the 'high' politics of independence and partition is self-limiting.

NOTES

[1] *See*, for example, M. Ayoob, *The Politics of Islamic Reassertion* (London, 1981).

[2] *See*, for example, A. Zolberg, 'The formation of new states as a refugee generating process', *The Annals*, vol. 467, 1978, pp. 24-38.

[3] Reformist thought arose as a result of the efforts of the Delhi scholar, Shah Waliullah (1703-62). He stressed study of the Koran and Hadith and (*tatbiq*) reconciliation between Sunnis and the Shias. His concern for Islamic reform and revival was taken up in the nineteenth century by the Deoband, Ahl-i-Hadith, and Ahl-i-Koran movements. Traditionalist Islam was upheld by the Barelvi movement of Ahmad Raza Khan of Bareilly (1856-1921) which was frequently at odds with the afore-mentioned reformists and revivalists. While modernist Islam was of course represented by the Aligarh movement.

[4] P. Hardy, *The Muslims of British India* (Cambridge,1972), p. 57.

[5] Titu Mir was a wrestler, but he campaigned in favour of a purified Islam from 1827 onwards. He was killed along with fifty of his followers in the military action of 1831.

[6] Congress claimed that democratic institutions would not result in Hindu domination and that it stood for the interests of all communities.

[7] Amir Ali's National Muhammadan Association called for separate electorates as early as 1884. *See*, F. Shaikh, *Community and Consensus in Islam, Muslim Representation in Colonial India 1860-1947* (Cambridge, 1989), p. 111.

[8] This was founded as a vehicle of the Aligarh movement in 1886.

[9] For details of its origins *see*, F.Robinson, *Separatism among Indian Muslims: The Politics of the United Provinces' Muslims 1860-1923* (Cambridge, 1975), pp. 69-76

[10] This was founded by Dayananda Saraswati in 1875. On its activities *see*, K.W. Jones, 'Communalism in the Punjab. The Arya Samaj Contribution', *Journal of Asian Studies* XXVIII, 1 (1968), pp. 39-54

[11] On his career see, R.L. Cashman, *The Myth of Lokamanya: Tilak and Mass Politics in Maharashtra* (Berkeley 1975).

[12] For details *see*, Muhammad Saleem Ahmed, *The All India Muslim League: From the Late Nineteenth Century to 1919* (Bahawalpur, 1988), p. 107 & ff.

[13] Ibid., (8) above p. 135 & ff.

[14] For details of the Khilafat movement consult G. Minault, *The Khilafat Movement: Religious Symbolism and Political Mobilization in India* (New York, 1982)

[15] For details consult S.F.Dale, *Islamic Society on the South Asian Frontier: The Mappilas of Malabar 1498-1922* (Oxford, 1980)

[16] For details of mass mobilization during the Khilafat movement, *see*, G. Minault, *The Khilafat Movement. Religious Symbolism and Political Mobilization in India* (New York, 1982) Chapter 3.

[17] For details concerning the controversy surrounding the appointment of the "all white" Simon Commission in 1927, consult R.J. Moore, 'The Making of India's Paper Federation, 1927-1935' in C.H. Phillips and M.D. Wainwright (eds), *The Partition of India: Policies and Perspectives 1935-1947* (London, 1970), pp. 54-76.

[18] P. Hardy, *The Muslims of British India* (Cambridge, 1972), p. 212.

[19] *See*, D. Page, *Prelude to Partition: The Indian Muslims and the Imperial System of Control 1920-1932* (Oxford 1982).

[20] These included the demands that India's future constitution should be federal with residual powers vested in the provinces and that Muslims should have one third of the seats in the Central Legislature. Separate electorates were also safeguarded as was the Muslim position in the majority provinces. The Congress's rejection of the 'Fourteen Points' has been seen by some writers as a significant turning point.

[21] For the background consult S. Wolpert, *Jinnah of Pakistan* (New York,

1984), p. 134.

[22] The reforms had introduced provincial autonomy, thus abolishing the system of dyarchy. The franchise had been extended to nearly thirty-five million. The 1935 Act also provided for the creation of an all-India federation of Provinces of British India and the Princely States, but this foundered on the demands of the States for accession.

[23] I. Talbot, *Provincial Politics and the Pakistan Movement: The Growth of the Muslim League in North-West and North-East India 1937-47* (Karachi, 1988), p. 39.

[24] Ibid. (19) above, p. 62.

[25] For details of the Congress performance, consult J. Brown, *Modern India. The Origins of an Asian Democracy* (Oxford, 1985), p. 286 & ff.

[26] This represented just 5.4 per cent of the Muslim seats. 'Return Showing the Results of the Election in India', 1937, Cmd. 5589.

[27] For details, consult Talbot, op.cit., pp. 82-107.

[28] P. Moon has termed this demand a fatal error and the prime cause of Pakistan. P. Moon, *Divide and Quit* (London, 1964), pp. 14-16.

[29] For details *see*, S. Sarkar, *Modern India, 1885-1947* (London, 1989), p. 353.

[30] *See*, G. Rizvi, *Linlithgow and India. A Study of British Policy and the Political Impasse in India 1936-43* (London, 1978), pp. 96-101.

[31] The Pirpur Report into Muslim grievances in Congress provinces was published in November 1938. The Shareef Report which dealt especially with Bihar followed a year later.

[32] *See*, Jamil-ud-Din Ahmed (ed), *Speeches and Writings of Mr Jinnah Volume 1* (Lahore, 1968), p. 169.

[33] Abul Hashim to Jinnah, 25 November 1944, SHC Bengal 1:43.

[34] Report of the Punjab Provincial Muslim League's work for June and July 1944 submitted to the All-India Muslim League Committee of Action, 28 July l944, SHC Punjab, Volume 1.

[35] The best biographical account of his career remains S. Wolpert, *Jinnah of Pakistan* (New York, 1984). The most controversial account is contained in A. Jalal, *The Sole Spokesman. Jinnah, the Muslim League and the Demand for Pakistan* (Cambridge, 1985)

[36] The Muslim League won only 17 out of 36 Muslim seats in the Frontier. For the background to this and the resounding vote for the Frontier's inclusion in Pakistan in the June 1947 Referendum, consult Talbot, *Provincial Politics and the Pakistan Movement*, op.cit., pp. 16-28.

[37] This phrase has been used by D.A. Low in his comment concerning the Congress performance, in the 1937 elections, but it can be used just as well for the Muslim League's nine years later. D.A.Low, *Eclipse of Empire* (Cambridge, 1991), p. 94.

[38] In Karachi, the Jamaat-i-Islami and latterly the Mohajir Qaumi Movement have garnered the refugee vote. In the inaugural Delhi State

elections in November 1993, the Bharitya Janata Party did well in the Punjabi-dominated wards.

[39] Works by British Officials include: P. Moon, *Divide and Quit* (London, 1961); H.V. Hodson, *The Great Divide: Britain, India, Pakistan* (London, 1969); Sir Francis Tucker, *While Memory Serves* (London, 1950). The nationalist Muslim view is provided by Maulana Abul Kalam Azad, *India Wins Freedom.* (Bombay, 1959).The Muslim League perspective is reflected by such writers as C. Muhammad Ali, *The Emergence of Pakistan* (New York, 1967), and C. Khaliquzzaman, *Pathway to Pakistan* (Lahore, 1961). A pioneering biography of Jinnah was provided by H. Bolitho, *Jinnah* (London, 1954). This was written without the access to archival material which informs the more recent work by Stanley Wolpert: S. Wolpert, *Jinnah of Pakistan* (New York, 1984). Two pioneering studies of the Pakistan movement, again written without access to Official records are, K.K. Aziz, *The Making of Pakistan — A Study in Nationalism* (London, 1967); and K. B. Sayeed, *Pakistan: The Formative Phase 1857-1947* (London, 2nd ed. 1968).

[40] A classical exposition is found in A. Mehta and A. Patwardhan, *The Communal Triangle in India* (Allahabad, 1941).

[41] This is reflected in such works as H. Malik, *Moslem Nationalism in India and Pakistan* (Washington, 1963); and I.H. Qureshi, *The Struggle for Pakistan* (Karachi, 1965).

[42] *See,* for example, the early work of Francis Robinson and the studies of Ayesha Jalal, David Page and Peter Hardy. F. Robinson, *Separatism Among Indian Muslims: The Politics of the United Provinces' Muslims 1860-1923* (Cambridge, 1974); A. Jalal, *The Sole Spokesman: Jinnah, the Muslim League and the Demand for Pakistan* (Cambridge, 1985); D. Page, *Prelude to Partition: The Indian Muslims and the Imperial System of Control 1920-1932* (Delhi, 1982); P. Hardy, *The Muslims of British India* (Cambridge, 1972).

[43] P. Brass, *Language, Religion and Politics in North India* (Cambridge, 1974) and 'Elite Groups, Symbol Manipulation and Ethnic Identity among the Muslims of South Asia' in D. Taylor and M. Yapp (eds), *Political Identity in South Asia* (London, 1979), pp. 35-77. F. Robinson, 'Islam and Muslim Separatism' in D. Taylor and M. Yapp (eds), op. cit., pp. 78-112.

[44] *See,* for example, B.N. Pandey, *The Break-up of British India* (London, 1969), pp. 191-211. B.R. Nanda, 'Nehru, the Indian National Congress and the Partition of India, 1935-47' in C.H. Philips and M.D. Wainwright (eds), *The Partition of India. Policies and Perspectives 1935-1947* (London, 1970), pp. 148-87. K.B. Sayeed, 'The Personality of Jinnah and his Political Strategy', ibid., pp. 276-93.

[45] F. Shaikh, *Community and Consensus in Islam: Muslim Representation in Colonial India 1860-1947* (Cambridge, 1989).

[46] In addition to Ranajit Guha's pioneering work on peasant insurgency, Stephen Henningham, Kapil Kumar and David Hardiman, to name just a few, have contributed to the 'subaltern studies' approach to Indian history

from below. R. Guha, *Elementary Aspects of Peasant Insurgency in Colonial India* (Delhi, 1983); S. Henningham, *Peasant Movements in Colonial India: North Bihar 1917-42* (Canberra, 1982); D. Hardiman, *The Coming of the Devi: Adivasi Assertion in Western India* (Delhi, 1987).

[47] Study of gender has now become a cottage industry. A large number of works have been produced during the past decade, as for example, H. Papanek and Minault (eds), *Separate Worlds. Studies of Purdah in South Asia* (Delhi, 1982); B.R. Nanda (ed), *Indian Women: From Purdah to Modernity* (Delhi, l990); T. Mandal, *Women Revolutionaries of Bengal 1905-1939* (Calcutta, 1991).

[48] T. S. Hamerow, *Reflections on History and Historians* (Madison, 1987); AHR Forum, 'The Old History and the New' *The American Historical Review* 94, 3 (June 1989), pp. 654-99.

[49] Criticisms have been made of its contributors' tendency to attach a timeless quality to the actions and collective traditions of subaltern groups. The term subaltern has not been adequately defined according to some critics. Finally the group's over concentration on acts of 'resistance' has drawn adverse comment. For a lively critique, consult R. O'Hanlon, 'Recovering the Subject, Subaltern Studies and the History of Resistance in South Asia', *Modern Asian Studies*, 22, 1 (February 1988), pp. 189-224.

[50] Sarkar, *Modern India 1885-1947* (London, 1989), p. 8.

Section 1

Popular Participation in the Pakistan Struggle

Chapter 1

Popular Participation in the Pakistan Struggle

The Role of the Crowd

The All-India Muslim League took its political campaign from the drawing room on to the streets, following its shattering set-back in the 1937 provincial elections.[1] Jinnah drew even larger crowds than those seen at the height of the Khilafat campaign as he travelled the length and breadth of the subcontinent popularizing the League's demands. Hundreds of thousands of Muslims joined processions, demonstrations and strikes as the Pakistan movement gained momentum. They were also caught up in the riots which scarred the drive to independence. Such crowd activity is, however, overlooked altogether by many accounts of Pakistan's emergence.

Historians have frequently concentrated on the 'high' politics of constitutional negotiations between the Muslim League, the Congress and the British. Even with the rise in interest in the politics of the region and the locality, they have tended to focus upon the elite levels of the Muslim League organization. Much attention has been devoted to factional rivalries.

This scholarly appproach neglects both the nature and significance of popular participation in the achievement of Pakistan. What common features lay behind such crowd activities? How did pressures from beneath influence elite factional realignment behind the Muslim League in the key Punjab region during the period 1944-46? How important were the mass civil disobedience movements in the Punjab and the

Frontier early in 1947 in finally breaking the power of the
Muslim League's rivals in these Muslim majority areas?

This chapter seeks to address these questions by focusing on
the nature and the role of the crowd in the Muslim League
struggle for Pakistan in the 1930s and 1940s. It attempts to
uncover the faces in the crowds, to understand how they were
mobilized and to assess their significance. The 1947 Direct
Action movements in the Punjab and the Frontier provide a
major part of the study. Before turning to this and other
historical material, however, it is necessary to discuss the
methodology and approaches which have emerged in the study
of crowd behaviour.

I

Methodologically, the sources for uncovering the role of the
crowd in history must be treated with extreme care. Neither
colonial nor vernacular sources can be taken at face value as an
accurate 'text'. They are likely to be highly polemical and to
explain from their differing viewpoints what was thought to
have happened, rather than what actually transpired.
Furthermore, such written sources focus on the speeches and
actions of elite leaders of crowds, leaving the historian to assume
that their followers shared this agenda and motivations. The
problematic character of the source material has undoubtedly
encouraged some historians to leave the study of Indian crowd
behaviour well alone. Sandria Freitag, however, has
demonstrated how crowd behaviour as 'discerned through
judicious interpretation of administrative accounts' can provide
our historical 'text'.[2]

Early studies of collective action were influenced by Le Bon's[3]
contention that crowds were emotional, capricious and ruled
by passions. More recently, an opposite image has emerged
that crowds are rational, disciplined and ruled by reason. This
perception has coincided with the burgeoning interest in history
from below. George Rudé pioneered the view that crowd activity

involved social purpose and provided a valuable approach to the study of popular politics.[4]

The most authoritative analysis of the role of the crowd in history has however been provided by Elias Canetti. In the work, *Crowds and Power*,[5] Canetti deploys an elaborate typology. The four essential attributes of crowds are classified as growth, equality, density and direction. The physical characteristics of crowds are described in four opposed types, open and closed, rhythmic and stagnating, slow and quick, and visible and invisible. Finally, Canetti divides crowds into five emotionally influenced categories: baiting crowds, prohibition crowds, reversal crowds, feast crowds, and double crowds. This analysis is not only more detailed than Le Bon's but is in stark contrast to his belief that crowds were empty-headed and dominated by leaders.[6]

Crowd studies from the outset emphasized themes of social protest: for example, food riots, machine breaking, and religious riots were rapidly added to this repertoire. Janine Estebe's study of the St. Bartholomew's Day Massacre of 1572 paved the way.[7] It understood Catholic crowd violence against the Huguenots primarily in economic terms. Conflict between poor Catholics and rich Protestants rather than pathological religious hatreds lay behind the popular disturbances. Natalie Zemon Davis has added further sophistication to the understanding of religious riot.[8] She has linked violence with the religious calendar, rather than with vague economic backgrounds such as rising food prices. Events like the St. Bartholomew's Day Massacre are motivated by the need to safeguard the true doctrine and to free a community from the 'pollution' of opposing sects. Finally, she has maintained that the different beliefs of Protestants and Catholics resulted in varying patterns of violence.[9]

Crowd studies have been increasingly extended to areas outside Europe. Sandria Freitag,[10] Anand Yang,[11] Max Harcourt,[12] Sugata Bose,[13] and Suranjan Das[14] have all written on the crowd in the setting of the colonial Indian state. Numerous studies have been produced on communal and ethnic riots in contemporary South Asia.[15] It is dangerous, however, to project backwards insights from such examinations, for the scope, temporal sequence of riots, and the response of the State have all been influenced by the changes in communications which have occurred since Independence.

Freitag and Yang both reject a primordialist understanding of Hindu-Muslim violence. They paint a much more complex picture in which conflict is connected with cultural and religious developments, changes in social mobility and in the political arena, and finally with competition within religious communities. Freitag has demonstrated the importance of the leadership of various *mohallas* (urban localities) and the *akhara* organization in mobilizing crowds, whether for ceremonial processions or riots.[16] She has developed a threefold typology of collective activities: public performances, collective ceremonies and collective protests. The second type she sees as the most sustained collective experience which sets the patterns and symbolic 'rhetoric or vocabulary for all public activities'; while the third particularly prompts a definition of identity as against an 'other'.[17] By far her most important finding, however, is the contention that collective action in public arenas facilitated the transition from localized, relational expressions of community to a 'more ideological and broad-based definition of the collectivity' or 'communalism'.[18]

Yang's study of the 1893 Basantpur anti-cow killing riot closely follows Rudé's approach in examining the social composition of the crowd, its aims and targets.[19] Max Harcourt's work displays a similar methodological debt. Sugata Bose's detailed study of the 1930 Kishoreganj riots in rural Bengal is, however, more concerned with causation. He sees the disturbances as having primarily economic roots. Significantly, Suranjan Das who has produced the most comprehensive analysis of Bengali riots to date, has declared that the Kishoreganj riot 'can be legitimately considered as the last major communal outbreak of twentieth century Bengal possessing strong class connotations'.[20] His thesis is that there was a definite shift in the nature of communal rioting in Bengal between 1905 and 1947. The first phase of riots, for example Calcutta

(1918,1926), and Dhaka (1930), were relatively unorganized, and displayed a strong class orientation. The 1941 Dhaka Riot, however, marked a turning point. Thereafter, riots were more organized and reflected antagonisms arising from communal politics, rather than class interests.[21] Common to all these three latter approaches is a concern with protest or violence. Despite the rich ritual life of the Indian subcontinent, comparatively little has been written about festive, ceremonial or celebratory crowds in which group sentiment and community values are perpetuated.

Potential crowd subjects of the Muslim League movement might be analyzed according to Canetti's typologies; the open crowds of public rallies as opposed to the closed crowds meeting in mosques and shrines, or the baiting crowds of communal riots as opposed to the flight crowds of the mass migrations of August 1947. There again the taking out of black flag demonstrations against the Khizr regime in the Punjab could be fitted to Canetti's reversal crowd category, while *hartals* (strikes) are a clear example of his prohibition crowd type. It would be foolish, however, to bundle willy-nilly all episodes of crowd activity into a rigid typology, even if in the case of Canetti the strait-jacket is fastened with chains of gold. This analysis, nonetheless, accepts Canetti's contention that equality is the fundamental characteristic of the crowd. There are important consequences stemming from this, for in a real sense a 'subaltern' element can thus be seen in all crowd activity, regardless of how crowds were mobilized, or the intended uses to be made of them by power elites.

Two additional premises undergird this examination. Firstly, there is the belief that crowd violence cannot be solely explained in economic terms. Secondly, the necessity to 'deconstruct' the colonial narrative on communal riots is openly acknowledged. Such writers as Gyan Pandey have now clearly established that a discourse became fixed in which the significance of popular disturbances was reduced to that of a 'law and order' problem. Furthermore, the actions of the participants were understood in terms of 'natural' characteristics—'bigotry', 'criminality' and so on—thereby distancing the 'rational' colonial state from the 'irrational' native Other.[22]

Official reports of riots frequently displayed this stereotypical construction. The Bengal government characterized the Muslim crowd during the 1906-7 Mymensingh disturbances as consisting of *badmashs* (criminals) when in fact it was made up of labourers and servants.[23] The Bengal Governor, Sir Frederick Burrows, peppered his report on the Calcutta disturbances of 16 August 1946 with references to the 'mob', 'mob violence' and 'hooliganism'.[24] General Sir Roy Butcher, the acting army commander, in his report on the ensuing disturbances in the Noakhali and Tippera districts of East Bengal, talked of 'gangs of hooligans' and 'gangsters' going round the villages, beating up Hindus and converting them to Islam.[25] The emptying of social content and significance from popular disturbances in this manner reduced them to an instinctive criminal violence. This legitimized the coercive power of the colonial state. The 'deconstruction' of the latter's discourse should not, however, blind one to the existence of criminal elements in crowds. These took advantage of the breakdown of order to loot, rob and burn. Moreover, there is growing evidence that both the Congress and Muslim League employed *goondas* (thugs) during communal disturbances in Bengal. Half of the Muslims arrested following the 1941 Dhaka riots were known criminals. Some of these had been 'imported' from outside the province. Notorious *goondas* from the Muslim slums of central and north Calcutta and from the Hindu-run brothel areas of its central districts were encouraged by politicians to cause mayhem during the Great Calcutta killings of August 1946. According to one report, there were 402 known *goondas* amongst the 3,553 persons arrested on rioting charges by the first half of September.[26] Indeed, Bengali disturbances during the 1940s share many characteristics with post-independence communal riots in which the participation of politicians, police, and criminals has been clearly documented.

The remainder of this chapter will focus on four types of crowd activity: namely, processions, *hartals* (strikes), such acts of civil disobedience as picketing and trespass, and communal violence. Despite their variety, these activities shared common features. They were all events which influenced the perceptions and aspirations of those who participated in them. They reaffirmed community identity and values as against the 'other'. This was as much the case in the disciplined behaviour of the *hartal* as in the intensive violence of a riot. For this reason it is justified to include the former in an analysis of crowd activity.

II

Political processions were daily occurrences during the closing period of British rule in India. All parties organized them and they sometimes merged imperceptibly with the crowds which marked important moments in the religious calendar. The morning *prabhat pheris* (nationalist processions) taken out by *mohalla*—ward—level Congress committees in north Indian towns adopted such religiously symbolic behaviour as song, prayer and bathing in the Ganges.[27] Where historians have remarked upon these processions at all, they have taken their cue from the official record which maintained that they were the work of agitators. This abstracts such gatherings from their physical and social context, ignoring the importance of local focal points such as mosques, temples, tea-shops and bazaars, all of which could draw crowds together. It further neglects the role of caste, kinship, and sectarian networks in mobilizing crowds. This section will demonstrate how these were all at work in forming processions during the Muslim League's Direct Action campaigns. It will turn, first, however, to a quite different kind of procession in which celebratory rather than protest themes were predominant. These were the crowds which accompanied Jinnah's peripatetic political tours. Typical examples will be given, before an attempt is made to assess their significance.

One such procession occurred in October 1938, when Jinnah arrived in Karachi to preside over the Sindh Muslim League

Conference. He was conveyed through the streets in a procession which stretched for three miles.[28] There were contingents of Muslim National Guards and mass bands amongst the crowds. On another occasion five years later, an estimated fifty thousand persons swept Jinnah through Quetta city. The Quaid-i-Azam came and saw and conquered.

In July 1944, Jinnah journeyed by road from Rawalpindi to Lahore to attend an All-India Muslim League Council Meeting. Ceremonial gates and *pandals* (tents) for meetings were constructed by the Punjab Muslim Students Federation along the roadside villages and towns of the entire route. Such was the press of the crowds that the journey took all of twelve hours. When an exhausted Jinnah arrived at his destination of Mamdot Villa, his car overflowed with hundreds of ornamental garlands and thirty or so framed addresses of welcome.[29] This type of reception was not, of course, confined to Jinnah. Gandhi and Nehru received similar welcomes, and were, if anything, greater crowd pullers. India's teeming population enabled crowds to gather which were huge by European standards. What, then, was the significance of this type of crowd activity?

It was certainly more than a splash of local colour as far as the Muslim League movement was concerned. Such processions played a key role in strengthening community solidarity. Their overall effect was to confirm and reinforce group sentiment. In Durkheim's terminology, they upheld and reaffirmed 'the collective sentiments and collective ideas' which make up all societies, 'unity and personality'.[30] They achieved this by outpourings of loyalty directed towards Jinnah who symbolized the community's aspirations. The slow pace at which such processions moved also aided the expression of community. For as Sandria Freitag has commented in the context of the Muharram procession, 'onlookers had much time to observe and participate, to be incorporated into the process'.[31] Furthermore, the processional routes themselves aided integration by demonstrating the value which they attached to the areas through which they passed. Routes invariably symbolically laid claim to the main bazaars and thoroughfares as well as taking in centres of Muslim community such as mosques, schools and *Anjuman-i-Islamia* Halls. When Jinnah was about to address a public meeting at Patna late in October 1937, the procession which accompanied him pointedly stopped at places on the route which symbolized either his leadership or the community's claim to unity. During one such halt the *Imam* of the Juma Masjid, Bankipore presented Jinnah with a sword and addressed him as *Mohib-i-Millat, Fakhr-i-Qaum* and *Mohib-i-Watan*.[32]

Muslim community values were also perpetuated in other types of crowd activity, notably in religious assemblies at mosques and shrines, or in electioneering rallies and meetings which were often held there.[33] The processions which accompanied Jinnah, however, did far more than reaffirm Muslim social solidarity. They also made important statements about political sovereignty. Jinnah was accorded the honour given to a head of state. The British report of the occasion in Karachi, in October 1938, stated that Jinnah was conveyed in a manner 'befitting a king'.[34] Even the anti-League *Sindh Observer* admitted in its columns that it was a reception 'a Prince might well envy'.[35] Again in June 1943, Jinnah was described by the British as being borne through Quetta city like a 'royal potentate'. His entire route was decorated with welcome arches and gateways named after Muslim heroes.[36]

Such welcomes bear unmistakable similarities with coronation crowds using public places to honour the head of state. Despite the reality of the Raj, Muslims were greeting Jinnah as their king. Much of the ceremonial deliberately re-enacted Mughal spectacle. Jinnah, it is true, did not ride on an elephant like a Mughal potentate, nor was he accompanied by slaves, servants and treasure chests, but the roads were all cleared, shops and houses decorated, and small tents and canopies erected to provide refreshments for spectators as had been the practice when the Emperor had left his palace for Friday prayers or at festival time.[37] Furthermore, like the Mughals, Jinnah paraded his own uniformed bodyguard, musicians, horses and camels. Mughal processions were designed to generate a sense of pride and loyalty to the dynasty by displaying the Emperor's wealth and power. Those which acccompanied Jinnah had a similar psychological impact, heightening the Quaid-i-Azam's (The Great Leader's) symbolic role as the embodiment of Muslim unity and aspirations. Moreover, his processions symbolized claims to the locale through which they passed. This is the key to understanding the meaning of Jinnah's 'slow and dramatic production' of a journey through the Punjab. In the late 1930s such demonstrations were mere straws in the wind, but by 1944 they presaged a turn of events which Jinnah's Muslim opponents most feared. Politicians in the Punjab who had carefully hedged their bets between the Muslim League and the Unionist Party noted the new wind direction and fell in with the Quaid-i-Azam.

In addition to 'state' processions, celebratory themes were emphasized by gatherings during the Muslim League calendar. Its national anniversaries included Pakistan Day, Jinnah Day, and Iqbal Day. Not to be outdone, Muslims in the Princely states held their own celebrations, such as Tipu Sultan Day, which was annually observed on 24 November by the Muslims of Mysore.[38]

Processions, rallies, and flag salutations all formed part of these 'national' days. Muslim houses were also illuminated, and bedecked with Pakistan flags. Thirty-seven meetings were held in the Bombay district alone to celebrate Pakistan Day in 1942.[39] When freedom finally arrived, celebrations were muted in comparison, because of the violence which accompanied Partition. There was a flag hoisting and offering of prayers in Lahore, but no illuminations; while at Chakwal, a march past was organized in which Hindu and Sikh officers participated.[40] Jinnah's birthday was enthusiastically celebrated annually on 25 December. His sixty-seventh birthday celebrations in the city of Mysore in 1942 were typical. The Muslim League, Muslim Students' Federation, and Muslim League Civil Defence Council, all had a hand in the arrangements. The day finished with a five thousand strong procession and rally.[41]

Alongside these regular celebrations, there were special occasions linked to contemporary political developments.

Deliverance Day on 22 December 1939 was pre-eminent amongst these. Jinnah had called for its celebration by way of thanksgiving for deliverance from the 'tyranny, oppression and injustice' of the Congress provincial ministries. Deliverance Day was marked in cities, towns and villages throughout British India as well as in the Princely State of Hyderabad.[42] Joint meetings were held with Indian Christians, Parsis, and members of the Scheduled Castes. At Jinnah's express behest, they were not accompanied by *hartals* or processions.[43] Meetings either in mosques or public spaces followed the offering of the special Deliverance Day prayer[44] after the Jumma prayers. Ceremonial activity included the hoisting of the Muslim League flag and the presence of detachments of Muslim National Guards.

Large crowds attended meetings across the length and breadth of India. Ten thousand Muslims packed into Madras's main mosque. A similar number offered prayers at Bhagalpur town in Bihar. Twenty thousand assembled in the local mosque compound at Barisal. Elsewhere in Bengal, five thousand strong crowds were reported at Comilla Town Hall and at the Bhanga Idgah Maidan. Public meetings at Azad Park in Peshawar, Aminudaullah Park in Lucknow, the Ochterlony monument Maidan in Calcutta, and Govind Park in Sylhet attracted large numbers.[45] The biggest gathering, however, was in Bombay where the Untouchable leader, Dr Ambedkar, joined the Muslim League President on the platform. Preparations for the Bombay meeting had been set in hand from early on the Thursday evening. Muslim *mohallas* (wards) were decorated, as were all the mosques. A 'Minorities Gate' was erected before the main entrance of the Jumma Masjid. Flags, ceremonial gates and arcades were set up along the entire length of Mohammad Ali Road which was to form the venue. Loudspeakers relayed the speeches to the forty thousand crowd which thronged the road and perched on the adjacent buildings. The drama of the occasion was heightened by the illumination of the mosques on either side of the meeting place.[46] This was one of a number of occasions when the League carefully stage managed its meetings. In November 1937, for example, the venue of a keynote address by Jinnah was carefully chosen to heighten its theatre. He spoke to a crowd of some fifteen thousand Muslims in Patna to the majestic backdrop of the confluence of the Ganges and the Trihut river at 'Kila ki Masjid'.[47]

There were also victory day celebrations following electoral successes. Here too there was a re-enactment of Mughal ceremonial: the *Jashn-i-Fath* (festival after victory). Such festivals were celebrated on a grand scale for several days and included the recitation of *Qasida-i-Fath* (Victory Odes).[48] Muslim League victories were celebrated in verse in 1946, although the venues for victory festivals had changed. Mosques and shrines were frequently used for such occasions. The Ajmer shrine of the great Muslim saint, Khwaja Muin-ud-Din Chishti, was the venue of a large gathering early in 1946 to celebrate the Muslim League's victories in the Central Legislative Assembly elections.[49]

Processions protested as well as celebrated events. Usually the crowds' grievances were localized, but on 16 August 1946, the Muslim League organized a national day of protest following hard on the heels of the collapse of the Cabinet Mission's proposals. The protests passed off peacefully with the tragic exception of Calcutta. In Bombay, the largest procession and rally drew a crowd of around twenty thousand. This trumped the Congress's sparser rally a week earlier, during its Quit India Day celebrations.[50] Large parades also occurred in Bangalore, Cuttack, Madras and Karachi.[51] Elaborate arrangements had been made for the cavalcade in Calcutta. *Kafelas* (processions), *akharas* (groups of wrestlers) with bands and *tabaljungs* (mounted drums) were organized from all the Muslim *mohallas* in Calcutta and its hinterland. They converged at the foot of the vast Doric column raised on the maidan in honour of Sir David Ochterlony (a traditional gathering point for demonstrations), where a mass meeting was scheduled from 3.00 p.m. onwards.[52]

The taking out of protest processions was a major weapon in the Muslim League's assault on its opponents in the Punjab and the Frontier early in 1947. Both campaigns were rooted in local grievances,[53] but they rapidly developed into struggles for control of the government in these 'Pakistan' areas. They provide the historian with glimpses of the Muslim League's growing support from below at this juncture. Previously marginalized groups such as women, small shopkeepers, labourers, and tribesmen were all heavily involved. Such groups not only lent the Muslim League valuable support, but began to set their own agendas.

Processions during the civil disobedience campaigns displayed elements of both social solidarity and protest. The latter was graphically demonstrated by the carrying of black flags and the deliberate flouting of government bans on public assembly. The crowds challenged the authority of their opponents and successfully isolated them. The Unionist Premier, Khizr, was dared to take repressive action which would alienate the whole Muslim population of the Punjab, or bow to the force of the Muslim League's campaign. The League was in a weaker position to 'dare' the Red Shirt Congress government in Peshawar, but here too it sought to provoke an unpopular reaction. Hence the prominent role which women played in many processions. In both provinces, the regular routine of protests wore down opponents and encouraged waverers to desert a sinking ship.

The first procession in the Punjab was taken out on 24 January 1947 in defiance of the Public Safety Ordinance.[54] Two days later, Khizr removed the ban on the Muslim National Guards, which had been the League's initial grievance, but the genie was now out of the bottle and the campaign escalated. There was a ten thousand strong procession in Lahore on 30 January. Ten times that number surged towards the civil lines in Amritsar a fortnight later. The crowd was only held back by police baton charges and tear gas. A thousand Pathans paraded through the streets of Jullundur on 13 February in defiance of the law. Around ten thousand Muslims marched the fifty-odd miles north-east from Lyallpur to Sheikhupura the following week.[55] A large procession of men and horses, said to number thirty thousand, moved through Muzaffargarh on 18 February. The same day a huge crowd wound its way through the provincial capital of Lahore headed by a man on a donkey impersonating Khizr.[56]

The police struggled to control such gatherings. Five hundred people were arrested in Gujarat alone on 1 February. This was the largest single round-up of Muslims in the Punjab's history. A week later, the Lahore constabulary had to call up additional lorries to cope with the rush of arrests. By the middle of February, independent sources put the province-wide number of arrests at over eight thousand.[57] Clashes between police and demonstrators became increasingly violent. In one incident alone in Lahore, five hundred rounds of tear gas were fired. On 13 February the police lathi-charged processions as far afield as Sargodha, Ferozepore and Wazirabad. Sixty people were seriously injured in clashes with the police at Gujarat, three days later.[58] The first death occurred in Simla. When the news spread, angry crowds gathered in many of the Punjab's towns on 18 February. The police also killed processionists in Gujarat and Amritsar. The nervous and disillusioned Unionist Premier, Khizr, quit office less than a week later.

How did the Muslim League mobilize such large numbers of people in a previously politically backward province? It could call on a dedicated band of student workers. Ordinary Muslims were generally sympathetic because they believed that the British had unfairly restored Khizr to power, after the Unionist party's defeats in the 1946 elections. But the influence of Muslim landowners and *pirs*—spiritual guides—was also important in gathering demonstrators. Tenants and kinsmen of the Nawab of Mamdot, Sardar Shaukat Hayat, and Firoz Khan Noon swelled the protests. *Pirs* also encouraged their disciples to join processions. Ten thousand of *Pir* Sial's *murids* camped outside his cell, when he was arrested and taken to Sargodha's Central Jail.[59] Khizr was hoist with his own petard, for his imprisonment of his own *pir* confirmed his moral bankruptcy in the eyes of many Punjabi Muslims.

Students led many processions. Those from Islamia College, Lahore were particularly eager to abandon their books in favour of the wider political struggle. During one sit-down demonstration, they succeeded in blocking the Mall for three hours.[60] On another occasion, two hundred students were arrested outside the Civil Secretariat which was the scene of a number of struggles between demonstrators and police. The Muslim National Guards also played a leading role in the League's heady campaign. When the *Salar* (Chief) of the Delhi Guards came to cheer on the campaign in Ferozepore, the local police could stomach it no longer. They broke sixty Guardsmen's heads and arrested anyone they could lay their hands on.[61]

It is no easy task to identify all the faces in these crowds. Contemporary disturbances in South Asia are far better documented. There is no equivalent of the *Who are the Guilty* report into the 1984 Delhi violence. Detective work using newspaper reports suggests, however, that a wide cross-section of Muslim society was involved. Craftsmen, butchers, traders, and even *tongawallahs* swelled the funeral procession of a victim of police brutality in Lahore. Nearly two hundred thousand Muslims marched to the graveyard at Miani Saheb. After the burial, the crowd retired to the Mochi Gate, where an impassioned rally took place.[62]

Punjabi women were not backward in coming forward to lend their support to the campaign. Half a dozen women's parties merged into a large parade in Lahore on 25 February. This proceeded to the Civil Secretariat, where it was met by volleys of tear gas. The police meted out similar treatment to women on numerous other occasions. When this did not do the trick, they lathi-charged. This happened not only in Lahore, but in such district towns as Ferozepore and Dera Ghazi Khan.[63] This was grist to the mill of the Muslim League press. *Dawn's* edition of 26 February, for example, included a photograph of victims of police assault. It was mainly the wives of prominent Muslim Leaguers who were captioned, such persons as Begum Shah Nawaz, Begum Shaukat Hayat, Begum Bashir Ahmed, and Begum Hidayatullah, the wife of the Sindh Muslim League Premier. It was not only elite women who braved the tear gas. Wives of craftsmen and traders, many of whom were in purdah, swelled the processions The largest recorded crowd numbered around twenty-five thousand as it slowly wended its way down the Mall in Lahore.[64]

The civil disobedience campaign in the Frontier moved along similar tracks. There was a daily routine of protests and demonstrations. The police, as in the Punjab, responded with tear gas, lathi charges and bullets from time to time. Crowds were gathered by tribal chiefs, *pirs* and students. Women also played a prominent role. Violence, as ever, however, was a more common fact of life in the Frontier region than its neighbour. Students and National Guardsmen blew up government property and communications; while there were the stirrings from below of communal disorder. The Dera Ismail Khan district became a dangerous powder keg.

There were large processions in all of the Frontier's towns. The following incidents plucked from newspaper reports capture the flavour of the events. Eighteen thousand Muslims marched through Kohat on the evening of 12 March 1947. Eight days earlier, around twenty thousand Muslims drawn mainly from the surrounding villages proceeded through the bazaar at Dera Ismail Khan to the post office, where a group led by an advocate, Muhammad Rustam Khan, were arrested. On 22 March, over fifteen thousand Muslims assembled in front of the League's headquarters in Bannu before setting off in procession. Just a few days earlier, Bannu had been the scene of a large parade of Waziri tribesmen. During the morning of 5 April, an estimated twenty thousand Muslims marched through the provincial capital, Peshawar, in defiance of a twenty-four-hour curfew.[65] By the middle of the month, *Dawn* claimed that thirty-five thousand people had been arrested and six thousand injured in police action.[66] The campaign continued unabated, however, for a further seven weeks. Repression in fact sustained it, rather than slackened its momentum. Huge processions and rallies were, for example, held on the tenth of every month to commemorate the victims of police firing in Peshawar on 10 March.[67]

The campaign was directed at the top by a Provincial War Council. Its members included Mian Abdullah Shah, the

President of the Peshawar district Muslim League, Mian Muhammad Shah and the *Pir* of Manki Sharif.[68] Beneath it, there stretched a chain of command which reached down to district and town 'dictators' who recruited volunteers and planned processions and demonstrations. The Peshawar Muslim Students Federation formed another coordinating network. Students organized demonstrations, picketed buildings and engaged in sabotage. One underground cell eagerly sought instruction in the use of explosives from a chemistry teacher at Islamia College.[69] Finally, there was the unpredictable presence of Major Khurshid Anwar, the chief commander of the Muslim National Guards.

Most 'dictators' derived their power from their local standing rather than rank in the Muslim League. Muhammad Ramzan Khan, a Dera Ismail Khan 'dictator' was, for example, a leading *jagirdar* (landholder) and Chief of the Utmanzai tribe. His Bannu counterpart, Habibullah Khan, headed the Mina Khel clan of the Marwat tribe. Malik ur Rahman Kiyani, who directed operations in the Kohat district, was a large landowner and came from a locally prominent Shia family.[70] Such persons were able to mobilize large numbers of followers for direct action. Khan Saifullah Khan, Chief of the Ghazi Khel Marwats, exported truckloads of tribesmen fifty miles to Bannu to court arrest.[71] The Nawab of Tonk brought the big batallions of his followers into the campaign in the Dera Ismail Khan district. On 11 April, he led a huge procession through the district headquarters. The *Pir* of Manki Sharif and *Pir* Zakori were also key figures. They both exhorted their numerous disciples to join in the protests.

It should thus be crystal clear by now that these were not the work of aimless mobs. The protestors possessed clear political goals. Many crowds had been drawn together through highly structured traditional networks. Does this mean, then, that all we are dealing with is top-down mobilization in order to legitimize the Muslim League struggle? The answer is no. For the crowds were able to set their own agendas and did not necessarily reflect the values and aims of their leaders.

Furthermore, we need to delve below the physical descriptions of their mobilization to fully understand their significance. At the psychological level they provided for their participants the experience which Victor Turner has dubbed 'communitas' that 'intervening liminal phase betwixt and between the categories of ordinary social life...the direct, immediate, and total confrontation of human identities which tends to make those experiencing it think of mankind as a homogeneous, unstructured and free community.'[72] Canetti deploys different terminology, but points to the same psychological experience. He calls this 'the blessed moment of discharge' when all distinctions were cast off. These processions fit particularly well his typology of the stagnating crowd.[73]

III

Hartals played an increasingly important role during the Pakistan movement. The *hartal* or strike was a traditional demonstration of protest and mourning which was directed against a third party, rather than an employer. The Congress employed *hartals* during the 1919 Rowlatt *satyagraha*. Thereafter they became a feature of all Gandhian campaigns. A complete *hartal* closed all educational institutions, and halted public transport, as well as shuttering shops and businesses. This not only paralyzed normal activity, but freed people to demonstrate. During the direct action campaign in the Punjab, for example, Muslim shopkeepers in Kasur closed daily between one and four to attend public meetings held in defiance of Government orders.[74]

The Muslim League ordered its first All-India *hartal* on 16 August 1946. The best response came in Bombay where schools and businesses closed, mill-hands went on strike and even tongas and hack-victorias no longer plied for hire. Nor was there the vandalism which had accompanied the strikes of February 1946 in support of the Royal Indian Navy mutiny.[75] This was not the case everywhere. In Karachi, for example, Muslims used force

to halt the trams.[76] There was some support for the *hartal* in
the Princely States. Muslim mill-hands struck in Indore.[77]
Crescent flags fluttered proudly over closed shops in Mysore.[78]
Traders also shut up shop in the Muslim quarters of Rampur.[79]

Hartals mattered most, however, during the Muslim League
campaigns in the Punjab and the Frontier. Complete stoppages
of work occurred in Muslim Lahore on 10, 16 and 24 February
1947. The first of these freed Muslims to join a huge funeral
procession for a victim of the disturbances. The vegetable,
mutton and beef markets were all closed, although Hindu
shopkeepers continued to trade unmolested. Muslim schools
and colleges were on holiday. Streets were blocked and all
Muslim shops closed. In such leading bazaars as Delhi Gate
bazaar, Kashmiri bazaar, Bazaar Hakiman, Dabbi Bazaar, and
Bhati Gate bazaar.[80] Even the small roadside tobacconists,
paanwallahs and tea stalls packed away their wares. The last
(24 February) had been designated 'National Struggle Day' by
the Punjab Muslim League Committee of Action. This
commemorated the opening month of struggle against the Khizr
Government. Stoppages and strikes spread from Lahore to
Amritsar, Multan, Kasur, Rawalpindi, Jullundur and
Ludhiana. There was very little in all this to cheer the Unionist
leader.

There were numerous *hartals* in the Frontier. Nowshera, for
example, shut down on 20 February.[81] Five days later, it was
Peshawar's turn. There was a complete *hartal* there again on
10 May as part of the ongoing commemoration of 'Martyrs'
Day'. There were strikes in most towns on 5 April in protest at
Pir Manki's arrest. Many of Peshawar's traders and artisans
downed tools to join a large procession which *Dawn* numbered
at twenty thousand, the British at half that figure.[82] Support for
the stoppages spilled over into violence against Hindu and Sikh
traders who refused to close their businesses. On 21 March,
for example, the Hindu-controlled main bazaar in Mansehra
was looted and razed to the ground.

Historians of the Muslim League movement have consistently
ignored *hartals*. Yet even this brief exploration demonstrates

their value in uncovering the scope and character of crowd activity. The large number of successful *hartals* during 1946-7 eloquently attests to multi-class involvement in the freedom struggle's closing stages. For a complete *hartal* could not be achieved without support from casual labourers, industrial workers, shopkeepers and artisans, as well as the professional classes. *Hartals* also lay bare the purposeful nature of crowd behaviour. They could not be further removed from generic depictions of crowd activity as mindless disorder. They were highly disciplined and orchestrated protest movements. Like processions, they displayed both social protest and social solidarity. They spontaneously threw up their own organizational structures of marshalls, pickets and messengers. They were authentic subaltern events in that in the moment of stopping work, all became equal in the Pakistan struggle.

IV

This section briefly explores two other types of crowd activity, namely picketing and trespass. Both were from early on a part of the weaponry directed against the colonial state by the Indian nationalists. Such action was not merely symbolic, but deliberately hit at government revenues and attempted to obstruct its day to day workings. The Muslim League's preference for constitutional methods meant that for many years, these weapons were kept securely shut away in its locker. But in the heat of its struggle with the Punjab Unionists and the Frontier Congress in 1947, they were quickly brought out for use.

Picketing and trespass soon badly disrupted public life in Lahore. On 22 February, a band of around a thousand women forced their way into Government House. One intrepid female in a *tour de force* clambered on the roof to plant a Muslim League flag. The police tear-gassed the trespassers. Undeterred, a small group of amazons broke into the premises of All-India Radio on their way back to Empress Road. A few days earlier, some women had entered the Lahore District Court and delayed its proceedings for several hours.[83] Such disruption was not confined to Lahore. Forty veiled women forced their way into the Central Jail compound in Jullundur on 29 January and performed a mock funeral of the Unionist leaders. In this instance the police stood their ground.[84]

Members of the Frontier Zenana (Women's) Muslim League broke into courts, jails, radio stations, and railway booking-offices. Their campaign was strongest in Peshawar, but district towns did not escape unscathed. It was more effective than that of their Punjabi sisters, as the authorities pussyfooted about when it came to force. Officials took the afternoon off if female trespassers could not be persuaded to leave, with predictable consequences for efficiency. Nevertheless, youthful enthusiasm occasionally resulted in female injury. On 15 April, five women were hurt when they attempted to halt the Peshawar to Bombay express at Qila Bala Hasar.[85] Female volunteers had earlier entered the Peshawar Cantonment Railway Booking Office and distributed free 'Pakistan tickets'.

The train incident resulted in one of the few successful attempts by the Provincial War Council to intervene in the women's campaign. It was conducted independently of both the All-India Zenana Muslim League and the men's Frontier League. Even the Frontier Zenana League, which received a fresh lease of life because of the agitation, possessed little real influence over activists, who went their own way. Women used the constraints of purdah to limit male authority over their actions. A belated attempt in May to reimpose the control of the Provincial War Council was defeated by a threat of mass resignation from the female leaders.[86]

The freedom and autonomy displayed by women during the direct action campaign stands in stark contrast to their traditional status in Frontier society. This was summed up by the Pushtu proverb, 'For the women, either the house or the grave'.[87] Male dominance was almost complete in public life. When the Frontier Zenana League was founded in 1943, there was little deviation intended from this traditional pattern. It was clearly subordinate to the men's organization, and its members took on the roles permitted by their male relatives. By May 1947, women had been freed from the taboos which constrained them. They were free to move around outside the house, they demonstrated alongside men and defined their own agendas. Most importantly, they developed their own autonomous leadership.

Women along with their male counterparts mounted successful pickets of courts and liquor stores as part of the direct action campaign. Early in March, five thousand volunteers picketed the Civil Courts in Kohat.[88] When a repeat performance was attempted later in the month, the police were prepared and made over four hundred arrests. The courts in Peshawar and Bannu came in for similar attention. On 10 April, around ten thousand Meetakhel tribesmen blockaded the courts at Bannu.[89] The familiar ritual of raising the Muslim League flag on to the roof of the District Courts at Peshawar occurred on 3 March.[90]

The Congress Ministers had seen it all before, although in a different setting. They were now arresting volunteers for the same kind of acts of civil disobedience in which they had engaged in the past. Early in October 1942, for example, groups of Congressmen had picketed the District Courts in Mardan for six consecutive days.[91] Perhaps because they were now the poachers turned game keepers, they kept police violence to a minimum.

Muslim League volunteers also picketed liquor stores both to reduce government revenue and as a gesture to Islamization. On 11 March, large crowds blockaded the stores in Mardan. Three days earlier, a leading Waziri Chief, Khan Nasrullah Khan, had been arrested at the head of a crowd outside the shop in Bannu. The unfortunate store was the scene of another mass picket a fortnight later. The police unceremoniously carted away over two hundred volunteers, including a large number of Muslim National Guardsmen.[92]

V

The riots which ravaged India during 1946-7 appear to belie those analyses of crowd activity which stress its social purpose. What rationality can be discerned in a massacre of the magnitude of, say, the October 1946 Bihar killings, in which according to the Muslim League forty thousand people died?[93] Such extreme violence encourages thoughts of collective madness, frenzy and blood lust. Even in such horrifying episodes, however, it is possible to discern structure and purpose. The perpetrators were not deviants or crazed, and believed that their actions were 'legitimate'. The politics of crowd violence will be largely examined in this section through material relating to attacks on the minorities in the Frontier in 1947. This is not intended to imply that the Muslims were the sole aggressors in the disturbed circumstances of 1947. The Bihar killings mentioned above underline the point that all communities had blood on their hands.

Concerted attacks on non-Muslims in the Frontier began as early as December 1946. Black Mountain tribesmen raided villages in the Hazara district and razed many bazaars. The violence quickly spread to the mountainous regions in the Abbotabad tehsil. Before order returned, around a hundred Hindus and Sikhs had been killed, while ten times that number had been driven from their homes.[94] An uneasy calm ensued which lasted until March, when there was a further eruption of violence during which the main bazaar in Mansehra was burnt down. The storm centre, however, was in the Dera Ismail Khan district to the south. Eighteen people were killed and nine hundred shops destroyed in three days of mayhem in its district headquarters. The aggressors were Mahsuds and Bhittanis who had crossed over from the adjoining tribal territories of South Waziristan.[95]

What lay behind these attacks? Were they the result of blood lust and a desire for loot? Had they been caused by class conflict between 'poor' Muslim tribesmen and 'rich' Hindu and Sikh traders and moneylenders? Evidence exists that Muslims accused

Hindu shopkeepers at the time of diverting scarce supplies of food and cloth on to the black market.[96] But such grievances do not appear to have caused or legitimized the violence. Far more important was, first, the tribesmen's strong sense of Muslim brotherhood and, secondly, their conviction that it was a religiously sanctioned duty to raise *lashkàrs* (tribal war parties) against the Hindus and Sikhs.

The raids in December 1946 followed hard on the heels of serious rioting in Bombay city and in Bihar, in which thousands of Muslims had perished. Firsthand[97] accounts by relief workers and Pathan survivors of the killings in Bombay shocked and then angered the tribesmen who crossed into the settled districts to attend Muslim League meetings in Dera Ismail Khan and Tonk.[98] These were chaired by *Pir* Manki who possessed vast numbers of Waziri disciples. *Mullahs* (preachers) called similar meetings in other areas south of the Kurram river. Shortly afterwards, the tribesmen attacked Hindu houses and shops in the Hazara district.

The incursions in March 1947 share a similar background. Mohmand shopkeepers who had fled Amritsar caused a stir on returning to their ancestral homes. The Toru *mullahs* confirmed their harrowing accounts in a meeting held at a Ghaziabad mosque on 14 February. The congregation pledged support for the Muslim League's cause.[99] Thereafter, *Pir* Manki toured Mohmand territory calling on disciples to court arrest in the direct action campaign. He then journeyed to North Waziristan where, on 16 and 17 March, he addressed packed meetings at Miran Shah. Mahsuds, Ahmadzai Waziris, and Bhittanis crossed over to Tonk a couple of weeks later, to attend a secret meeting called by *Pir* Wana. It was decided to hold a general tribal council (*Marakka*) at Miran Shah to resolve whether a *jihad* should be launched.[100] On 7 April, over three hundred Waziri *maliks* (chiefs) attended the *Marakka*. Resolutions were passed demanding the resignation of the Congress Premier, Dr Khan Sahib, and calling for the creation of Pakistan. Maula Khan, *faqir* of Shewa and the Council's President, pledged that he would raise a *lashkar* to fight for their fulfilment.[101]

The attack on Tonk which followed was thus not a spontaneous raid in which 'deviant' tribesmen sated their lust for booty. It was carefully conceived and was a morally 'legitimate' action. The *Paktunwali* code of honour allowed for the taking of revenge (*badal*) for every hurt and insult to a kinsmen who had been killed. Many Pathans had died in Bombay and Amritsar. Moreover, the events in Bihar had greatly enhanced the Pathans' sense of community with other Muslim victims. Further still, Islamic as well as ethnic values sanctioned their action. This was symbolized by the presence of *pirs* and *mullahs* as well as *khans* at the tribal conference. The Koran sanctions jihad both for the purpose of advancing Islam and for repelling evil from Muslims.

Is it possible to discern purpose in the pattern of violence as well as in its instigation? The tribesmen's preferred target appears to be property, rather than people. Although much of Tonk and Dera Ismail Khan was gutted during April 1947, only just over a hundred Hindus and Sikhs were killed. Similarly, there were just fifty-five victims in the earlier Hazara disturbances, despite the total destruction of Hindu shops and homes in such villages as Battal and Oghi.[102]

Frontier tribesmen do not normally possess a reputation for squeamishness. Interestingly, if we examine communal violence elsewhere in India, a similar pattern of Muslim violence emerges. Sugata Bose's study of the 1930 Kishoreganj riots reveals, for example, that 'personal violence was on the whole eschewed... the wrath of the (Muslim) rioters was directed against property, in general, and loan bonds, in particular'.[103] Similar patterns of behaviour were displayed during riots in Dhaka at this same period. Again, during the so-called 'communal war of succession' in Lahore in the spring of 1947, Muslim attacks were largely on property. Hindus responded with bomb throwing and stray stabbings.[104] Muslims did on occasion kill many Hindus and Sikhs. Three thousand perished in the West Punjab early in 1947.[105] This was a mere prelude to the blood-letting of the Partition period. Hindus and Sikhs, for their part, did sometimes attack Muslim property. Four thousand Muslim shops and homes were destroyed in the walled area of Amritsar during a single week in March 1947.[106] But were these exceptions which prove the rule? It appears that casualty figures were frequently higher when Hindus rather than Muslims were the aggressors. More Muslims died in Bihar than Hindus in Noakhali. Again, during the last two weeks of March 1941, 2,734 rioting incidents were reported in Dhaka city and its suburbs: nearly 3,000 people were rendered homeless, Hindu-owned shops blazed, 'so furiously that it was impossible to get near enough to fight the flames'. Yet only 58 Hindus lost their lives.[107] What then lies behind the different patterns of crowd disorder?

Muslim emphasis on the destruction of Hindu property could be understood in terms of class motivated violence—the poor pillaging the shops, warehouses and stores of the rich. Economic motives certainly lay behind attacks on moneylenders' homes because by making a bonfire of their documents, Muslims were freeing themselves from the *bania's* (moneylender's) grip. Suranjan Das tellingly reveals that at the height of the 1930 Dhaka Riot, 'When a moneylender's house was raided, the first aim of the looters was not to commit physical violence on the owner, but to search for his account books and burn them'.[108] But there was no direct correlation between scarcity and Muslim violence in 1946-7. Moreover, it was not just the poor and dispossessed who made up the crowds which attacked Hindu property. They also included prosperous traders and professional elites.

A cultural explanation would see community values lying behind not only the motives for crowd violence but its pattern. The greater incidence of Hindu assaults, for example, could be linked with the concept of pollution. Muslims were 'unclean' and a personal source of pollution which death alone could eradicate. Muslims, on the other hand, regarded Hindus as infidels and thus lacked the incentive to attack individuals as sources of impurity.[109] Nevertheless, they were highly sensitive 'to the wrongful use of material objects in worship'. From the earliest times, they had smashed the idols of infidels and destroyed the paraphernalia associated with the worship of false gods. The sacking of the great Shiva Temple at Somnath in AD 1025 still remained a byword for unyielding resistance to idolatry at the close of the colonial era. Can the Muslim violence thus be understood in terms of this iconoclastic tradition?

Certainly, there were few great temple complexes in North India by the twentieth century. But each Hindu locality possessed numerous small shrines and mandirs (temples). All its dwellings housed shrines and images where the obligatory daily offerings were made to the gods, to the house spirit dwelling in its north-east corner and to deceased ancestors. Stall-holders sold rice, sweetmeats, and flowers as well as statues and prints of the Hindu pantheon which were all essential to this daily worship. They also set up their own shrines in adjoining rooms. Was the destruction of this incubus of idolatry by fire, following the Prophet's own traditions, the motive impelling attacks on Hindu shops and residences?

There is considerable evidence of desecration of Hindu temples in Bengal during communal rioting from the 1920s onwards. Eleven temples and *gurudwaras* were attacked in the early stages of the 1926 Calcutta riots.[110] Muslim attacks on the wealthy Basak mercantile community in Dhaka in September 1926 may well have been rooted, not in economic grievances, but in the fact that it sponsored the Janamastami procession which had occasioned the riots.[111] 'Large numbers of small personal temple-huts have burnt out,' an official reported during the 1946 communal violence in the Tippera district, 'images have been pulled down and smashed and at least one large and brick-built temple has been looted and desecrated'.[112]

There are, however, a number of problems with this explanation. Hindus defiled mosques as frequently as Muslims desecrated temples. An equal number of mosques and temples (fifty-two) were attacked during the violence in Calcutta in August 1946.[113] Islamic libraries and burial grounds were also assailed.

Indian Christians and Untouchables were as 'polluting' as Muslims, but were not attacked by Hindus at this time. Muslims destroyed and looted property which possessed economic value, but which by any stretch of the imagination could not be considered as an 'incubus of idolatry'. During the 1926 Calcutta riot, for example, Muslim fruitsellers from Peshawar suffered badly. In a single attack on a Peshwari fruit stall in central Calcutta, Rs. 10,000 worth of fruit was pillaged.[114] Moreover, why was communal violence limited in time and geographical extent? This latter question points to the main weakness in any cultural theory; it abstracts the disturbances from their political and historical context.

One does not in despair have to fall back on the colonial discourse of 'mob' violence. Local political, economic and social variables undoubtedly lay behind different patterns of violence. The presence, for example, of a large, 'socially unstable' immigrant population in Calcutta and its industrial suburbs is a key factor in understanding the full-blooded violence in August 1946. Further work is required on the linkages of riotous crowds with the world of organized politics and on the impact of the circulation of rumours during disturbances. It may also be fruitful to assess patterns of violence from the cultural perspective of community 'honour'. The increasing incidences of abductions and attacks on women in 1946-7 undoubtedly reflect attempts to expose the most protected aspects of rivals' honour and self-identity.[115] Certainly, as the British departure approached, force was used in boundary demarcation. This was clearly evident in Punjab and the Frontier, but was also present in Bengal. During the Noakhali riots, for example, one British observer spoke of a 'determined and organized' Muslim effort to drive out all the Hindus.[116] Commercial communities whose capital was mobile would have required less 'persuasion' to flee than immobile peasantry or embedded professional elites. This may well account for the greater Muslim casualties in Bihar, in comparison with the Hindu and Sikh victims in the Frontier. It may be unwise, however, to go for too 'neat' an explanation.

VI

For such writers as Sumit Sarkar, evidence of mass action during the Pakistan movement is as elusive as the snark of Lewis Carroll's nonsense verse. This study has, however, introduced an array of crowd activity into the historical discourse. In doing so, it has demonstrated the multi-class character of the freedom struggle: a fact which has been obscured by the tendency of accounts to concentrate on the politics of elites.

It has proved possible to identify at least some of the faces in the crowd. Light has also been shed on how they were gathered and what they signified. It is clear that crowds possessed both 'associational' and 'communal' features, in that they were mobilized through the Muslim League's formal institutions as well as traditional social networks. This questions the adequacy of the 'pre-industrial/industrial' dichotomy which is present in much of the methodology of crowd study.[117] The extent to which crowd activity reinforced group sentiment also raises doubts about the wisdom of studies which have made the crowd synonymous with social protest. We have seen that such 'protest' activities as *hartals* also possessed important integrationist aspects. Even in the case of communal violence, 'mob' characterizations of crowd activity have been revealed as totally inadequate. Disturbances were not the product of pathological disorder. It is possible to discern structure and purpose within them.

Crowd activity contributed significantly to the creation of Pakistan. Personal experiences of processions, strikes and riots strengthened communal identity. Local loyalties and interests were superseded by a heightened consciousness of Islamic brotherhood. Individuals thought of themselves as Muslims first and then Punjabis, Pathans and Bengalis. The crush of crowds in confined spaces added to the sense of theatre and self-importance of Muslim League political events.[118] Crowd activity not only involved symbolic integration, but territorial claims. The movement of processions through Muslim quarters, market places and 'sacred space' reaffirmed their centrality to the community's cultural and political entity; whilst the use of public arenas by Muslim minorities carried echoes of the auspicious action of Hindu religious processions. Thus the Muslims of Patna asserted their rights to 'alien' urban space when they decorated the long stretch of land running from Bankipore to Patna city with flags, festoons and ceremonial gates when Jinnah came early in November 1937 to rally support for the League.

Crowds not only influenced their participants, however, but played to a wider audience. The reception at Patna emphatically underpinned Jinnah's message to 'rally round' the Muslim League and 'enroll in *lakhs*' in the face of Congress oppression.

Crowds legitimized the Muslim League's claims from the late 1930s onwards. The Congress, ironically, was less required to demonstrate its public backing at this time, following its victories in the 1937 provincial elections. Crowd activity, as we shall see in more detail in Chapter 3, played as important a role as factional struggles within the Unionist Party in encouraging Muslim elites in the Punjab to transfer their loyalties to the League. Evidence drawn from the Unionist fieldworkers' accounts points to a groundswell of opinion in favour of Pakistan which hindered their activities and resulted in demoralizing losses of support.[119] Khizr shored up the Unionist citadel after the 1946 elections by forming a coalition government with the Congress and the Sikh Akalis. But the tide of opinion had turned against him. The mass protests early in 1947 ensured that the Unionist power, once the envy of its rivals, collapsed like a mud fort in the monsoon.

Crowd activity was also important in undermining the Muslim League's opponents in the North-West Frontier Province. Here, as in the Punjab, it had failed to form a government after the 1946 provincial elections. Yet the imminent British departure made it essential for the League to demonstrate that it commanded the allegiance of the Pathans. Attlee's announcement of 20 February 1947 created added urgency, as it held out the possibility that power might be handed over to the existing provincial governments if agreement could not be reached at the Centre by the June 1948 deadline. Coincidentally, the Frontier League's civil disobedience campaign was launched on the day of the Premier's announcement, although there is no evidence that this was at the instigation of the League High Command.

The constant demonstrations, picketing and processions resulted in many desertions from the Frontier Congress. Even more importantly, it convinced Sir Olaf Caroe, the governor, that fresh elections were imperative as the Congress Ministry no longer represented public opinion. Lord Mountbatten resisted this idea, but insisted instead that a referendum be held to decide the province's future. The Muslim League's orchestration of the civil disobedience campaign thus reaped rich dividends. The Frontier Congress conceded that Pakistan was inevitable by boycotting the referendum.

It would be wrong to assume, however, that crowds were merely tools in the hands of the Muslim League elite. It never fully controlled the popular forces it sought to unleash. Crowds could tragically run out of its 'control', as in the Great Calcutta Killings. They could also set their own agendas, as we have seen most clearly in the case of the women's campaign in the Frontier. Finally, even hierarchically mobilized crowds created a sense of 'communitas'. Their participants, albeit temporarily, were freed from the 'burdens of distance' and patterns of authority existing in everyday life.

NOTES

[1] In the three Muslim majority areas of the Punjab, the Frontier and Sindh, the Muslim League captured just one seat.

[2] S.B. Freitag, *Collective Action and Community. Public Arenas and the Emergence of Communalism in North India* (California, 1989) p. 17.

[3] G. Le Bon, *The Crowd* (London, 1952).

[4] G. Rudé, *The Crowd in History, 1730-1848* (New York, 1964).

[5] E. Canetti, (C.Stewart, trans.) *Crowds and Power* (Harmondsworth, 1981).

[6] For an excellent comparison of Le Bon's and Canetti's views, consult, J.S. McCelland, *The Crowd and the Mob. From Plato to Canetti* (London, 1989), p. 293 & ff.

[7] J.Estebe, *Tocsin Pour un Massacre. La Saison des St. Barthélemy* (Paris, 1968).

[8] N.Z. Davis, 'The rites of violence: religious riot in Sixteenth Century France', *Past and Present* LIX (May 1973), pp. 51-91.

[9] Ibid., (8) above pp. 75-84.

[10] S.B. Freitag, 'Sacred Symbol as Mobilizing Ideology: The North Indian Search for a "Hindu" Community', *Comparative Studies in Society and History*, 22, (1980), pp. 597-625.

[11] A. Yang, 'Sacred Symbol and Sacred Space in Rural India: Community Mobilization in the "Anti-Cow Killing" Riot of 1893', *Comparative Studies in Society and History*, 22, (1980), pp. 579-596.

[12] M. Harcourt, 'Kisan Populism and Revolution in Rural India: The 1942 Disturbances in Bihar and East United Provinces', in D.A. Low (ed.), *Congress and the Raj: Facets of the Indian Struggle 1917-47* (London, 1977), pp. 315-348.

[13] S. Bose, 'The Roots of communal violence in rural Bengal: A Study of the Kishoreganj riots of 1930', *Modern Asian Studies*, 16, 3 (1982), pp. 463-491.

[14] S. Das, *Communal Riots in Bengal 1905-1947* (Delhi, 1991).

[15] *See*, for example, V. Das (ed.), *Mirrors of Violence. Communities, Riots and Survivors in South Asia* (Delhi, 1990).

[16] Freitag, *Collective Action*, op. cit., pp. 39;122;140.

[17] S.B. Freitag, (ed.) *Culture and Power in Benaras: Community, Performance and Environment, 1800-1980* (California, 1989), pp. 27-8.

[18] Freitag, *Collective Action*, op. cit., p. 96.

[19] Yang. op. cit., p. 590 & ff.

[20] Suranjan Das, op. cit., p. 131.

[21] Suranjan Das op. cit., p. 207 & ff.

[22] G. Pandey, 'The Colonial Construction of "Communalism": British Writings on Benaras in the Nineteenth Century' in Das, op. cit., pp. 94-135.

[23] Suranjan Das, op. cit., p. 53.

[24] Governor of Bengal to the Viceroy. Telegram, 18 August 1946. L/P&J/8/577. 117/B/5/6, IOR.

[25] Note on Wavell's Interview in Calcutta, 31.10.46. L/P&J/8/577. 117/B/5/6, IOR.

[26] Suranjan Das, op. cit., p. 156-7; 183-5.

[27] Freitag, *Collective Action*, op. cit., pp. 224-5; 234-5.

[28] I. Talbot, *Provincial Politics and the Pakistan Movement: The Growth of the Muslim League in North-West and North-East India 1937-47* (Karachi, 1988), p. 56.

[29] Zia-ul-Islam, A Historical Background of the Majlis Karkunan-e-Tehrik-e-Pakistan', unpublished paper (Lahore, n.d.), p. 3.

[30] E. Durkheim, *The Elementary Forms of Religious Life* (London 1961), p. 427.

[31] Freitag, *Collective Action*, op. cit., p. 134.

[32] *Star of India*, (Calcutta), 28 October 1937.

[33] For details, consult, for example, Talbot, op. cit., pp. 75, 97-9.

[34] Talbot, op. cit., p. 56.

[35] K.A. Jones, 'Muslim Politics and the Growth of the Muslim League in Sindh 1935-41'. Duke University, unpublished Ph.D Thesis, 1977, p. 161.

[36] Talbot, op. cit., p. 118.

[37] For details of Mughal ceremonial consult Mubarak Ali Khan 'The Court of the Great Moghuls', unpublished Ph.D dissertation, Bochum University, 1976, p. 70 & ff.

[38] See, for example, Mysore Residency FR 2nd Half of November 1946. L/P&S/13/1303, File 1 (6), IOR.

[39] Bombay FR 1st Half of April 1942. L/P&J/5/163, IOR.

[40] Report on the Situation in the West Punjab, 31 August 1947. L/WS/1/1037, IOR.

[41] Mysore Residency FR 1st Half of January 1943 L/P&S/13/1303, File 1 (4), IOR.

[42] The most useful source for details of the activities is the *Star of India* (Calcutta) which published between 22-29 December a daily compilation of reports which it had received from all over the subcontinent.

[43] Jinnah's writ did not extend as far as the Frontier, where the Provincial Muslim League took out processions in Peshawar and Dera Ismail Khan. *Star of India* (Calcutta), 23 & 25 December 1939.

[44] The full text of the prayer can be found in, *The Times of India* (Bombay), 23 December 1939.

[45] *Star of India* (Calcutta), 23, 25, 26 December 1939.

[46] *The Times of India* (Bombay), 23 December 1939.

[47] *Star of India* (Calcutta), 3 November 1937.

[48] Khan, op. cit., p. 56.

[49] Ajmer FR 1st Half of January 1946, L/P&J/5/287, IOR.

[50] Bombay FR 1st half of August 1946, L/P&J/5/167, IOR.

[51] Mysore Residency FR 2nd Half of August 1946, L/P&S/13/1305, File 1 (6); Orissa FR 2nd Half of August 1946, L/P&J/5/236; Madras FR 1st Half of August 1946, L/P&J/5/209; Sindh FR 21 August 1946, L/P&J/5/262, IOR.

[52] Bengal Affairs, L/P&J/8/655, File 1 (9), IOR.

[53] The background in the Punjab was the Unionist Government's banning of the Muslim National Guards and the arrest for obstruction of leading Muslim figures during a search of the Guards' headquarters in Lahore. The immediate cause in the Frontier was the Muslim League's outcry over the case of a woman who, it claimed, had been forced to revert to Sikhism by Dr Khan Sahib just a month after her conversion to Islam. The woman had originally been abducted from her Hazara village. When she had been rescued by the authorities, she was taken to Dr Khan Sahib's house in Peshawar.

[54] Report on the Punjab Situation, L/P&J/8/663, IOR.

[55] *Dawn* (Delhi), 15, 13 & 25 February 1947.

[56] *Dawn* (Delhi), 19 February 1947.

[57] *Dawn* (Delhi), 16 February 1947.

[58] *Dawn* (Delhi), 11, 14 & 17 February 1947.

[59] *Eastern Times* (Lahore), 7 February 1947.

[60] *Dawn* (Delhi), 11 February 1947.

[61] *Dawn* (Delhi), 9 February 1947.

[62] *Dawn* (Delhi), 11 February 1947.

[63] *Dawn* (Delhi), 9 February 1947.

[64] *Dawn* (Delhi), 25 February 1947.

[65] *Dawn* (Delhi), 5, 23, & 17 March & 6 April 1947.

[66] *Dawn* (Delhi), 16 April 1947.

[67] Governor of the Frontier to the Viceroy, Telegram, 13 March 1947, L/P&J/8/660, IOR.

[68] Mian Abdullah Shah was in fact a veteran of the Afghan Jirga's 1931 civil disobedience campaign. For further details, consult, S.A. Rittenburg, 'The Independence Movement in India's North-West Frontier Province, 1901-47', Columbia University, unpublished Ph.D Thesis 1977, pp. 364-5.

[69] The Frontier League in fact conducted a campaign of sabotage calculated to paralyse the province's administration. On 27 May, for example, a bridge was burnt on the Abbotabad–Nathiagali road disrupting traffic. On 3 March, all the telephone and telegraph lines between Peshawar and Nowshera were cut. The following month, extensive damage was done to telegraph lines in the Dera Ismail Khan district. On 17 May, two canal rest houses were attacked and records were destroyed in government offices in the Mardan district. Ten days later there was a spate of bomb blasts which the British attributed to Khurshid Anwar, *Naib-i-Salar* of the Muslim National Guards, who had entered the Frontier from the Punjab on 28 February. Governor of the Frontier to the Viceroy, Telegrams of 31 March; 14 April; 28 May 1947. L/P&J/8/660, IOR.

[70] Rittenburg, op. cit., pp. 358, 230.

[71] *Dawn* (Delhi), 17 April 1947.

[72] Quoted in Freitag, *Collective Action*, op. cit., p. 91.

[73] Canetti, op. cit., p. 33.

[74] *Dawn* (Delhi), 14 February 1947.

[75] Bombay FR 2nd Half of August 1946, L/P&J/5/167, IOR.

[76] Sindh FR 21 August 1946 L/P&J/5/262, IOR.

[77] Indore Residency FR 31 August 1946 L/P&S/13/1181, File 155(2), IOR.

[78] Mysore Residency FR 2nd Half of August 1946, L/P&S/13/1305, File 1(6), IOR.

[79] Gwalior Residency FR 3 September 1946, L/P&S/13/1197, File 5, IOR.

[80] *Eastern Times* (Lahore), 11 February 1947.

[81] *Dawn* (Delhi), 22 February 1947.

[82] Governor North-West Frontier Province to the Viceroy, 5 April 1947, L/P&J/8/660, IOR.

[83] *Dawn* (Delhi), 17 & 23 February 1947.

[84] *Eastern Times* (Lahore), 29 January 1947.

[85] *Dawn* (Delhi), 15 April 1947.

[86] Rittenberg, op. cit., pp. 381 & 378.

[87] Rittenberg, op. cit., p. 376.

[88] *Dawn* (Delhi), 1 March 1947.

[89] *Eastern Times* (Lahore), 12 April 1947.

[90] *Dawn* (Delhi), 4 March 1947.

[91] Rittenberg, op. cit., p. 283.

[92] *Dawn* (Delhi), 12, 10 & 23 March 1947.

[93] The Muslim League produced a detailed report on the disturbances which began on 27 October. This was compiled by leading figures from Bengal and the Punjab such as Khwaja Nazimuddin, Firoz Khan Noon, Mian Mumtaz Daultana, and the Nawab of Mamdot. Khwaja Nazimuddin et al., *Report on Disturbances in Bihar & U.P* (Muslim Information Centre, 1946), P/T 3363, IOL.

[94] Rittenberg, op. cit., p. 351.

[95] Rittenberg, op. cit., p. 374.

[96] Weekly Intelligence Survey 16 November 1946 L/P&S/12/3200, IOR.

[97] They returned brandishing blood-stained clothing and even the skulls of Muslim victims. North-West Frontier Province FR 2nd Half of January 1947, L/P&J/5/224, IOR.

[98] Weekly Intelligence Survey, 4 & 11 January 1947 and 8 March 1947, L/P&S/12/3201, IOR.

[99] Weekly Intelligence Report 22 March & 22 February 1947, L/P&S/12/3201, IOR.

[100] Weekly Intelligence Survey 22 March & 5 April 1947, L/P&S/12/3201, IOR.

[101] Weekly Intelligence Survey 12 April 1947, L/P&S/12/3201, IOR.

[102] Jansson, op. cit., p. 190.

[103] Bose, op. cit., p. 480.

[104] Punjab FR 2nd Half of May 1947, L/P&J/5/250; Punjab Governor's Report 25.6.47, R/3/1/91; Report by John Eustace, Deputy Commissioner Lahore, n.d., R/3/1/91, IOR.

[105] Jenkins to Wavell 17 March 1947, R/3/1/176, IOR.

[106] *Civil and Military Gazette* (Lahore), 16 March 1947.

[107] Suranjan Das, op. cit., p. 149 & 143.

[108] Suranjan Das, op. cit., p. 113.

[109] An English observer of the 1946 violence in the Tippera district of East Bengal in fact remarked that its object 'had been conversions to Islam

and not extermination of Hindus'. Quoted in Suranjan Das, op. cit., p. 197.

[110] Suranjan Das, op. cit., p. 86.

[111] Suranjan Das, op. cit., p. 88.

[112] Quoted in, Suranjan Das, op. cit., p. 198.

[113] Suranjan Das, op. cit., p. 174.

[114] Suranjan Das, op. cit., p. 85.

[115] Suranjan Das, op. cit., p. 198.

[116] Suranjan Das, op. cit., p. 199.

[117] For a critical discussion of this methodology, *see*, R.J. Holton, 'The Crowd in History: some problems of theory and method', *Social History* 3, 2 (May 1978), p. 229.

[118] Interestingly, collections of Jinnah's statements are prefaced with detailed descriptions of the crowd setting and enthusiasm. *See*, for example, W. Ahmad, *Quaid-i-Azam Muhammad Ali Jinnah: The Nation's Voice Towards Consolidation. Speeches and Statements March 1935–March 1940* (Karachi, 1992).

[119] *See*, for example, Bashir Husain, District Organizer, Jhelum Zamindara League, to Mian Sultan Ali Ranjha, 2 January 1946, file D-48, Unionist Party Papers. This area is explored in further detail in Chapter 3 below.

Chapter 2

Crowds, Ceremonial and State Symbolism

The Role of the Muslim National Guards in the Pakistan Movement

The formation of the Muslim National Guards coincided with its parent organization's 'appropriation'of public spaces to demonstrate the growing support for the Pakistan campaign. Meetings, processions and demonstrations all articulated a Muslim community discourse centred on a sense of solidarity and separateness. The League's use of public arenas, however, contained the possibility of disorder. The public passions which spilled over during the Shahidganj agitation in Lahore in 1936 provided a clear warning of the damaging effects of disorder. This not only invited government repression, but opened up serious divisions in the Muslim community. Indeed, the once powerful Ahrar movement never recovered its influence after the agitation.[1]

The Muslim National Guards movement was accordingly created with the purpose of reconciling popular participation with public order, but the original roles assigned to Guardsmen as marshalls and gate-keepers were rapidly transcended. The volunteers increasingly demonstrated both attachment to the 'national' symbols of Pakistan and embodied the 'new' Muslim who was self-disciplined and self-consciously devoted to the ideals of Islam.

This chapter sets out to examine not only the actions of the Muslim volunteers but also their symbolic significance for the

Pakistan movement. Despite their importance, they have been largely neglected. The Muslim National Guards have commanded in fact little more than a footnote in the historical discourse of the freedom struggle. Yet their first *Salar-i-Ala*, Nawab Siddique Ali Khan, in his autobiography puts their strength in Bengal alone at three hundred thousand.[2] This figure is clearly too generous. Even more conservative British estimates, however, indicate that in many districts more Muslims were enrolled in the Guards than in the Muslim League itself. Any attempt to uncover the role of the people in the creation of Pakistan must therefore consider the Muslim National Guards' history. Before turning to such an analysis it is necessary, however, to set the movement's development within the context of other Indian volunteer organizations in the late colonial era.

I

It was a common sight in the Indian dawn to see young men[3] drilling on the *maidan* of large towns, or marching in singing parties through the labyrinth of tortuous lanes of *mohallas*. Whether drilling with dummy rifles, spades, or lathis, or wearing the red of the Khudai Khidmatgars, the khaki of the Rashtra Seva Dal, the blue of the Majlis Ittehad-i-Millat, or the green of the Muslim Guards, they revealed the proliferation of quasi-paramilitary volunteer organizations.

Their emergence coincided with the rise of fascist movements in troubled inter-war Europe. But the sound and fury of the storm troopers was only a faint whisper in the *mohallas* of India.[4] Its volunteer movements were rooted in the practice of landlords and *rais* employing *goondas* in factional disputes and in the tradition of proficiency in *lathi*-bearing practiced in open spaces and gymnasia by youths and professional wrestlers. Communities and political parties institutionalized the employment of volunteers, as communal conflict increased in India's towns and cities during the early 1920s. Thus the scheduled castes formed the Samata Sainak Dal, whilst the Arv

Samaj established the Arya Vir Dal. Subhas Chandra Bose, the nearest equivalent to a budding Indian Mussolini, set up the Azad Hind Dal of the Forward Bloc following his spat with Gandhi in 1939.

The Rashtriya Swayam Sevak Sangh was a giant amongst these pygmies. It took on an especially fearsome appearance to Muslim minority communities. Significantly, Nawab Siddique Ali Khan and other Muslim National Guards leaders came from the RSS's Nagpur heartland. It is justified, therefore, to slightly digress by considering the RSS's development.

The RSS was founded in the mid-nineteen twenties by Dr Keshav Hedgewar, a Brahmin from the Nagpur district. Hedgewar was profoundly influenced by the militant Shivaji cult which Bal Gangadhar Tilak popularized in the 1890s.[5] The movement's anti-Muslim appearance was reinforced by the patronage it received from such figures as B.S. Moonje, an old supporter of Tilak, and the Hindu Mahasabhite leader, V.D. Savarkar. Hedgewar employed full-time publicists (*pracharaks*) to establish local RSS branches (*shakas*). These consisted of a tightly disciplined corps of physically fit volunteers. The RSS programme included drills, training camps, discussion sessions, and offering of prayers. The RSS ideology was most clearly articulated by Madav Sudashev Golwalker, who became its leader following Hedgewar's premature death. Golwalker published his seminal work, *We, or Our Nationhood Defined*, shortly before the outbreak of the Second World war. It talks of the Hindu Race Spirit, ideal and mission. Its exultation of the Hindu race is accompanied by a contempt for the 'debased and degenerating' Islamic and European civilizations. The idea of a future Hindu state is clearly implied. Non-Hindus are presented with a stark choice of assimilation or complete subordination, 'claiming nothing, deserving no priviliges'.[6]

The activities of the RSS undoubtedly spurred the formation of the Muslim National Guards. But the example of earlier Muslim volunteer movements also played a part. Indeed, recruits were drawn from former Khilafat volunteers and to a lesser extent from the Khaksar movement of Allama Mashriqi.[7]

The Khilafat volunteer corps emerged during the struggle by the 'Young Muslim party' to support the power of the Ottoman Sultan and Caliph at the end of the First World War.[8] By 1920 virtually every Khilafat Committee or Congress branch possessed a volunteer corps. Their membership was predominantly, but by no means exclusively, Muslim. The volunteers policed meetings, escorted political leaders, and picketted liquor shops. Their well organized campaigns in such regions as Bihar[9] eventually forced the British, late in 1921, to ban all volunteer organizations. This was the first of a number of such restrictions.[10]

Allama Mashriqi founded the Khaksar movement at Lahore in April 1931. Thereafter, parades of khaki-clad Khaksars carrying their movement's flag and brandishing their *belchas* (spades) became an everyday spectacle in the city. The latter conveniently served as fearsome weapons when sharpened, as well being put to their intended use to clean gutters as part of the movement's social welfare projects. By 1938, the crusading zeal fuelled by Mashriqi's speeches and publications in the weekly newspapers, *The Radiance*, *Al-Askariat* and the *Iqbal* [11] enabled Khaksar branches to spread from the Punjab to neighbouring Sindh, Balochistan, and the Frontier.[12] Special volunteers known as *janzabes* signed a pledge in their own blood to place their 'life, wealth, and everything else' at the disposal of the central Khaksar organization.

The Khaksars differed immensely from such nineteenth century Muslim reform movements as the Deobandis and the Ahl-i-Hadith in their attitude to the state and the *Shariat*. But they drew on the tradition of self-improvment and disciplined devotion to spiritual excellence which has been termed a 'protestant' form of Islam. The dominant Khaksar beliefs were the need for active struggle to win freedom, and devotion to public service. The latter was vividly demonstrated during the famine which devastated Bengal in 1943, when Khaksars ferried destitutes to the Relief Camps which they had established elsewhere in India.[13] The former resulted in the tragedy of the police firing on the Khaksars in Lahore on 1 March 1940[14] and in the wartime bans and arrest of Mashriqi.[15]

The Khaksars' ideology of Hindu-Muslim unity precluded cooperation with the Muslim League volunteers. Rafiq Sabir's attempt to assassinate Jinnah on 26 July 1943 naturally intensified the Muslim League's aversion to the movement. Mashriqi stridently opposed Pakistan, but to an ever dwindling band of listeners. By 1946, the Khaksars were all dressed up with nowhere to go, even in their Punjabi heartland. Nevertheless, their popularity during the heyday of the late 1930s revealed that a volunteer organization could tap a large reservoir of support amongst the Muslim masses.

II

The growth of the RSS, the Khaksars and other Muslim volunteer organizations challenged the Muslim League to move into this field of activity. The nettle was grasped by the youthful Raja of Mahmudabad, who convened a committee early in 1937 to draft the ground rules for a Muslim League National Guards organization. These combined discipline, truthfulness and social service with a concern to meld together a cohesive Muslim community.[16] The emphasis on self-discipline and socio-political activities carried echoes of Mashriqi's programme, but whilst non-Muslims could join the Khaksars, they could not apply for membership of the Muslim National Guards. Literacy, along with physical fitness, was required of the volunteers. The minimum age for membership was 15, compared with 12 for the RSS. Disciplinary procedures owed in fact more to the kindergarten than the Army. Miscreants would be punished for minor misdemeanors by fines and the wearing of arm bands with the word 'defaulter' or 'punished' emblazoned on them. Summary dismissal was the sanction for more serious offences. Other subjects covered in the exhaustive aims and objectives drafted by Mahmudabad included the establishment of a Muslim National Guards Fund, details of rank and uniform and regulations for Staff conferences, and finally the proposal for an 'in-house' newspaper which was to be entitled *Amal.*

The Muslim League spared a little time at its historic October 1937 Lucknow session to ratify the aims and objectives. Perspicacious as the delegates no doubt were, they could not foresee the rapid deterioration in the communal situation. This shifted the Guards' emphasis from social welfare to protection activities. It also convinced the Working Committee of the All-India Muslim League that the Muslim volunteers should be tied more firmly to its leading strings. Thus a new constitution was drawn up in 1940, which stated unequivocally that the aims and objectives of the Muslim National Guards were identical to those of the All-India Muslim League. This was not, however, the final word on the matter, for in May 1944 the Council of Action of the AIML fine-tuned the Guards' constitution once more. It now emphasized the organization's role in the social and physical development of Muslims, and in creating a spirit of self sacrifice and service. The Muslim volunteers were called upon not only to organize public meetings and processions, but to perform duties of self defence, and in particular to render all kinds of services in case of 'natural calamities, or government pressures'.[17] A renewed emphasis was simultaneously placed on volunteers wearing uniform, and attending the mosque and monthly flag salutation ceremonies.

Siddique Ali Khan, who became the new Commander-in-Chief, provides in his autobiography a brief but illuminating insight into the Muslim National Guards during the final stage of the Pakistan struggle. He possessed both the physical and political credentials for the task of reorganizing the movement. Although a political lightweight, he was likeable and immensely devoted both to Jinnah and Nawabzada Liaquat Ali Khan. He had represented the Muslim League in the Central Legislative Assembly in the early 1930s. His Nagpur background and the personal tragedy of his father's death in a communal riot alerted him to the dangers posed by the RSS. He had been taught wrestling, archery, and shooting on the family estate. He had also developed his physique playing both hockey and cricket at school. Indeed, he acquired an enthusiasm for the latter pastime which he sustained into adulthood.

Siddique Ali Khan provides useful insights both into the organizational structure and the activities of the Muslim National Guards. What is of particular interest concerning the former is the extent to which 'civilian' control was built into it. Thus he could only nominate Provincial Commanders on the recommendation of its Muslim League President. The Provincial League's Action Committee was similarly empowered in the selection of district and city level leaders.[18] These safeguards were intended to ensure that the Muslim League had not created a frankenstein monster. Nevertheless, there were isolated instances of rivalries between the Muslim volunteers and the parent organization. In the Amraoti district of the Central Provinces, one section of the Muslim National Guards acted independently of the Muslim League organization and code of conduct.[19] In Delhi, Muslim National Guards set up rival *mohalla* committees to the City Muslim League, and formed their own publicity and propaganda department.[20] Similar rivalries were reported from Broach and Godhra in the Bombay Province.[21]

According to Siddique Ali Khan, the largest contingent of Muslim National Guards came from Bengal. He supplies a membership figure of 300,000 but does not indicate the year for which this applies. British records seem to tell a rather different story. They reckon an All-India membership of just 118,152 in February 1947.[22] An Intelligence Bureau report of August 1940, moreover, assigns a figure of just 4,000 Guardsmen in Bengal, with Bihar leading the way with a membership of just two-and-a-half times this number.[23] It should not, however, be automatically assumed that the British figures are more accurate. Serious discrepancies exist between the numbers quoted in the Provincial Fortnightly Reports and those compiled at the All-India level. It is a well known fact that the CID's efficiency sharply declined in a number of provinces by the end of the Second World War. Furthermore, the 1939 Intelligence Bureau report itself admitted that for such provinces as Bihar, 'reliable statistics are not available'.[24] All that can be said in the absence of sufficient data is that

British figures undoubtedly underestimate the strength of the movement, whilst Siddique Ali Khan probably exaggerates it.

The worsening communal situation in 1946-7 indisputably encouraged a mushrooming of support for the Muslim National Guards. Twenty-two branches were established in the Central Provinces during the second half of 1946. A similar advance was reported from Lucknow, Aligarh, Muzaffarnagar, Bareilly and Cawnpore in the United Provinces.[25] Maulvi Latifur Rahman, President, Orissa Muslim League, cited the 'present communal tension' while advocating the formation of a Muslim National Guards organization at a League Working Committee meeting in Cuttack on 27 October 1946.[26] Bombay and Bihar also witnessed increased National Guards activity following serious communal disturbances late in 1946 which claimed many Muslim victims.

Sizable Muslim volunteer corps were established in Muzaffarpur and Champaran in Bihar in January 1947.[27] Shortly afterwards, the publicity officer for the Bihar Guards appealed for mass enlistment and asked each district to send three volunteers to Phulwari Sharif for training.[28] Further efforts to strengthen the Guards' presence involved sending students into the villages to drum up support, and the wooing of Khaksars. Following the serious disturbances in November 1946, a number of local units were also established in Bombay Province. The ball was set rolling with a successful Muslim National Guards conference, held in January 1947 at the textile finishing centre of Broach City.[29] This was followed up by a tub thumping tour of the Surat district by local Muslim League and National Guard leaders.[30]

The Muslim National Guards marched indefatigably into Princely India, where communal tensions were also increasing. Volunteers began to be enlisted in Bharatpur in April 1946. Sufficient progress had been made within two months to provide a procession of over 200 Guardsmen armed with *lathis* and swords to lend muscle to a Muslim conference held within the State.[31] A unit of the Muslim National Guards was formed in the town of Ujjain in Gwalior State following riots there in

November 1946.[32] Some of its members were drawn from a volunteer force which had been active in the locality at the beginning of the decade.[33] When the RSS stepped up its activity in the State in May 1947, Muslim volunteers responded by parading at such places as Bhilsa, Guna and Mornea. By the eve of the British departure from the subcontinent, even such tiny States as Nandgaon in eastern India could boast their own Muslim volunteer units.[34]

Unfortunately, neither Siddique Ali Khan nor colonial sources provide more than fragmentary evidence on the Muslim National Guards' membership. Evidence pieced together from British reports indicate, however, that a wide range of individuals was recruited. Intelligence Bureau investigations reveal, for example, that drill instructors were drawn from such varied backgrounds as University Training Corps, the Police, the Army, and the Khaksars.[35] A letter written by the Bengali Muslim Leaguer, M.A.H. Ispahani, to Jinnah in March 1940 strengthens this insight. It incidently includes information on the Belguam Corps, which clearly numbered in its ranks, technicians, college students, traders, clerks and even mill-hands.[36]

Evidence is easier to come by on the Muslim National Guards' training and activities. Training camps were less lavish than either those of the Khaksars or the RSS.[37] The Guards were volunteers and had to organize time off work to attend them. Much time was taken up with drilling in order to improve physical fitness and instill discipline and *esprit de corps*. Guards were trained in club-handling and exercised with dummy rifles. During the exceptionally tense period of May 1947, illegal training with live ammunition was given in some camps in the western districts of the United Provinces.[38]

In the early 1940s, the Guards' activities consisted mainly of crowd control and ceremonial duties. They formed guards of honour at rallies, escorted speakers, and unfurled the Muslim League flag. These concerns gave way to the relief of refugees and the protection of Muslim lives and property in the communally disturbed period at the close of the Second World War. It is here that the paucity of the data on the composition of the Guards is especially frustrating, as it is impossible to ascertain whether these circumstances led to a new breed of tougher and lower class recruit. The Muslim National Guards were also increasingly involved in popularizing the Pakistan message. Finally, as we have noted in the preceding chapter, they played an important role in the direct action campaigns in the Frontier and Punjab.

Siddique Ali Khan gives a graphic account of his men's involvement in both propaganda and relief work activities. He recalls that in order to popularize the Pakistan demand, the Nagpur Muslim National Guards sent out a group of 'eleven, tough, crazy cyclists' under the 'enthusiastic, brave and sincere' leadership of Abdul Hamid Khan Ghanvi. 'It is quite obvious', he avers, 'that the spirit of self sacrifice and hard work of these people gave a very good name to the Muslim League, and its name reached the houses where previously people talked of nothing but the local landlord, lack of rains, land taxes, cattle diseases, festivals and marriages. But now in every house, people talked of Mr Jinnah and the Muslim League.'[9] The romanticized image of cycling the dusty village lanes of Nagpur to spread the Muslim League word must be juxtaposed, however, with the scene which Siddique Ali Khan portrays on the preceding page.

> They (the Muslim volunteers) rendered services to this extent, that when in the district of Kulab in Bombay, the Hindus began to set Muslim houses on fire and killed Muslims, the Muslim National Guards discovered and removed corpses which had been decaying for four to five days. They removed the dead bodies with their own hands, dug graves and buried them.[40]

Such actions became all too common in the dying days of the Raj. Volunteers protected Muslims who were injured in the clashes which disfigured Jabbulpore in the Central Provinces in May 1947.[41] They also helped in relief work during the disturbances which simultaneously swept the Gurgaon district of the Punjab.[42] Muslim National Guardsmen ran many of the refugee camps which were established in Bihar following the communal massacres of late Autumn 1946. They also organized the defence of beleaguered Muslim localities. Night-time patrols by steel helmeted National Guardsmen had become commonplace in Bombay, Delhi and elsewhere in North India by the beginning of 1947.[43] Indeed, when the Unionist Ministry raided the Muslim National Guards' headquarters in Lahore on 24 January 1947, thereby precipitating the direct action campaign which led to its downfall, over a thousand steel helmets were taken away by the police.

The question inevitably arises whether the Muslim National Guards instigated the mounting violence, or merely responded to it. Punjabi Hindus and Sikhs charged them with responsibility for the vicious 'communal war of succession' which began in the province as early as March 1947. Congressmen in both the Frontier and Assam maintained that Muslim National Guards intimidated voters during the referenda campaigns on the Pakistan issue in June 1947. Investigations by the Muslim governor of Assam failed to find evidence to substantiate these claims concerning the voting in Sylhet.[44] But the final Muslim League meeting in Peshawar on the eve of the ballot was hardly held in a tea-party atmosphere. The prominent contingent of Muslim National Guards discharged volleys of shots into the evening air and tore up the Congress flag.[45] It could, of course be argued that Pathans do not frighten that easily.

The British authorities in the Punjab were, however, growing increasingly concerned about the threat to public order posed by the Muslim National Guards. Whilst the Unionist Premier was attending the Paris Peace Conference, the new Governor, Sir Evan Jenkins, pushed through the Punjab Public Safety Ordinance which banned drilling and parading in uniform in public. He later encouraged Khizr to ban both the Muslim National Guards[46] and the RSS.

Liaquat Ali Khan protested strongly to the Viceroy about this. He maintained during the course of an interview with Wavell that there was no similarity between the Muslim National Guards and the RSS. He reiterated that the Muslim National Guards' aims were entirely peaceful and were limited to the organization and management of political meetings. He further

retorted that the Muslim equivalent of the RSS was not the
Guards but the Khaksars.[47] Liaquat, who by now had become
the Guards' main patron within the AIML, was being slightly
disingenuous, as their actions had moved far beyond this original
aim. Nevertheless, it was only after the Unionists repressed them
that the Guards became involved in illegal activities. They
stockpiled weapons, some of which were distributed to the
beleaguered Meos of Gurgaon.[48] Under the leadership of Major
Khurshid Anwar, Siddique's second in command, they blew
up bridges and railway lines during the civil disobedience
campaign.[49] The Punjab Muslim National Guards were not,
however, involved in communal 'mischief-making' until the
very eve of Partition, despite the general atmosphere of hatred
and the collapse of the administration.[50]

An analysis which concentrates solely on the culpability of
the Muslim National Guards in the communal violence of the
Partition period is, however, rather self-limiting. Besides which,
it is questionable whether the historian's role is to apportion
blame. It is in fact far more interesting to ask the question what
was the symbolic significance of the Muslim volunteers activity?
This concluding section of the chapter will address a few remarks
to the question.

III

The original role assigned to the Muslim National Guards was
the maintenance of order during the Muslim League's
utilization of 'public' space to demonstrate the existence of a
'Muslim' community with its separate political interests.
Detachments of Muslim volunteers accompanied and marshalled
the huge crowds which attended the processions of Jinnah and
other high-ranking League officials. Such events, as we have
noted earlier, recalled Mughal court ceremonial. The Muslim
National Guards indeed acted as the modern day equivalents
of the *yassawals* and the uniformed soldiery which preceded
the Emperor. The mace-bearing *yassawals'* role was to clear

the streets and ensure that the shops and doors of houses on the route of the royal procession were suitably decorated. The uniformed soldiery provided the Emperor's escort. Their fearsome weapons and fine apparel reflected the ruler's power and wealth. Echoes of this past can be discerned in the Guardsmen's ceremonial. Mounted officers accompanied the motorcades of the Muslim League. Detachments of the ordinary volunteers marched resplendent in their khaki and green uniforms, or stood silently to attention at important places along the route. The *Star of India* provides a colourful account of this ceremonial in its report of Jinnah's arrival in Patna on 24 December 1938 to attend the annual Muslim League Session. The Quaid-i-Azam proceeded into the city from the station in a decorated car, 'thousands of volunteers on foot and horseback …with drawn swords escorted the President's car', the paper recounts, 'while cyclist guards who had arrived from Nagpur and other guards from Sindh and Delhi under generals Zafar Hussain, Yusuf Hasan and Muhammad Hasan in beautiful green uniforms were most conspicuous.'[51] The Mughal connotations of such actions were surely not lost on all of the onlookers.

If the assembled Guardsmen did not summon up Mughal glories, they undoubtedly physically manifested Jinnah's contemporary clarion call for 'unity, faith and discipline'. This was not just a catchy slogan, but arose from the tradition established by nineteenth century reformers, and which Muhammad Iqbal popularized, that self-discipline was essential for the assertion of communal solidarity under the conditions of colonial rule.[52] For Iqbal, personal Islamic self-realization and transformation could be powerfully aided by public symbolic cultural expression. The Muslim National Guards' flag salutation and uniform itself in fact carried symbolic significance. The uniform contained a deeper meaning than the 'surface' show of smartness and discipline. It also epitomized a commitment to a sense of Islamic community which transcended loyalties to particularist identities. Turbans, caps and clothes which bespoke of regional or *biraderi* allegiances were replaced by the common uniform and Jinnah cap of the Muslim volunteer. Siddique Ali

Khan significantly informs us that at the same time as a new
emphasis was placed on Muslim National Guardsmen attending
Friday prayers,

> *Nawab Mohammad Ismail Khan Sahib nay, bahaysiat-e-Sadar, U.P.*
> *Muslim League, yay kar dia tha kay subai Muslim League ki majlis-*
> *e-amal ka har rukan uniform pahn kar majlis-e-amal mein sharik*
> *hua karay.*

Nawab Mohammad Ismail Khan Sahib had made it a rule, as the
President of the U.P. Muslim League, that members of the
Provincial Muslim League Action Committee (who were also
members of the Muslim National Guards) will attend its meetings
wearing the uniform.[53]

The uniforms helped to dramatize the Muslim League's
commitment to a uniformity among the populace which was
free of the UP's well known sectarian divisions. It also sought
to transcend the 'tribal' groupings of the Frontier or the Punjab.
The Guards' de-particularization of identity reflected the goal
of a new Muslim citizen of Pakistan, bereft of local affiliation.
Social cohesion was to be underpinned by attachment to
national symbols which were themselves rooted in Islamic
awareness.

Flag salutations significantly formed an increasingly important
part of Muslim League ceremonial. Four hundred Muslim
National Guards, for example, attended a Pakistan Day flag
salutation in Poona in 1947.[54] The green Muslim League flag
with its Islamic crescent had been unfurled for the first time at
the same Lucknow League Session which had ratified the
proposal for a volunteer movement. Its adoption symbolically
rejected the Congress's claim to represent all the Indian
communities, as reflected by its own tri-colour flag.[55] When
the League flag was flown over meeting places and government
buildings it stated a claim to sovereignty.

The formation of a guard of honour at the unfurling of the
flag on such 'public' occasions as Pakistan Day or Jinnah or
Iqbal Day, borrowed heavily from British ceremonial. Muslim

National Guardsmen were the equivalent of the Black Watch when it was the Union Jack which was being hoisted. But it was not merely a cheap imitation of British power that was on offer. This is clearly brought out by the following description of a flag-hoisting ceremony performed on the *maidan* at Patna at the time of the 1938 League Session.

> The flag-hoisting ceremony was performed by Mr M.A. Jinnah at 12:30 p.m. in the presence of about 50,000 Muslims at the main gate of the *pandal*....Mr Jinnah, with Miss Jinnah, Syed Abdul Aziz and Mr Shareef, arrived at the *pandal* escorted by magnificently uniformed body guards with drawn swords. The party was greeted with cries of 'Allah-o-Akbar', 'Jinnah Zindabad', 'Muslim League Zindabad'. Mr Jinnah first inspected the Guard of Honour formed by the National Guard, representing different provinces and districts. Qari Syed Zahir Ahmad recited a verse from the Holy Koran, and Mr Muhammad Hanif sang most melodiously Dr Sir Muhammad Iqbal's national anthem, *Chin-o-Arab Hamara*, which visibly moved all hearts and many eyes to tears. Mr Jinnah then hoisted the beautiful green Crescent–Star flag amidst cries of 'Allah-Akbar'. Mr Muhammad Hanif of Allahabad sang the flag salutation song, *Purcham Rahey Buland Hamara* (May our flag fly high) in chorus.[56]

The ceremony was intended to affirm the Muslim League's claim on the loyalties of individual Muslims as a result of the Pakistan 'national' ideology. Those who saluted the flag demonstrated their 'citizenship' of Pakistan, although the Muslim state had yet to achieve its fulfillment. The enactment was of itself, however, believed to hasten the actualization of the Pakistan ideal.

Historians have surprisingly paid little attention to this ceremonial. Yet it was an important symbolic underpinning of the freedom movement. This was spelled out by Jinnah himself following the Patna flag-salutation ceremony. 'By inviting me to hoist this flag of Islam, you have done me the greatest honour', he told the packed crowd. 'This is the flag of the Muslim League. It means that all Muslims should rally under it. When Muslims will be united under the flag of Islam, no earthly power will defeat them. Victory and success will be theirs. Let every Muslim come under this flag and realize the mission of Islam in the world.'[57]

Jinnah was always at pains to link the Muslim League flag with the flag of Islam. This was a constant theme of his public addresses.[58] Indeed, he openly disagreed with the Punjab Premier, Sikander, on this issue at a flag hoisting ceremony at Bombay early in June 1938. Sikander had compared the flag to an army's regimental colours and had said that every regiment had its own standard besides having a common flag. Sikander had continued to argue that there was, therefore, no reason why the various political parties in India should not have their own individual flags, in addition to a common flag. The Premier went on to lament the failure to agree upon a national flag, and to recall that all party flags in the Punjab were accorded equal respect, although, as 'party' insignia, they could not be flown over public buildings.

Sikander had hardly finished his remarks before Jinnah snapped back that the League flag was not a 'new' flag. It had, he declared, been given to them by the Prophet. The 'disorganization' among the Muslims made them forget their own flag, but a 'new awakening' had come about, which had kept the flag afloat. No 'power on earth' could bring their flag down, which was there to 'demonstrate to the world that the Muslims were united.'[59] Both speakers' attitude to the flag reflected, of course, their underlying conception of Muslim 'community'.

The symbolism of flag salutation exercised a powerful emotional effect on onlookers. 'Quaid took his seat,' Begum Ikramullah writes in her autobiography of another occasion, 'and Maulana Akram stepped forward and read the verses from the Koran in a voice charged with emotion, and then the League flag, white crescent and stars on a green ground, was unfurled, and the strains of the popular song, 'This moon is not one that shall ever remain in eclipse', floated in the air. The crowd took up the refrain.'[60]

IV

A speaker at a public meeting in Hyderabad (Sindh) on 4 July 1947 hailed the Muslim National Guards as the 'sepoys of Islam'.[61] Siddique Ali Khan recalls that at a time when Indian politics was a 'life of battle', the *salars* of the Guards served with 'devotion' and 'zeal'. With the passage of time, they played a variety of roles in addition to their original duty of maintaining order in public meetings. In Bengal, a Muslim National Guard ambulance brigade was established under the supervision of qualified doctors and nurses.[62] The Ajmer corps assisted the throng of pilgrims proceeding to the leading Sufi shrine of Hazrat Moinuddin Chishti.[63] More usually, Muslim National Guardsmen were involved in popularizing the Pakistan message, perhaps with decisive effect during the June 1947 referenda.[64]

The growth of the Muslim National Guards in such regions as the Punjab both reflected and contributed to the growing communal polarization. Their presence undoubtedly reassured beleaguered Muslim minorities at the height of the riots which soured India's pathway to freedom. The relationship between some local Muslim League branches and the Muslim corps was ambivalent. This fact and the issue of the Muslim National Guards' culpability in communal violence partly explains their historical neglect. Yet any movement which claimed upwards of a million members cannot be treated as inconsequential. It was, however, not just the numbers of the Muslim volunteers which lend them importance. The Muslim National Guards in fact provide valuable clues to the cultural definition of power and its symbolic 'representation' during the freedom struggle.

The Muslim volunteers symbolized the self-disciplined commitment to Muslim 'community' which Iqbal claimed was the key to Islamic fulfillment in India, but the underlying significance of their role does not stop there. It may be argued that the student volunteers from Aligarh and Lahore more clearly understood Iqbal's philosophy of the power of Islam in individual lives bringing about the community transformation upon which the foundations of the Pakistan State should be laid. It could also be maintained that the sufis were more appropriate models of the realization of Islamic principles in the north Indian countryside. But the Muslim volunteers were the group most closely associated with the public power of symbols which focused on the state as both the expression and guarantor of the cultural identity of the Indian Muslims. This was demonstrated most vividly in their role at flag salutation ceremonies. The Muslim National Guards both embodied the tradition of active devotion to Islam and provided the outward political trappings of a Pakistan State. It has been largely lost to historians, but the Muslim volunteers were as much a symbolic underpinning of Pakistani 'nationalism' as the new flag and anthem which also emerged at the Lucknow Session.

The Guards' 'life of battle', which stood in such marked contrast to the Muslim League's traditional 'calling card' politics, provides further glimpses into the freedom struggle as seen from the 'bottom up.' It reveals the devotion, sincerity and above all the emotion which countless Muslims invested in the freedom struggle.

The Muslim National Guards' symbolic identification with Pakistani 'nationalism' exerted its greatest impact in the urban milieu of north India. The material conditions of communal competition and the intellectual background of reformist Islam popularized through a vibrant press, created a wide audience for their message. This situation was in marked contrast to the countryside, where kin-based communities predominated. Significantly, a Muslim volunteer movement never struck deep roots in the rural areas of the Punjab, Sindh or the Frontier. The Muslim League message in these areas was mediated through the different idiom of the *piri-mureedi* relationship. The role of popular participation in the Pakistan movement in the vastly different environment of the rural West Punjab will form the focus of our next chapter.

NOTES

[1] For a brief background on the Ahrar and the Shahidganj agitation, *see*, D. Gilmartin, *Empire and Islam. Punjab and the Making of Pakistan* (Berkeley, 1988), p. 96 & ff.

[2] Siddique Ali Khan, *Be Tegh Sipahi* (Lahore, 1971), p. 236.

[3] Whilst the overwhelming majority of volunteers were young men, women and even children were also involved. The Azad Hind Dal, for example, which was organized by Subhas Chandra Bose as the paramilitary arm of the Forward Bloc, boasted a Bala Sena for children and a Laksmi Pathak organization for women.

[4] Fascist influence was more evident in the extra-parliamentary parties which grew up in the Middle East. The most extreme example was the Syrian Social Nationalist party whose leader, Antun Saada, was known as *al-zaim* (the Fuhrer) and whose party anthem, 'Syria, Syria, uber alles', was sung to the same tune as the German national anthem. M.E. Yapp, *The Near East Since the First World War* (Harlow, 1991), p. 113.

[5] For details, *see*, R.L. Cashman, *The Myth of Lokamanya: Tilak and Mass Politics in Maharashtra* (Berkeley, 1975), pp. 98-122.

[6] M.S. Golwalker, *We, or Our Nationhood Defined* (Nagpur, 1939).

[7] Allama Inayatullah Khan Mashriqi (1888-1963) was born in Amritsar. After a brilliant academic career, he joined the Indian Educational Service. He quit this in 1919 to involve himself in nationalist politics. In 1931 he founded the Khaksar movement. This was a disciplined volunteer movement of largely lower-middle-class Muslims. Khaki-clad Khaksars drilled with spades and engaged in social welfare activities. Mashriqi is an extremely complex and controversial personality. His British and Unionist opponents dubbed him a fascist and a megalomaniac. The extent to which Mashriqi may have been inspired by Hitler's storm-trooper movement following a meeting between them in Berlin in the mid-1920s still remains open to question.

[8] For a brief study of the Khilafat volunteers which places them within the wider context of the Khilafat campaign, *see*, G. Minault, *The Khilafat Movement: Religious Symbolism and Political Mobilization in India* (New York, 1982).

[9] Ibid., 164-6.

[10] In August 1940 under the Defence of India rules, the British prohibited the performance of drill 'of a military nature' and the wearing of uniforms by volunteers which resembled, in colour, police or military dress. A further order issued in 1944 required 'political' and 'communal' organizations to seek the permission of the District Magistrate before holding camps and parades, whether in public or in private.

[11] *The Radiance* was published in Aligarh, *Al-Askariat* was produced in Lucknow, and the *Iqbal* in Rawalpindi.

[12] I.H. Malik, *Sikander Hayat Khan. A Political Biography* (Islamabad, 1985), p. 65.

[13] The Khaksar Movement. File 28/5/43–Poll (I) & KW, NAI.

[14] For an emotional account of the incident, *see*, A. Ata, *Kutch Shikasta Dastani, Kutch Pareshan Tazkarey* (Lahore, 1966), p. 220 & ff.

[15] A Mashriqi Day was held on 2 May 1941 to secure his release, but the government only finally acted in January 1942. Malik, op. cit., p. 73.

[16] Muslim League National Guards. F. 762 Quaid-e-Azam Papers. IOR, Microfilm Pos 10791.

[17] Quoted in Siddique Ali Khan, op. cit., p. 233 & ff.

[18] Siddique Ali Khan, op. cit., p. 231.

[19] Central Provinces Fortnightly Report, 1st Half of May 1947, L/P&J/5/196, IOR.

[20] Chief Commissioner Delhi Fortnightly Report, 2nd Half of May 1947, L/P&J/5/287, IOR.

[21] The dispute at Broach centred over whether the National Guards should campaign for Muslim League candidates in the Local Board elections of February 1947. The tensions at Godhra resulted in the dissolution of the National Guards' branch and fresh enrolment. The new recruits had to swear allegiance to a committee of five persons which included representatives of the City Muslim League. Bombay Fortnightly Report 2nd Half of April 1947, L/P&J/5/168, IOR.

[22] Political Organizations and Private Armies. File 333/47/P/l9, Appendix B.2. High Commissioner and Consular Archives India 1947, Do. 133.58, PRO.

[23] Volunteer Organizations and Volunteer Movements, Intelligence Bureau report 23 August 1940, L/P&J/8/678, PJ., Coll 117/c81, IOR.

[24] Volunteer Organizations and Volunteer Movements, Intelligence Bureau Report for the 2nd half of 1939, L/P&J/8/678, PJ. Coll 117/C81, IOR.

[25] There was almost constant communal violence in Allahabad and a large number of Muslims were killed in a serious affray at Garhmuktesar. United Provinces Fortnightly Report 1st Half of November 1946, L/P&J/5/257, IOR.

[26] Orissa Fortnightly Report 2nd Half of October 1946, L/P&J/5/236, IOR.

[27] There were 400 members in Muzaffarpur and over 100 in Champaran. Bihar Fortnightly Report 1st half of January 1947, L/P&J/5/182, IOR.

[28] Bihar Fortnightly Report 1st Half of April 1947, L/P&J/5/182, IOR.

[29] Bombay Fortnightly Report 2nd Half of January 1947, L/P&J/5/168, IOR.

[30] Bombay Fortnightly Report 2nd Half of April 1947, L/P&J/5/168, IOR.

[31] Rajputana Agency Fortnightly Report 15 July 1946, L/P&S/13/1442, IOR.

[32] Gwalior Residency Fortnightly Report 14 February 1947, L/P&S/13.197, file 5, IOR.

[33] Gwalior Residency Fortnightly Report 2nd Half of July 1940, L/P&S/13/197, file 5, IOR.

[34] The Muslim merchants of Rajnandgaon had organized a 50-strong corps in Nandgaon State by February 1947. Chattisgarh States Agency Fortnightly Report 2nd Half of February 1947, L/P&S/13/962, IOR.

[35] Volunteer Organizations and Volunteer Movements Intelligence Bureau Report 23 August 1940, L/P&J/8/678, PJ Coll. 117/C81, IOR.

[36] Ispahani to Jinnah 15 March 1940, Muslim League National Guards F. 762, Quaid-e-Azam Papers. IOR Microfilm Pos 10791.

[37] Over 6,000 RSS volunteers attended a training camp in the Nagpur district in April 1947. A hundred tents were pitched and 'all the paraphernalia of a military camp was maintained, for example, bugle calls, guards'. Central Provinces Fortnightly Report 2nd Half of April 1947, L/P&J/5/196, IOR.

[38] United Provinces Fortnightly Report 2nd Half of May 1947, L/P&J/5/276, IOR.

[39] Siddique Ali Khan, op. cit., p. 235.

[40] Siddique Ali Khan, op. cit., pp. 233-34.

[41] Central Provinces Fortnightly Report 2nd Half of May 1947, L/P&J/5/196, IOR.

[42] Chief Commissioner Delhi Fortnightly Report 2nd Half of June 1947, L/P&J/5/287, IOR.

[43] Chief Commissioner Delhi Fortnightly Report 2nd Half of March 1947, L/P&J/5/287, IOR; Bombay Fortnightly Report 2nd Half of April 1947, L/P&J/5/168, IOR.

[44] Sir Muhammad Saleh Akbar Hydari to Nehru, Telegram, 14 July 1947, *Transfer of Power*, xii, p. 156.

[45] Governor of the North-West Frontier to the Viceroy, 21 June 1947, R/3/1/151, IOR.

[46] Jenkins to Wavell, 26 January 1947, *Transfer of Power*, ix, p. 558.

[47] Wavell interview with Liaquat Ali Khan, 27 January 1947, *Transfer of Power*, ix, p. 563.

[48] Chief Commissioner Delhi Fortnightly Report 2nd Half of June 1947, L/P&J/5/287, IOR.

[49] E. Jansson, *India, Pakistan or Pakhtunistan? The Nationalist Movements in the North-West Frontier Province 1937-47* (Uppsala, 1981), p. 196 & ff.

[50] Jenkins to Mountbatten, Telegram, 12 August 1947, R/3/1/171, IOR.

[51] Star of India (Calcutta), 24 December 1938, quoted in Waheed Ahmad (ed.) *Quaid-i-Azam Mohammad Ali Jinnah: The Nation's Voice Towards Consolidation. Speeches and Statements, March 1935–March 1940* (Karachi, 1992), p. 320.

[52] Iqbal built on this tradition to eventually come to the understanding that Islamic 'community' depended on the discipline and Islamic worth of

'self-concentrated' individuals. M. Iqbal, *The Reconstruction of Religious Thought in Islam* (Lahore, 1971), p. 146 & ff.

[53] Siddique Ali Khan, op. cit., p. 235.

[54] Bombay Fortnightly Report, 2nd Half of April 1947, L/P&J/5/168, IOR.

[55] This of course included saffron for the Hindus, green for the Muslims, and white for the other minorities.

[56] Waheed Ahmad, op. cit., p. 321.

[57] Waheed Ahmad, op. cit., p. 321.

[58] *See*, for example, his speeches at Gaya, 11 January 1938; Bijnor, 23 October 1937; Patna, 24 December 1938. Waheed Ahmad, op. cit., pp. 221, 183, 321.

[59] Waheed Ahmad, op. cit., p. 261.

[60] Begum Ikramullah, *From Purdah to Parliament* (London, 1963), p. 108.

[61] Sindh Fortnightly Report, 1st Half of July 1947, L/P&J/5/263, IOR.

[62] Siddique Ali Khan, op. cit., p. 236.

[63] Chief Commissioner Delhi and Ajmer Fortnightly Report 2nd Half of May 1947, L/P&J/5/287, IOR.

[64] *See*, for example, Siddique Ali Khan, op. cit., p. 237 & ff.

[65] *See*, Gilmartin, op. cit., p. 208 & ff.

Chapter 3

Popular Participation in the Pakistan Struggle

Muslim Politics in the Punjab 1944–46

Historians have largely neglected popular participation and initiatives in the Pakistan struggle. Most scholars at first focused on constitutional negotiations at the rarefied All-India level of politics. More recently, scholars have been sceptical of such an approach, however, and have turned their attention to the provinces. Nevertheless, their writings have still centred on the activities of factional leaders. They have side-stepped the issues of how their followers understood the Pakistan demand and why they responded to it. Such accounts assume that clients almost automatically followed the lead of their patrons.

This understanding achieved its baldest statement in the work of the Manchester-based political scientist, Hamza Alavi. 'The reason for the decision of the provincial magnates to accept the Muslim League label is (not) obvious', he maintains. 'It was not the vote-pulling power of the League, for it was the landed magnates themselves who controlled the mainly rural vote.'[1] This view of course reduces the Muslim masses to the role of passive observers rather than active participants in the making of history.

This chapter seeks to question this interpretation. It aims to discover whether pressures from 'beneath' influenced either the political choices of faction leaders, or the methods by which the Muslim League transmitted information about its Pakistan demand. Muslim political mobilization in the rural Punjab will form the focus for this analysis. This is an area which has been the subject of considerable recent research and which possesses a wider historical significance because of its key importance to the Pakistan struggle. The examination will in particular centre around the tussle for power between the Unionist Party and the Muslim League in the period 1944-6. We shall turn first, however, to a brief characterization of the distribution of political and economic power within the local community.

I

It is important to acknowledge at the outset that there were considerable variations in the Muslim landholding and social structure within the Punjab. The further the historian delves into conditions at the village level, the more highly localized these appear. The established pattern of interpretation still holds good, however, that society in the East Punjab was 'flatter' than in the West. When considering political mobilization, there has been a tendency to assume a uniformity of social structure which clearly did not exist. This has underestimated the importance of the role of the collective context in political activity.

It is well known that Muslim rural society in the West Punjab was extremely complex and highly segmented. In the southwestern areas, many Punjabis led a pastoral existence in which village communities were largely absent. Social and economic power was wielded by a heterogeneous cluster of dominant landed elites. Local politics revolved around factional struggles for control of economic resources. The special nature of religious influence in the West Punjab has also been carefully examined by such writers as David Gilmartin and myself.[2] We have both assumed that the religious influence of the *pirs* and *sajjada nashins* reinforced the power of the landed elites. For the purposes of this study, however, the angle of perspective will be on their ability to embody individual commitment to the political demands of the Muslim community which transcended the factional rivalries of the leading magnates. This made them indispensible to the Pakistan movement in the rural areas, as it enabled it to aquire a mass orientation.

There were other groups within the locality who were also capable of generating popular responses and initiatives independently of the landowners. These included village elders, *hajis*, retired soldiers, schoolmasters and students. Ex-servicemen were particularly important politically because of the respect in which they were held and the fact that they were enfranchised. Literate individuals were also significant 'opinion formers' within the community because they read aloud to the vast majority of the unlettered the reports of 'public events' contained in vernacular newspapers and party pamphlets. Students from Punjabi colleges and as far afield as Aligarh flooded the countryside with Muslim League propaganda during the vital 1946 election campaign.

It should thus be clear that even in the West Punjab, power relationships based on land ownership had to compete with other sources of political influence. Moreover, the 'crisis' situation of 1946, which required Muslims to forget their internal differences, allowed for the exercise of power by those who stood outside the hierarchical pattern of influence. To understand political mobilization at this juncture as solely a 'top down' process is therefore a gross over-simplification.

Nevertheless, the Pakistan movement did not entirely displace or proceed without reference to traditional patterns of rural influence. It expanded into the Punjab countryside by tying itself into the extensive network of local factions.[3] Despite its commitment to a community based on faith, it worked through *biraderi* loyalties.[4] The flow of influence was naturally not one-way. The impact of the larger cultural and political issues brought by the League altered long-standing factional alignments in some localities.[5] The Muslim League's accommodation to rural realities meant that there was still a place for mobilization around factional loyalties. This type of politics has been evident in Pakistan's elections since independence, but we should not as a result deny the fact that in 1946 popular mobilization occurred

on a scale never previously witnessed in the Punjab. This made
the creation of Pakistan inevitable, but did not sweep away the
local structure of political power, because the Muslim League
lacked the rural organization to institutionalize this support.[6]

Thus, to sum up, even in the West Punjab, the relations of
power based on economic dependence were not the only factor
in popular mobilization. Authority based on notions of respect
was exercised by a range of individuals within the locality. In
certain contexts, a different kind of authority than that based
on economic wealth could come into play. The crisis of the
1946 elections was particularly likely to result in popular
initiative and participation. We shall now turn briefly to the
background of this case study of Muslim political mobilization.

II

The nature of the Unionist Party and its success in the 1937
Punjab elections has now been well established by historians.[7]
The reason why the Muslim League was no more than an urban
phenomenon has also been a subject for scholarly analysis. What
I should like to emphasize here is that despite the Unionist
Party's stance as the champion of the 'backward' agriculturalists,
it never achieved a mass base of political support. It owed its
success in 1937 to strategic local factional alliances.[8] Not all
Unionist leaders, of course, accepted this situation. Chhotu
Ram, the leading Hindu Jat politician, encouraged the
formation of district-wide Zamindara Leagues based on the
political organization he had founded in his own Rohtak region
in the 1920s.[9] But this attempt to bring about popular
participation met with little success. The Zamindara Leagues
were either captured by local landlord factions or failed to survive
at all. This represented a missed opportunity for the Unionists,
particularly as the legislation which they introduced in 1938 to
curb the problem of rural indebtedness was popular with both
the large landowners and the peasant proprietors.[10] Early in
September, over one and a half *lakh* agriculturalists attended

the Zamindara Conference which Chhotu Ram and the Unionist Premier, Sikander, organized at Lyallpur to explain the benefits of their policies.[11]

The Unionist Party's failure to achieve a mass base of support ironically resulted from the source of its underlying strength in the 1930s. This was the structure of rural factional politics based on the social and economic power of the rural elites. Thus, even at the height of its influence, it lacked the ability to establish face-to-face relationships with localized communities. The contradictions between its ideology and the basis of its power were to become a major source of weakness as the Muslim League mounted a challenge to the Party's rural predominance.

III

The struggle for power between the Muslim League and the Unionist Party has attracted considerable historical interest because of its wider political implications. We have, of course, David Gilmartin's excellent analysis of the factional weakness of Malik Khizr Hyat Khan Tiwana, who succeeded to the Unionist Premiership following Sikander's sudden death in December 1942.[12] My own work has revealed how British food policy undermined the position of their Unionist allies during the war years.[13] It would serve little purpose to belabour these points. I should like, instead, to turn to a narrative of the key period from Khizr's expulsion from the Muslim League in May 1944[14] to the 1946 elections. This should illustrate the role of popular participation and initiative at a vital stage in the Pakistan movement.

The Muslim League launched a campaign of extensive touring beginning in the summer of 1944. Its aim was to open local branches down to the tehsil level, and to transform the structure of rural power by appealing to the peasantry over the heads of the rural elite. 'It is becoming quite clear', wrote Mian Mumtaz Daultana, the Punjab League's General Secretary in July 1944, 'that in view of the determined government opposition, our basic strength must come, not from the landlords or the *Zaildar-Lambardar* class, but from the masses of the Muslim people.[15]

During June and July, a team of propagandists headed by Daultana and Sikander's son, Shaukat Hayat, toured all five of the province's Divisions. Muslim League conferences were held at Montgomery, Lyallpur, Sheikhupura, Sargodha, Jhang, Sialkot and Rawalpindi. These attracted large audiences: over 15,000 attended the meeting at Multan and 10,000 at Montgomery.[16] For the first time ever, primary League branches were established in rural Sargodha and Mianwali. Four-and-a-half thousand members were enrolled in the former district.[17] The Muslim League organizer for Mianwali reported that 17 primary Leagues with some 2,000 members had been established in July alone.[18]

As the elections drew nearer, the Muslim League stepped up its rural propaganda. Much of the work was done by students. During the 1945 Christmas vacation, there were 1,550 members of the Punjab Muslim Students' Federation and 250 Aligarh students touring on the League's behalf. Their role was to drive home and personalize the Muslim League message which was flooding off the printing presses. They achieved the latter, not only by holding public meetings, but by going from door to door in the villages which they visited.[19] The Aligarh workers made a virtue out of their unfamiliarity with the peasants by stressing that they had covered such large distances out of love for Islam.[20] They had all attended a Worker's Training Camp before they left for the Punjab, where lectures were given on such topics as the religious background to the Pakistan demand.[21] Whenever they visited a village, they joined in the prayers at the local mosque and gained its *imam's* permission to hold a meeting there. Students from the Punjab Muslim Students' Federation were similarly advised to follow the Prophet's example in all things, all of the time they were in a village. They were to join in the prayers at the mosque or lead them like 'Holy Warriors'. Their speeches were to be filled with emotional appeal, and always to commence with a text from the Koran, invoking God's protection and praising His wisdom.[22]

The extent of such student activity on the Muslim League's behalf was novel, but its principle was not. The Punjab Muslim Student's Federation had supported the Pakistan demand from the outset. Indeed, it had organized a conference at Lahore in March 1941, at which Jinnah had presided. At this conference, a Pakistan Rural Propaganda Committee was established with the prominent student leader, Hameed Nizami, as its Secretary. In May 1941, it embarked on a twenty-day-tour of the Sheikhupura district, during which it visited fifty villages, in each of which it opened a primary branch of the Muslim League.[23] Although this effort represented only a tiny drop in the ocean, it had important consequences, for the experience of approaching rural communities led to a significant refinement in Muslim League propaganda. Its activists found that support for the Pakistan demand at the grassroots was greatest when it was linked with the realities of the villagers' lives. This insight was enshrined in the advice which was subsequently enjoined to propagandists when they visited a village: 'Find out its social problems and difficulties. Tell them (i.e., the villagers) that the main cause of their problems was the Unionists (and) give them the solution—Pakistan.[24]

My earlier work has revealed how this advice was put into effect. I do not want to repeat here how the League's activists attempted with considerable success to crystallize rural opposition to the requisitioning of food grains which the British had forced on the Unionists but rather to emphasize the Muslim League's appeal to Punjabi servicemen as part of this strategy. We noted in our introductory remarks, the importance of servicemen as 'opinion formers' and voters. They had traditionally been loyal supporters of the Unionist Party. The reasons for this were summed up during a conversation between Mian Sultan Ali Ranjha and Lt. Colonel Sir Sher Mohammad Khan in August 1944. 'In spite of his conviction in Pakistan', the Zamindara League Secretary noted in his Tour Report, 'he (Sher Mohammad Khan) seems to think that a population of soldiers like that in the Jhelum area must always side with the government in order to protect their economic interests both as a soldier and as a Zamindar'.[25] By 1928, over 140 *lakhs* of rupees (one *lakh* represents 100,000) was in fact being annually paid out in pensions, and there were 16,000 military pensioners in the Rawalpindi district alone.

During the Second World War, the Unionist Party endeavoured to maintain the accustomed loyalty of the recruiting areas. Free medicine and schooling was given to the dependents of soldiers on active duty. As during the 1914-18 conflict, remissions of land revenue were made for villages with especially good recruiting records.[26] The Post-War Five Year Development Plan drawn up by the Khizr Cabinet enshrined the specific purpose of benefitting the recruiting areas and providing employment for demobilized soldiers.[27] Again as after the First World War, rich irrigated land in the Canal Colonies was earmarked for both commissioned and non-commissioned officers. But these plans were thrown out of gear by the speedy end to the war in Asia.

The slump which had hit the Punjab's trade and industry as a result of the fall in the high wartime levels of demand meant that many servicemen returned home to face unemployment. Even by the end of 1946, less than twenty per cent of the demobilized soldiers registered with employment exchanges had been found work.[28] The Muslim League adopted the cause of the servicemen and cleverly linked its campaign with their grievances. Shaukat Hayat, who had served in the Indian Army before his return to the Punjab, delivered a series of hard-hitting speeches against the Unionist Party in the main recruiting areas in September 1945.[29] He hammered home the point that despite the Unionists' promises, there was no reward for the soldiers' wartime efforts. The League also addressed itself, however, to the servicemen's wider areas of concern which included such issues as the Palestine Question, the use of Muslim troops in Indonesia, and the fate of Punjabi members of the Indian National Army. It was the result of pressure 'from beneath' articulated by local branches that the League decided to follow

the Congress example and establish a Defence Committee for
I.N.A. members who were on trial. This step was well received
by ex-servicemen.[30]

Significantly, the Muslim League's greatest electoral success
in 1946 in the Rawalpindi Division came in the two major
recruiting areas of Rawalpindi and Jhelum. It won all thirteen
of the constituencies in these former Unionist strongholds, and
polled over seventy-five per cent of the popular Muslim vote,
some thirteen per cent above its average for the Division as a
whole. Undoubtedly, the influence exerted in the League's
favour by Pir Fazl Shah of Jalalpur contributed to this success,
but it also owed much to grassroots support. This was seen not
only in the polling booths, but in the difficulties which faced
the Unionists throughout this period.

The Zamindara League fieldworker for the Rawalpindi
district, Shahzada Sadiq Bukhari, frequently reported to Mian
Sultan Ali Ranjha that he encountered hostility during his tours
of the villages in the summer of 1945.[31] Significantly, the
Zamindara League Secretary had been unable to find an
organizer for the Rawalpindi Division during his tour the
preceding autumn. The most dramatic evidence of pressure from
below, however, came in the defection of the sitting Unionist
member for Rawalpindi East, Major Farman Ali. Some of the
thirty Unionists who crossed the floor in the period 1944-6
may have been prompted by political opportunism based on a
reading of All-India developments. But in the case of Farman
Ali, and indeed that of his fellow Rajput member for Gujar
Khan, it was the result of growing hostility to the Unionist
cause in his own villages.[32]

The Muslim League not only extended its influence in the
Punjab countryside by taking up local issues and causes, it also
put across its message through the idiom of rural Islam. This
gave it familiarity and conviction. The role played by *pirs* and
sajjada nashins in the Pakistan movement in the Punjab has
been well documented.[33] *Pirs* not only produced *fatwas*[34] on
the Muslim League's behalf, which were published in the
vernacular press, but gave these commands a personal presence

during the tours of their *murids* (disciples). The *urs* ceremonies
at the leading Sufi shrines formed a ready-made channel of
communication for the Muslim League, as thousands of
Muslims attended these important events in the religious
calendar. They were drawn from a wide area, and took back to
their own villages the Muslim League messages which they had
seen and heard. The ground was thus often prepared for the
League before its propagandists reached the local communities.

The *pirs* not only provided the Muslim League with access
to their vast chains of disciples, but also sanctified its cause
with their great moral authority. This authority enabled them
to transcend the faction based rural power structure of which
they themselves were part. They made appeals to individual
Muslim voters to personally identify with the cause of Islam by
supporting the Pakistan demand. 'Your vote is a trust of the
community' (*qaum*), warned the *sajjada nashin* of the leading
Chishti shrine at Ajmer, 'No question of someone's caste (*zat*)
or conflicts of *biraderis* should at this time come before you.'[35]

Not all *pirs* of course supported the Muslim League in 1946.
The Qadiri *Pir*, Mian Syed Badr Mohy-ud-Din, was in fact
narrowly defeated as the Unionist candidate for the Batala
constituency. Some pirs continued to stress their local influence,
rather than identification with the wider Islamic community. 'I
command all those people who are in my *Silsilah*' warned the
sajjada nashin of the shrine of Hazrat Shah Nur Jamal, 'to do
everything possible to help the Muslim League and give their
votes to it. All those people who do not act according to this
announcement should consider themselves no longer members
of my *Silsilah*'.[36] Moreover, even such influential *Pirs* as *Pir*
Golra and *Pir* Sial were unable to undermine Khizr's factional
support in the Shahpur district, but in many other regions, the
intervention of leading *pirs* and *sajjada nashins* did prove
decisive.

The Muslim League attempted to coordinate the pirs'
activities in a *Mashaikh* committee, but they were not easy to
organize. Few *pirs* attended the Jamiat-ul-Ulema-i-Islam
Conference which the Punjab Muslim League held in the

Muslim League Working Committee Meeting, Bombay, November 1941 (*National Archives of Pakistan*).

Mohammad Ali Jinnah in procession, Allahabad, 1942 (*National Archives of Pakistan*).

Mohammad Ali Jinnah and Miss Fatima Jinnah, Quetta, 1943
(*National Archives of Pakistan*).

Balochistan Muslim National Guards (*National Archives of Pakistan*).

Ahmedabad Muslim National Guards (*National Archives of Pakistan*).

Muslim League procession, Delhi, 6 April 1947 (*National Archives of Pakistan*).

Mohammad Ali Jinnah, Miss Fatima Jinnah, Liaquat Ali Khan and Islamia College Students (*National Archives of Pakistan*).

Mohammad Ali Jinnah in procession, Peshawar, 1945 (*National Archives of Pakistan*).

The crowd at Lahore Railway Station awaiting Jinnah's arrival, 13 January 1946 (*National Archives of Pakistan*).

Independence Day, 14 August 1947 (*National Archives of Pakistan*).

grounds of Islamia College, Lahore in January 1946. The result was that the *Mashaikh* committee contained such unlikely Sufis as Pir Mamdot Sharif (Nawab of Mamdot), *sajjada nashin* of Wah Sharif (Shaukat Hyat), and *sajjada nashin* of Darbar Sargodha Sharif (Firoz Khan Noon).[37] Most of the Muslim League's dealings with the *pirs* had to be done at the local level, where it approached individuals and asked them to issue *fatwas* in its support. These were disseminated by means of small leaflets and wall posters as well as being published in such pro-League papers as *Nawa-e-Waqt* and the *Eastern Times*.

The Unionist Party's activists also attempted to make use of the *pir's* influence. The Montgomery district Zamindara League Organizer, Agha Barkat Ali Khan, set up a camp during the *urs* ceremonies at the shrine of Baba Farid at Pakpattan. Baba Farid was acknowledged as the Punjab's leading Sufi saint. Multitudes flocked to the shrine which was famous for its 'gate of paradise'. This was only opened once a year, on the final and most important day of the *urs* ceremonies, when it was believed that anyone who could squeeze through its narrow entrance was assured of a place in paradise.[38] Pakpattan was hell, however, for the Unionist workers. The large quantity of literature, gramophone records, and even the touring film van, counted for little in the face of the hostility of the *dargah* authorities. In marked contrast with the Muslim League, the Unionists were not permitted to hold a meeting in the shrine itself. Furthermore, the *sajjada nashins* who had gathered at Pakpattan refused to sign the Unionist manifesto which Agha Barkat Ali Khan had especially prepared. He attempted to gloss over many of these difficulties in his report to Mian Sultan Ali Ranjha, but one can well imagine the realities by reading between the lines of such statements as, for example, 'The camp life had cost a lot of worries and we had to be very vigilant to avoid any undesirable incident.'[39]

The Zamindara League Organizer for Rawalpindi was equally unsuccessful in neutralizing the *pirs'* support for the Muslim League. He visited Muhra Sharif at the express wish of the Unionist Premier, but only received the reply from *Pir* Nazir

Ahmad and *Pir* Nasir-ud-Din that *gaddi nashins* should not take
part in politics. His meeting with *Pir* Taunsa on 18 September
1945 was even less promising. When the *Pir* sahib was unmoved
by the recollection of the work the Unionists had done on behalf
of the Muslim zamindars, he played his trump card which left
'His Holiness surprised' but still committed to the Muslim
League cause. 'It was in a way explained to His Holiness that
when the Muslim League will come in power, the first Act which
will be passed will be Auqaf Bill, which will take away all their
properties and leave them almost destitute like the *mahants*
after the Gurdwara Bill.'[40] The Zamindara activist had in fact
raised this spectre in conversation with many other leading *pirs*.[41]
He optimistically maintained to Mian Sultan Ali Ranjha that
most of the *pirs* could be won over by regular propaganda along
these lines. He also counselled the payment of *nazrana* to the
pirs by the Unionists. This perfectly illustrates the extent to
which many Unionist activists had lost touch with popular
sentiment. They still thought solely in terms of the politics of
faction and local influence. Yet these were being challenged by
the religious stake which *pirs* and ordinary Muslims had invested
in the Pakistan campaign.

The Unionists' mindset is clearly revealed in the endeavours
which were made from 1944 onwards to reactivate the
Zamindara League. The intention was to fireproof the
countryside from the Muslim League's incandescent campaign
by establishing a modern political organization which stretched
down to the *tehsil* level. The local branches were to be assisted
in the task of mobilizing popular support by paid
propagandists.[42] These were personally selected by Sultan Ali
Ranjha, and had to provide him with a weekly report of their
activities,[43] but this attempt at formal organization coexisted
uneasily with both the realities of local power and the Unionist
leadership's attachment to them. Thus, the branches of the
Zamindara League still depended on the support of the rural
elite, with all too predictable results. 'What (can) the League
expect', lamented the Ludhiana Propaganda Secretary, 'from
office holders who are only in the field to further their names

and person with honours. In fact these office holders are political contradictions. It is alright to enroll members, but it is absolutely a different thing to utilize their strength for the support and success of the League.'⁴⁴ The Ludhiana case in fact well illustrates the limited impact of the attempt to transform the Unionist party into a popular organization. Despite the 'vigorous' work of the propaganda secretaries, who visited fifty-two villages during December 1944, only 167 members had been enrolled; whilst the city propaganda secretary had managed only a miserable 19 members.⁴⁵

Bashir Husain, the Jhelum district organizer, gave expression to the Unionist activists' approach to politics. He described to Sultan Ali Ranjha the operation of the Zamindara League at the local level in his monthly report for November 1945.

> The Zamindara League workers have been allotted different areas of the Tehsil. They always keep close touch with the influential people of their areas. The workers themselves are people of influence and have a link of brotherhood in their respective areas. They keenly watch the activities of the opponents—when they come to know that some persons somewhere have been misguided by the adverse propaganda of the Muslim League, they try to disinfect them of all such influences.⁴⁶

The concern both with knowledge of the Muslim League activities and with the influence of local *biraderis*, revealed in the above extract, increased as the elections approached. The Unionist Party headquarters requested that local workers supply them with the names of Muslim League office holders. It also provided detailed breakdowns of the tribal composition of individual constituencies. This ensured that members of its deputations included persons who could contact the dominant *biraderis*. Thus Chaudhri Abdul Rahim MLA, and Captain Mian Fateh Muhammad MLA, were specifically added to the tour party at the time of the July 1945 Hoshiarpur by-election because they were Gujars, and 'Gujars form a considerable proportion of the voters.'⁴⁷

Information on supporters and sympathizers of the Muslim League was especially valuable to a party which was beset by defectors, but which still controlled the machinery of government. Patronage could be withheld from such individuals as Chaudhri Faiz Ali, a Gujranwala Honorary Magistrate, who was wavering in his support.[48] Allegations of officials' support for the Muslim League could also be verified.[49] The strong police presence at Muslim League meetings was of course designed to limit their attendance.

The Unionists, in contrast, used the local administrative machinery to assist their own activities. Khizr, during a flying visit to Mianwali late in November 1945, intimated to Mohammad Aslam Khan, the Zamindara League District Organizer, that 'if any occasion arose, I would be given police help in convening meetings. The District authorities (DC) would also help in such cases.'[50] The Hoshiarpur District Commissioner accompanied the Zamindara League Organizer on a lengthy tour of the villages in January 1946. The latter noted that he addressed all the meetings 'in a charming and understandable manner', and absolved the government for the continuation of rationing.[51]

In a different political context, such official support for their rivals would have severely weakened the Muslim League. But it was able to turn this to its advantage in the circumstances of the 1946 elections. It strengthened its claim that it was the party of the ordinary Muslim, unlike the Unionists who represented the *Zaildari-Lambardari* class. The support of Hindu officials such as the Hoshiarpur DC, R.S.H.L. Khanna, for the Unionists also gave credence to its claims that the 'Khizri Muslims' were quisling enemies of Islam.

The Unionists did not rely simply on the politics of *biraderi* and the resources of government to defeat their rivals. Zamindara League activists toured the villages, addressing meetings and contacting individual voters. Even allowing for exaggeration, the report of Chaudhri Taj-ud-Din's tour of Hoshiarpur in January 1946 makes impressive reading. During it, he addressed meetings in nineteen different places and

estimated a total audience of well in excess of 36,000.[52] The
diaries of other Zamindara League workers indicate that this
was by no means exceptional. Mohammad Shafi from the Lahore
district, for example, toured seven villages during the course of
a single week in August 1944, 'conversing with notables and
peasant folk'.[53] Mohammad Aslam Khan sometimes addressed
two meetings in a day and travelled by tonga to the villages
surrounding Mianwali town. He also addressed meetings near
the jama masjid. He found it particularly profitable, however,
to interview people who had come from the *mofussil* in
connection with appeals to the DC Mianwali.[54]

The diaries of the Zamindara League activists reveal not only
the scope of their fieldwork but even more importantly the
message which they brought to the villages. Their most common
theme was the 'good that had been done by the present ministry
through the so-called Golden Acts that were passed In the
Legislature'. The Unionist government was linked to the
region's era of prosperity, when the rights of the Zamindars
found true representation. The need for communal harmony
was also stressed and the Unionists were depicted as the only
politicians who could form a stable ministry. The propagandists
devoted little attention to the Muslim League. Mohammad
Aslam Khan, during the course of a speech in Mianwali town
on 5 December 1945, did nevertheless dwell on the misdeeds
of the Frontier Muslim League Ministry of Aurangzeb Khan.
'The control of the central authority over the Muslim League
ministries', he declared, 'is very meagre, with the result that
they become irresponsible and unscrupulous.'[55]

The propagandists' message lost some of its impact because
nearly seven years had elapsed since the passage of the Golden
Acts. During the intervening period, through no fault of its
own, the Unionist government had to bear the brunt of the
unpopularity created by wartime controls and restrictions. More
importantly, the activities of the *pirs* had ensured that the
election was about far more than bread and butter issues and
the formation of a stable ministry. 'Wherever I went', reported
a Zamindara League worker from Jhelum, 'everyone kept saying,

bhai, if we did not vote for the League, we would have become kafir'.[56]

In the face of the pressure of the *pirs'* public support for the Muslim League, the Unionist Party began to introduce a religious content into its own propaganda. Malik Khizr Hayat Khan Tiwana began to garnish with quotations from the Koran his discourses on the economic benefits which the Unionist Party had brought to the rural population. In a speech at Gujrat, he used the first verse of the Sura Fatiha to prove that the Unionists had a greater Islamic justification than the Muslim League.[57] The Unionist Party also employed as speakers, *ulema* drawn from the Jamiat-i-Ulema-i-Hind, who were hostile to the Muslim League and its Pakistan demand. Local Zamindara League workers pleaded that the fiery Ahrar[58] orators, Sayed Ataullah Shah Bokhari and Maulana Mazhar Ali Azhar, be despatched to their districts to counteract the influence of the *pirs*.[59] Such reformist ulema had always been highly critical of the religious leadership provided by *pirs*, but they had also been hostile to the Unionists because of their close ties with the British. They were not the only strange bedfellows to whom Khizr turned in his moment of desperation, he also enlisted the support of the Khaksars, who had been bitter enemies of the Unionist Party during the time that his predecessor, Sikander, had held the premiership. They nevertheless possessed the virtue of outspoken opposition to the Pakistan demand. A lorry load of Khaksars was duly despatched to do election work in the Unionist Premier's own constituency; they were also deployed in the Ferozepore district, the political base of the Punjab Muslim League President, the Nawab of Mamdot.[60]

The Unionist Party, however, profited little from this strategy. There was a glaring inconsistency between its professed non-communal stance and the employment of *ulema*. Moreover, the latter, along with the Khaksars, were strangers in the districts to which they were sent. They lacked the local moral authority of the *pirs* and their networks of followers which provided ready-made channels of communication. Nor were they naturally able to relate their messages to the actual experience and rhythm of life of their hearers. The poets and singers which the Party also deployed with its propaganda lorries were more successful in this respect.

In the end the Unionist Party was faced, not only with the loss of many of its Assembly members to the Muslim League, but the defection of large numbers of its Zamindara organization workers. Chaudhri Nur Khan, the Unionist candidate for Chakwal in 1946, had to completely replace all the workers in his tehsil as they 'had changed colours'.[61] The problems in the Jhelum district,[62] however, started right at the top, as the chief worker, Mohammad Iqbal, divulged secrets to the Muslim League and obstructed operations until his final dismissal. The situation was little better elsewhere. By the beginning of November 1945, the presidents of the Ludhiana, Rawalpindi and Lyallpur branches of the Zamindara League had all decamped to the Muslim League. Another tell-tale sign of demoralization was the reluctance of some local activists to work in Muslim majority areas of their districts.[63] These difficulties were brought home forcibly to Khizr during his election tour of the Jhelum district. He unsuccessfully interviewed 120 people in an attempt to find someone willing to oppose the Muslim League candidate, Raja Ghazanfar Ali Khan,[64] in the Pind Dadan Khan constituency.[65]

Such situations suggest clearly a groundswell of rural Punjabi support for the Pakistan demand which has been previously denied by scholars.[66] This has been encouraged by the persistence of local political loyalties and the power of the rural elite in the post-independence period. The fact that the Muslim League's organizational weakness prevented it from bringing about a permanent transformation in the structure of local politics should not be allowed to obscure the existence of mass participation in the Pakistan movement. Its political success in 1946 resulted from the ability to link the Pakistan idea with popular aspirations and to anchor this message within the substratum of local rural Islam.

The results surprised even its own workers. 'The League is spreading even to the rural areas with what is seen to (by) the

League leaders here (as) *unexpected* rapidity', one Punjabi activist wrote to Jinnah in November 1945; 'our workers have not yet reached the villages in adequate numbers and yet one hears sensational stories of conversions to the League.'[67] Nazir Ahmad Khan, the local organizer for Montgomery, hailed a League rally at Shergarh in January 1945 as a landmark event, for it was attended both by ordinary Muslims and landowners, several of whom were '*Zaildars* and *Lambardars*, the class that is generally under the Unionist thumb.'[68]

Khizr shored up the Unionist citadel after the elections, forming a coalition government with the Congress and the Sikh Akalis, but the tide of events, both in the province and at the All-India level, had turned against him. His banning of the Muslim National Guards early in 1947 prompted the launching of a mass civil disobedience campaign. This second phase of popular participation, which we have explored in the book's opening chapter, marked the final advance of the Muslim League in the 'corner-stone' of Pakistan.

NOTES

[1] H. Alavi, 'Pakistan and Islam: Ethnicity and Ideology', in F. Halliday and H. Alavi (eds), *State and Ideology in the Middle East and Pakistan* (Basingstoke, 1988), p. 102.

[2] D. Gilmartin, *Empire and Islam. Punjab and the Making of Pakistan* (Berkeley, 1988), pp. 39-73; I. Talbot, *Punjab and the Raj, 1849-1947* (New Delhi, 1988), pp. 21-26.

[3] Gilmartin, op. cit., p. 201.

[4] Talbot, op. cit., pp. 208-210.

[5] Talbot, op. cit., p. 215-216.

[6] The absence of a grassroots Muslim League organization strengthened the hand of elite leaders who sought to limit political participation once the 'crisis' of 1946–7 had passed. Faiz Ahmad Faiz in his poem, 'To A Political Leader', reproaches such an attempt to curb mass mobilization.

> Long years those hands, unfriended and unfree,
> Have clawed into night's dark unyielding breast
> As straws might dash themselves against a sea,
> or butterflies assail a mountain-crest:

Till now that dark and flint-hard breast of night
Has felt so many gashes that all around
Look where you will, is woven a web of light,
And from far off the morning's heartbeats sound.

The people's hands have been your coat of mail,
Your wealth: what else has lent you strength, but they?
You do not wish this darkness to prevail,
Yet wish those hands lopped off, and the new day,
Now throbbing in its eastern ambush, doomed
Under night's iron corpse to lie entombed.

V. Kiernan (trans.), Poems by Faiz (London, n.d.), pp. 101-3.

[7] Talbot, op. cit., pp. 100-114.

[8] Gilmartin, op. cit., pp. 128-145.

[9] The Zamindara Leagues were cross-communal organizations designed to articulate the interests of the agriculturalists, and to form a popular base of support for the Unionist Party.

[10] For details of the so-called Golden Acts, *see*, Talbot, op. cit., pp. 118-119.

[11] Punjab FR 6 September 1938, L/P&J/5/241, IOR.

[12] Gilmartin, op. cit., p. 186 & ff.

[13] Talbot, op. cit., p. 145 & ff.

[14] For the background to this and its political implications, *see*, Talbot, op. cit., p. 170 & ff

[15] Report of the Punjab Provincial Muslim League's Work for June and July 1944 (Shamsul Hasan Collection, Karachi) Punjab, Vol. 1, General Correspondence.

[16] Talbot op. cit., p. 145 & ff.

[17] Report of Ghulam Mustafa Shah, Organizing Secretary, Rawalpindi Division Muslim League. Punjab Muslim League 1943-44, Vol. 162, Pt7, pp. 74 & ff, FMA.

[18] Report of Punjab Provincial Muslim League, op. cit.

[19] Bashir Husain, Zamindara League Organizer, Jhelum District, to Mian Sultan Ali Ranjha, Zamindara League Organizing Secretary, 2 January 1946 (Unionist Party Papers file D-48).

[20] Report of Ghulam Mustafa Shah, op. cit.

[21] Muslim University Union Aligarh and Muslim University Muslim League, Vol 237, p. 71, FMA.

[22] Punjab Muslim Students' Federation Election Board Pamphlet, Punjab Muslim Students' Federation, Vol 23, FMA.

[23] Report of Mohammad Sadiq: Sheikhupura Student Deputation, 22 July 1941. QIAP File 1099/64, NAP.

[24] Punjab Muslim Students' Federation Election Board Pamphlet, op. cit.

[25] Report of an Organizational Tour of the North & North-western Areas

of the Punjab, 21-24 August 1944, file marked 'Personal File of Mian Sultan Ali Ranjha', Unionist Party Papers file E-194.

²⁶ *The Eastern Times* (Lahore), 8 November 1942.

²⁷ *Government of India Five Year Postwar Development Plan* (Lahore, 1945). *See*, for example, p. 214.

²⁸ Punjab FR, 14 December 1946, L/P&J/5/249, IOR.

²⁹ *The Eastern Times* (Lahore), 29 September 1945.

³⁰ Resolution of the Montgomery District Muslim League (Shamsul Hasan Collection, Karachi), Punjab, Vol 2, General Correspondence.

³¹ *See*, for example, his letters of 28 May and 18 September 1945. Personal File of Shahdaza Sadiq Bukhari, Assistant Organizer, Rawalpindi Zamindara League, Unionist Party papers.

³² *See*, for example, Civil and Military Gazette (Lahore), 23 October 1945; also, Report of the Organizing Secretary, Rawalpindi Division Muslim League, Vol 162, Pt7, Punjab Muslim League 1943-4, p. 74 & ff, FMA.

³³ Gilmartin, op. cit., pp. 203-224; Talbot, op. cit., pp. 210-218.

³⁴ For examples of these, *see*, Talbot, op. cit., pp. 211-212.

³⁵ Cited in Gilmartin, op. cit., pp. 216-217.

³⁶ *Nawa-e-Waqt* (Lahore), 19 January 1946.

³⁷ K.B. Sayeed, *Pakistan, The Formative Phase 1857-1948*, 2nd ed, (London, 1968), p. 203.

³⁸ Montgomery District Gazetteer (Lahore, 1933), p. 66.

³⁹ Agha Barkat Ali, Organizing Director, Montgomery District Zamindara League, to Mian Sultan Ali Ranjha, 3 & 13 December 1945, file D-56, Unionist Party Papers.

⁴⁰ Zamindara League Divisional Organizer, Rawalpindi, to Mian Sultan Ali Ranjha, 1 October 1945, file E-l05, Unionist Party Papers.

⁴¹ These included the *Pirs* and *Sajjada Nashins* of Makhad, Mohra, Basal, Maira, Bhakra, Kundian, Bhor and Shah Daula. Ibid. (38 above).

⁴² Payment was in fact fixed at 100 rupees per month. The fieldworkers also received travelling allowances if they had to go further afield than their own district. As the number of workers increased with the advent of the provincial elections, salaries for new activists were reduced to 65 rupees per month.

⁴³ Sultan Ali Ranjha diligently read these reports and was quick to proffer advice or criticism. He rapped Khwaja Fakhr-ud-Din, the assistant organizer, Chiniot Zamindara League, firmly over the knuckles for only visiting one village during the week ending 9 June 1945. The previous December, he had strongly advised him to adopt a more methodical approach to his fieldwork activities. Mian Sultan Ali Ranjha to Khwaja Fakhr-ud-Din, Assistant Organizer, Chiniot Zamindara League, Jhang District, 20 December 1944 & 19 June 1945, file E-85, Unionist Party Papers.

⁴⁴ Propaganda Secretary, Ludhiana Zamindara League, to Secretary, Zamindara League, Ludhiana, n.d., file E-73, personal file of Agha Ghazanfar

Ali, Ludhiana Division Organizer, Unionist Party Papers.

[45] Report of the working of the District Zamindara League Ludhiana for the month of December 1944, file D-36, Unionist Party Papers.

[46] Monthly Report for November 1945 for the Jhelum District. Bashir Husain, District Organizer, Jhelum District Zamindara League, 5 December 1945, file D-48, Unionist Party Papers.

[47] Agha Ghazanfar Ali Khan to Mian Sultan Ali Ranjha, 14 & 19 July 1945, file F-28, Hoshiarpur By-Election, Unionist Party Papers.

[48] Aminullah Khan to Sultan Ali Ranjha, 8 July 1945, file E-99, Unionist Party Papers.

[49] *See*, for example, Sultan Ali Ranjha to K.B. Fateh Khan, Rawalpindi District Zamindara League Organizer, 6 October 1945, file D-40, Unionist Party Papers.

[50] Diary entry 28 November 1945, personal file of Mohammad Aslam Khan, District Organizer, Mianwali Zamindara League, file E-171, Unionist Party Papers.

[51] Report for the month of January 1946 of Chaudhri Taj-ud-Din, District Organizer, Hoshiarpur Zamindara League, file D-33, Unionist Party Papers.

[52] Sultan Ali Ranjha to K.B. Fateh, op. cit.

[53] Mohammad Shafi, Worker Lahore District Zamindara League, Diary 21–27 August 1944, file E-75, Unionist Party Papers.

[54] Diary entries of Mohammad Aslam Khan, District Organizer, Mianwali Zamindara League, 14, 16 & 17 November 1945, file E-171, Unionist Party Papers.

[55] Diary entry of Mohammad Aslam Khan, District Organizer, Mianwali Zamindara League, 5 December 1945, file E-171, Unionist Party Papers.

[56] Gilmartin, op. cit., p. 218.

[57] Khizr's point was that Allah is described in the Koran as *Rabb-ul-Alameen,* Lord of everything and everyone, not just the Muslims. In this light, the Unionist Party's non-communalism was more Islamic than the Muslim League's communal rhetoric.

[58] The Ahrar movement was an urban-based communal organization which had gained prominence in the Punjab in the early 1930s during its agitations in defence of Kashmiri Muslim rights and against the heterodox Ahmadiyah community.

[59] Mian Sultan Ahmad Ranjha, Sub-Register, to Sultan Ali Ranjha, 5 January 1946, file D-36, Unionist Party Papers.

[60] For more details of the Unionists' links with the Khaksars, consult file D-99, Unionist Party Papers.

[61] Bashir Husain, District Organizer, Jhelum Zamindara League, to Mian Sultan Ali Ranjha, 2 January 1946, file D-48, Unionist Party Papers.

[62] Bashir Husain, District Organizer, Jhelum Zamindara League, to Mian Sultan Ali Ranjha, 16 January 1946, file D-48, Unionist Party Papers.

[63] Mian Sultan Ali Ranjha to Sufi Abdul Haq, Assistant Organizer, Sargodha

District Zamindara League, 13 December 1944, file E-76, Unionist Party Papers.

[64] He was not only a prominent Leaguer and powerful opponent of the Unionists in the Provincial Assembly, but more importantly, the uncle of the leading Chishti revivalist, Pir Fazl Shah.

[65] *Dawn* (Delhi), 28 October 1945.

[66] *See*, for example, Gilmartin, op. cit., p. 187.

[67] Mian Bashir Ahmed to Jinnah, 14 November 1945, (Shamsul Hasan Collection, Karachi), Punjab Vol. 3.

[68] Nazir Ahmed Khan, 'Thoughts on Muslim League Speakers' Tour of Montgomery', 10 January 1945 (Shamsul Hasan Collection, Karachi), Punjab Vol. 3.

Section 2

The Human Face of Partition

Chapter 4

The Partition Experience
Literature, Meaning and Culture

The exploration of popular perceptions, cultures and consciousness has formed an important area in the study of 'history from
below'. Studies of Pakistan's emergence, however, have ignored
this issue, despite the fact that such a profound historical event
as the birth of a nation alters people's inward feelings and
emotions as well as their external situation. This theme can be
found in the works of many contemporary novelists. The aim
of this chapter is to utilize such sources to explore changing
sensitivities and collective representations. This forms part of
the wider task of introducing a human dimension to the
historical discourse on Pakistan's birth. Before embarking upon
it, however, it is necessary to briefly raise some of the problems
presented by the use of literary source material.[1]

I

Historical insights from fiction, whilst they can be profound,
are frequently elusive. The novelist's art is subjective by its very
nature. All literary sources must therefore be treated with the
utmost care and sensitivity. It must be remembered that they
have been produced by tiny literate elites within traditional
societies. The great writers can transcend their own experience
and echo the feelings of other classes and communities[2] but
lesser novelists frequently lack this empathy and produce merely
stereotypes and stylized emotional responses.

This style of writing is pervasive in much of the literature of partition, whether it has been produced by contemporaries or those distanced from the actual events. These were, of course, so emotionally powerful and have been surrounded by such polemic that this state of affairs is by no means surprising. Pakistani and Indian nationalist ideology runs through many novels. Equally didactic and influential is the approach of the school of progressive writers. Where this is more sophisticated, the result is a warm humanistic approach to communal violence. Even highly stylized works may be of value to the historian as they can reveal more than they intend when read between the lines. Moreover, the reception of such works lends valuable insights on conventional wisdom surrounding the events which they portray.

The language in which a text is written can also limit its meaning and perceptiveness as well as didacticism. This chapter mainly examines English and Urdu texts. These were the languages most widely used by Muslim novelists of Partition but Urdu works invariably stress the experiences of migration to the detriment of others. This stems from the fact that many Urdu writers were *mohajirs*. This 'bias' in the source material must be fully acknowledged, although it could be argued that this aspect of Partition was so powerful that it is rightly prominent in the literature. In the survey which follows, there is an attempt to set all literary sources in their historical and intellectual context. Material on the authors and the reception of the texts is also provided. The emphasis is on the value of the works for the historian, rather than on their literary style and merit. Prose sources are mainly utilized but poetry as represented by the works of Faiz Ahmad Faiz cannot be ignored because of its immense importance for Urdu speakers.[3] Significant works by non-Muslim writers are included where they shed light on the important themes of identity and representation. Most of the material is in Urdu, but the survey commences with a brief examination of some well known fiction which has either been originally written in English or translated from Punjabi or Hindi.[4] These are: Chaman Nahal's *Azadi*,

Khushwant Singh's *Train to Pakistan*, Mumtaz Shah Nawaz's *The Heart Divided*, Bapsi Sidhwa's *Ice-Candy-Man*, Kartur Singh Duggal's *Twice Born Twice Dead*, and Bhisham Sahni's novel, *Tamas*, and his collection, *We Have Arrived in Amritsar and Other Stories*. Each plot will be briefly outlined, before an assessment is made of its value for understanding the experience of Partition.

II

Chaman Nahal's *Azadi* and Khushwant Singh's *Train to Pakistan* are deservedly the most popular Indo-English works of fiction dealing with the events of 1947. Both display great compassion in their expression of the human tragedy arising from Partition. They carefully avoid the trap of apportioning blame in a partisan manner.[5] Thus, although they are written from the standpoint of the non-Muslim population, they yield insights into the feelings of the victims of the communal holocaust which can be universalized.

Azadi begins with the announcement of the 3 June Plan. It ends with Mahatma Gandhi's assassination. The story is built around one small group of people from Sialkot who are caught up in the violence and have to flee to India. The main characters, Lala Kanshi Ram, a grain merchant, his wife, Prabha Rani, and their student son, Arun, reach Delhi safely. But they have suffered considerable spiritual and emotional loss[6] in addition to the physical loss of their extensive property which will never be restored.[7] The Muslim aggressors, however, are also emotionally diminished, as they are coarsened by violence. Nahal excels in his depiction of the moral disintegration of Abdul Ghani, the hookah maker and shopkeeper neighbour of Lala Kanshi Ram. The novel's most useful insight for the historian, however, is its portrayal of Kanshi Ram's internal turmoil as a result of migration. The sense of uprootedness is laid bare in the following passages:

Refugee, refugee, indeed! he shouted. ... I was *born* around here, this is my *home*. How can I be a refugee in my own home.[8]

He would forgive the English and the Muslims all their sins, if only he could return. Return and die here and be cremated by the side of the River Aik! He shivered at the luxury of the thought. To be carried shoulder high on a bier through the streets of Sialkot, through all those streets in each of which somewhere sat a friend. ... Then at the last moment, for his Spirit to look at the Aik and the land of Sialkot from above, from the sky, or to come down and roll in the dust of the fields—that would be the very pinnacle of his delight.[9]

The novel concludes, however, with a different well of emotions in his heart following Gandhi's death.

What impressed Lala Kanshi Ram was the pride with which the men stood. ... He thought of pre-independence days. ... An Indian leader dying and the crowd feeling openly for him? Today the men stood in pride. ... Lala Kanshi Ram raised his head with pride and stretched back his shoulders. He was unrestricted now, he was untrammelled.[10]

Khushwant Singh's famous novel[11] examines the impact of communal violence on the small border village of Mano Majro. The murder of the moneylender, Ram Lal, signals an increasing external threat to the village's traditional harmony.[12] It emanates from refugees fleeing the massacres in Pakistan, from the Deputy Commissioner, Hukum Chand, who tries unsuccessfully to harness the external storms to his own interests, and most importantly from a train which arrives carrying the corpses of the victims of Muslim violence. These corrosive influences need, however, local assistance to triumph. This comes from the *badmash*, Malli, and his gang. The well-meaning but uneducated Sikh priest, Meet Singh, the stranger, Iqbal, and the *badmash*, Jugga Singh, are pitched into an unequal struggle against these destructive forces. Meet Singh is unable to dissuade Sikhs from Mano Majro joining in a deadly attack on a train carrying their former Muslim neighbours to Pakistan. Iqbal, the idealist revolutionary, also ultimately lacks the moral courage to prevent the attack. It is left to Jugga Singh to act. He is motivated by love for Nooran, the Imam's daughter. He lays down his life in order to cut the rope suspended over the bridge which the train to Pakistan must cross.

This absorbing narrative vividly illustrates the impact of Partition on ordinary people's lives. It clearly reveals how the collective destiny of communities dominated the individual's fate. The subtitle for the fourth part, *karma*, is significant in this respect. The train which links the village to the outside world and which brings the harrowing consequences of political decisions taken elsewhere to its tranquil life, is also highly suggestive. It is left to Iqbal Singh to express the hopelessness and cynicism which many must have felt at the time. He rejects an attempt to prevent the planned attack on the refugee train:

> It would be an utter waste of life! And what would it gain? A few were going to slaughter some of their kind, a mild setback to the annual increase of four million. ... In a state of chaos self-preservation is the supreme deity! Wrong triumphs over right as much as right over wrong. ... What happens ultimately, you do not know. In such circumstances what can you do but cultivate an utter indifference to all values.[13]

Khushwant Singh refuses, however, to leave the reader with this feeling of hopelessness. Instead, he affirms the heroic in the human nature with Jugga's thwarting the attack on the train.

Mumtaz Shah Nawaz's novel, *The Heart Divided*,[14] lacks the sophistication and literary quality of the works which we have so far examined. Its plot is predictable and verges on melodrama. The set-piece speeches of the leading characters are unconvincing. Nevertheless, it provides valuable historical insights into the social and political outlook of the upper class, urban, Punjabi Muslim society from which the author came. It lays bare, in particular, the frustrations of educated women as they sought self-discovery and liberation from the constraints imposed by purdah. Political activism was one important response to this situation.

The plot centres around the family of Sheikh Jamaluddin, the head of an old established *ashraf* family of Lahore. His eldest daughter, Sughra, suffers an unhappy arranged marriage with a cousin, Mansur Hussain, from the rural Multan branch of the family. Following the death of her son, Khalid, she leaves her dull but loyal husband and eventually comes to terms with herself through commitment to the political and social work of the Muslim League. Amidst the romantic setting of the Mughal monuments of Delhi, she falls in love with Syed Kamal Haider. He is a former playboy who has become active in politics following a failed marriage. Sughra, however, rejects romance to return to the family home in Lahore to carry on her work. She is finally reconciled with Mansur, following her discovery that he has become a zealous worker for the Muslim League.

Zohra, the youngest daughter, is depicted as the unconventional and spoilt darling of her father. She refuses an arranged marriage with a high ranking Indian official and teaches initially at her old college in Lahore and eventually in Amritsar, where she lives alone. There she forms a relationship with a radical political activist named Ahmed Hussain, who is the son of her father's Head Clerk. Despite the inevitable initial hostility, she secures permission for a betrothal. This coincides with her conversion to the Muslim League's cause.

Habib, Sheikh Jamaluddin's son, also switches political allegiance. He returns from schooling in England, committed to the Congress cause. Much to his family's consternation, he falls in love with a Congressite Hindu girl, Mohini. Her father, Pandit Sham Lal, is the head of a family of Kashmiri Pandits which has a long established friendship with the Sheikhs. Habib and Mohini's relationship is played out in romantic rendezvous in Shalimar Gardens. It is finally uncovered by a scheming aunt and her gossiping servants. There are heated discussions in both households. Mohini is conveniently stricken with tuberculosis and dies in distant Kashmir. Habib is thus freed to marry a

Muslim, albeit a divorcee, and to cast his lot with the Muslim League.

Despite the plot's artificiality and propagandist content, it is historically interesting because of its autobiographical influences. The writer came from the elite urban milieu of Lahore which she describes so acutely. Her grandfather, Sir Muhammad Shafi, a leading Muslim barrister, founded the Punjab Muslim League and was active in the Anjuman-i-Himayat-i-Islam. Her mother, Begum Shah Nawaz, was elected to the Punjab Assembly in 1937. The writer's career served as a model for Zohra. Mumtaz Shah Nawaz herself was attached, during the 1930s, to the secularist and socialist views of the Nehruvian wing of the Congress. She progressed, as does Zohra, from educational work to involvement with women's groups and trade unions in the factory area of Amritsar.[15] Finally, as a result of the wartime changes in Indian politics, she broke with the Congress and threw herself into the activities of the progressive wing of the Muslim League, an action which Zohra is poised to emulate, when the novel closes in 1942.

Mumtaz Shah Nawaz draws on her family's own experience to vividly portray the electioneering in the Lahore Women's Constituency, a part of the 1937 campaign which has been neglected by historians. The ambivalence of the Muslim elite before attitudes hardened against the Congress is also usefully explored through such characters as Habib and Zohra. Sughra, on the other hand, lends insights into the idealism generated by the Pakistan demand. It is left to the relatively minor figure of Syed Kamal Haider, however, to articulate this fully:

> Just think. ... our own State, to live in as free men and work and play and worship in our own way without let or hindrance. To develop once more our natural genius, to see again the blossoming of our language and our culture on true Islamic principles, whereby all men will be equal.[16]

The writer's own hopes shine through Sughra's immediate riposte, '(and) to build a society where women will get their birthright. ... and hunger and want and ignorance will be no more.'[17] Finally, through a conversation between the two sisters, the novelist hints at the emotions of many progressives who joined the Muslim League towards the end of the Pakistan struggle.

> Oh Apa you don't know how it is. ... I ...for so many years I've believed and trusted in the Congress leadership and now ... they should have accepted the principle of self-determination. I'm so unhappy. ...I feel I never want to do anything again. ...
>
> But your people need you. ... You believe in self-determination? Yes.
>
> You also sympathize with the Muslim women's struggle for their rights? ... Then don't you see your place is in the League. ... We need workers like you with energy and ideals.
>
> But Apa ... I ... I would be out of place.
>
> Nonsense, the doors of the League are open to all. It's a national organization. People of all ideas are there, socialists and democrats, fascists and communists, *maulvis* and modern men.
>
> But I've nothing in common with some Leaguers.
>
> Quite. But what have you in common with some congressmen, the representatives of big business and the fascist sympathizers ... And the League needs sincere workers to make it a living democratic people's organization and Pakistan will need people like you to make it a people's State.
>
> I see what you have in mind.[18]

We now turn to a very different work, Bapsi Sidhwa's *Ice-Candy-Man*.[19] It is ribald, fluent and realistic, whereas *The Heart Divided* is coy, stilted and stylized. Like *Train to Pakistan*, it depicts the tearing apart of a harmonious world by external political developments.

This world comprises of the family, friends and neighbours of Lenny, a young Parsee girl who lives in the affluent outskirts of Lahore. Life is carefree and unhurried, punctuated by the high spirited gambols of the servants, Imam Din, Yousaf, Hari, and Moti, while Hindu, Muslim and Sikh admirers swarm around Lenny's voluptuous *ayah*, Shanti. One of these is the ice-candy-man of the title. Gradually, the tensions borne of

communal violence elsewhere in India make themselves
apparent. The Muslim servants ostentatiously prepare
themselves for Friday prayers. The Parsees, Hindu and Sikh
neighbours pack up and leave. Shanti spends a small fortune
on the paraphernalia of Hindu devotionalism. Dissension even
intrudes into the ranks of her admirers. The ice-candy-man
temporarily adopts the garb of a 'lunatic holyman'. Like the
character, Abdul Ghani, in *Azadi*, he becomes corrupted by
the violence which eventually engulfs Lahore.[20]

Hari and Moti convert to Islam and Christianity respectively,
and thereby escape the attentions of a marauding Muslim mob.
But Shanti is abducted, despite the efforts of Imam Din to
protect her. Lenny's godmother eventually tracks her down to
the red light district of the city where she is married to the ice-
candy-man who has metamorphized into a *mandi* poet. She is
rescued and taken to the Recovered Women's Camp near her
old home. A penitent ice-candy-man pathetically idles outside,
hoping to catch a glimpse of her. Driven by 'private demons',
the novel concludes with his disappearance over the Indian
border in pursuit of his beloved.

Bapsi Sidhwa shrewdly observes the physical and
psychological turmoil of the Partition period. She picks up the
theme of the fear of being uprooted, which we have already
encountered in earlier texts, when describing the response of
Imam Din's relatives to the prospect of leaving the village of
Pir Pindo.

> Most of the villagers resisted the move. 'We cannot leave', they
> said, and like a refrain, I can hear them say: 'What face will we
> show our forefathers on the day of judgement if we abandon their
> graves?'[21]

The trauma of abduction is sensitively approached through the
characters of Shanti and Hamida. 'Where have the radiance
and the animation gone?' Lenny inwardly implores when she is
reunited with her *ayah*. 'Can the soul be extracted from its
living body?' Her vacant eyes are larger than ever: wide-opened

with what they've seen and felt. ... Colder than the ice that lurks behind the hazel in the Ice-candy-man's beguiling eyes.[22] Earlier we read concerning Hamida:

> (She) 'was kidnapped by the Sikhs', says Godmother seriously. ... 'She was taken away to Amritsar. Once that happens, sometimes, the husband—or his family—won't take her back.'
> 'Why? It wasn't her fault she was kidnapped!'
> 'Some folk feel that way, they can't stand their women being touched by other men.'
> It's monstrously unfair: but Godmother's tone is accepting.[23]

The most harrowing part of the work is contained in the sub-plot of Ranna's story.[24] Ranna, the great-grandson of Imam Din, lives in the Sikh dominated area, east of Amritsar. The account of his flight, following the destruction of his village of Pir Pindo, is based on the childhood experience of a friend of the author. Ranna is struck on the head and left for dead, but manages to flee across the canefields. The mayhem and destruction wrought by marauding bands of Sikhs and Hindus is seen through his childish acceptance and curiosity. The narrative reaches an almost unbearable climax as Ranna is confronted by a Sikh sepoy as he stands screaming for his relatives alongside the barbed wire cordon of a group of Muslim refugees outside Amritsar railway station.

> Ranna stayed his ground. He could not bear to look at the Sikh. His stomach muscles felt like choked drains. But he stayed his ground. 'I was trembling from head to toe', he says. ...
> 'Let the poor bastard be', Makran Singh said. 'Go on run along.' Taking Ranna by his shoulder he gave him a shove. ... A middle-aged woman without a veil, her hair dishevelled, moved forward holding out her arms. The moment Ranna was close enough to see the compassion in her stranger's eyes, he fainted.[25]

Kartar Singh Duggal is one of the most prominent Punjabi authors. He married a Muslim woman and settled in Delhi after migrating from the Rawalpindi district. His two novels,

The Blood-kins and *Twice Born Twice Dead* set in the Partition period, reflect the massacres and tragedy which befall this area.[26] The latter work has not only been translated into English, but also Urdu, Hindi, Sindhi and Malayalam. Duggal's own ancestral village, six miles from Rawalpindi, provides the location for his study of the impact of Partition. The Sikh village headman, Sohne Shah, loses his daughter, Rajkarni, in the communal riots. He wanders from refugee camp to camp with Satbharai. She is the daughter of his Muslim friend, Allahditta, who is killed when attempting to prevent the attack on his Sikh neighbours.

The book's first part opens with an almost lyrical description of rural communal harmony; Muslims and Sikhs are depicted as exchanging turbans and joining together to listen to *qawwali* performances at the shrine of the local pir. The image which Duggal seeks to portray is summed up in the description of Rajkarni and her friend Satbharai, following a wedding ceremony. Both girls appeared identical, 'even their *dupattas* were of the same colour.'[27] The tranquility of village life is brutally invaded by ousiders who incite the local Muslims to join in the attacks on their neighbours, despite Allahditta's courageous stand. Duggal unflinchingly describes the mayhem which followed the assaults on the village. He concludes this section of the novel with the safe arrival of Sohne Shah and Satbharai in a refugee camp.

The whole of the second part of the novel is taken up with the depiction of camp life through the eyes of the two principal characters. Satbharai is temporarily abandoned by her Sikh *chhacha* and grows fond of a young Sikh boy named Kuldip, who assists his fellow refugees by distributing medicine, milk and rice. It is in an endeavour to prevent any liaison between them that Sohne Shah takes Satbharai with him to begin a new life in Lyallpur.

Part three relates their hazardous journey to Lyallpur by way of curfew-stricken Lahore. This is followed by a temporary peaceful interlude in Lyallpur, where Sohne Shah buys land. Duggal paints a similar picture of communal harmony to that with which he began the novel. Once again, however, Sohne Shah and Satbharai are overtaken by events beyond their control. Partition forces them to flee once more into the relative safety of a refugee camp.

The concluding part of the novel describes Sohne Shah's and Satbharai's evacuation by plane to Amritsar. After a period in the Gandhi Nagar refugee camp in Jullundur, they settle down to a life of social service, assisting in the rehabilitation of abducted women. Sohne Shah takes Sita into his home. She is a pregnant Brahmin girl who is rejected by her own family. The novel ends on a poignant note. Satbharai's wish is granted to be reunited with Kuldip but this results, not in happiness, but tragedy overtaking their household. When Kuldip discovers her true religious identity, he insists that she be returned to Pakistan. Sohne Shah collapses as the police arrive to take her away, whilst a remorseful Kuldip plunges his hand into the lamp beside the niche where Satbharai had kept her copy of the Koran.

From a literary point of view, *Twice Born Twice Dead* is too flawed to be deemed a classic. Its conclusion is a little too melodramatic to entirely convince the reader, while the characterization of the key protaganists never moves beyond the conventional. The work is also marred by historical inaccuracies: the attacks on refugee trains and on the non-Muslim populations of the Rawalpindi district are portrayed as occurring before the fall of the Khizr ministry. Moreover, refugees from the March 1947 violence were entirely resettled in the Amritsar district. Sohne Shah would have been almost unique in heading westwards, instead, to the Lyallpur canal colony districts. Nevertheless, the novel yields valuable insights into the psychological scars created by communal violence. It also provides the reader with glimpses into the life of the refugees which are drawn from first-hand experience. The first extract describes the sheer size of the larger camps, whilst the second evokes the often desperate struggle for survival.

> The camp was like a small township. As far as the eye could see, there were only tents. Living quarters, bathrooms, offices, hospitals,

schools, gurdwaras, temples, the post office, and shops were all housed in tents. Roads, lanes and bylanes criss-crossed the camp. … Children were crying, men and women were shouting, there was uproar all around. Sohne Shah remembered the peace and quiet of his village. He could walk miles there without meeting anyone.[28]

And many days passed. Every instant flocks of refugees on bullock carts and trucks came to the camp under the protection of the army. Day and night the process continued. The College compound was congested. None dared set foot outside the gates. Those who had gone out without protection never returned. A few used to go out of the camp with the police. It transpired that a black market was flourishing—flour at ten rupees a *seer* and salt at a rupee. People were exchanging gold and ornaments for bicycles, bullock carts, *tongas* and camel coaches. It was rumoured that the only way to leave Lyallpur refugee camp was to march out in a caravan. Trains could not be trusted. And how could the railways transport the cattle of the farmers and the horses of the landlords?

The College principal gave small inducements and persuaded the refugees to pack library books into cases. People were amazed. Everyone was hoarding his valuables and yet this college principal was concerned about these musty volumes. Who would carry them?…

The radio was kept tuned the whole day. The stations of both India and Pakistan played gay music in honour of independence. The news was only of tyrannies committed on the Hindus and Sikhs in Pakistan and on the Muslims in India.[29]

Duggal, like Khushwant Singh, displays a depth of human compassion which transcends attachment to communal ideologies and identities. Towards the end of *Twice Born Twice Dead* he provides a poignant description of a Muslim refugee column passing through Amritsar which is unrivalled in the literature on Partition. It provides an appropriate high point at which to leave his work.

A caravan of Muslim evacuees was on the move. Whenever such a caravan was to pass, the police usually clamped down a curfew. At any rate, they would stop all the traffic on the road, so that the caravan could move without any hindrance. Policemen lined both sides of the road to prevent incidents. Still, the Hindu shopkeepers and their children poked fun at the cowed, miserable, hungry and emaciated evacuees.

The caravan was moving. Bullock carts were loaded with boxes, trunks and spinning wheels. On the top were charpoys, bedding and sacks. On the sacks were old men and women, carrying fowls, cats and lambs. From the bullock carts, hung hubble-bubbles, baskets, prayer mats, odds and ends. Holding on the bullock carts for imaginary support walked women with babies at their breasts. Muslim women nurtured behind seven veils ran the gauntlet of hostile glances. The men were wounded, they had seen their relations hacked to pieces with *kirpans*. There was not a single young man in the caravan. Where were the youths? There were small boys, bare-footed, bare-headed, walking fast or slowing down to cast a longing glance at the hot *jalebies* in the sweet shops. The most yearning look however was cast at the running tap. ... No Muslim even dared to take a drop of water from the Hindu tap. Men, women and children looked beseechingly at the water flowing from the tap and moved on.[30]

Bhisham Sahni[31] has published, several short stories set in the Partition period in addition to the Sahitya Akademi[32] award-winning novel, *Tamas*. Jai Ratan has recently translated them into English.[33] We shall briefly turn to these shorter works before examining Sahni's better known novel. They display, like *Tamas*, great compassion and humanity. The horrors of this period are realistically depicted and deplored without lapsing into didacticism.

In the short story, *We have arrived in Amritsar*, Bhisham Sahni addresses the brutality of communal hatred through the extended metaphor of a train journey through the Punjab to Delhi. Like Khushwant Singh, Kartar Singh Duggal, and Bapsi Sidhwa, he portrays the corrosion of human decency and harmony by fear, hatred and revenge. At the outset of the journey, the Muslim, Hindu and Sikh travellers sharing the same compartment happily gossip and laugh. Three Pathan traders playfully tease a Hindu clerk who, like them, is also travelling from Peshawar. The mood changes suddenly, however, when the train arrives at riot-torn Wazirabad. The Pathans eject a Hindu vendor from the carriage who tries to board the train to escape the violence. During the commotion, his wife is seriously injured. Thereafter, an oppressive silence sits over the compartment, and the passengers rearrange their seating on communal lines.

The greatest tension is felt between the clerk and his Pathan tormentors, who mock his lack of courage. When the train crosses what will shortly become the Indian frontier, the Babu turns on his persecutors and threatens to break their heads. At Amritsar, the division along communal lines is completed, when the Pathans leave the compartment to sit with some compatriots. This infuriates the clerk who has also got down from the train. All except the narrator are oblivious to the fact that he has returned carrying an iron rod in one of his hands. The story now builds to its horrendous climax in which the clerk beats to death a Muslim refugee who attempts to enter the compartment.[34]

The story's power derives from its simplicity and economy of style. The mounting tension and uncertainty amongst the passengers is deftly handled. The writer resists the temptation to moralize, leaving the reader to draw his own conclusions from the drama. The hateful lust for revenge which struck out blindly and claimed so many innocent victims in 1947 is both encapsulated and exposed in a single incident.

He gave a stunning blow on the man's head. ... Suddenly two or three tiny streams of blood burst forth and flowed down his face from under his turban. In the faint light of dawn I noticed his open mouth and his glistening teeth. His eyes looked at the Babu, half-open eyes which were slowly closing, as though they were

trying to make out who his assailant was and for what offence he
had taken such revenge.[35]

From a literary viewpoint, the short story, *Pali*, which is also
included in this collection, is even more impressive. With great
sensitivity and depth, it reflects on the fate of children who
were separated from their parents during the Partition upheavals.
Manohar Lal and his wife, Kaushalya, board a lorry for India,
only to discover that they have been separated from their tiny
son, Pali. The indifference of their fellow refugees to his fate is
as chilling a commentary on the brutalization brought by
Partition as the murder committed by the Babu.

> The refugees' hearts had dried of all sentiments. The same Pali
> had once got lost and the whole *mohalla* had gone out in search of
> him. And here someone kept crying repeatedly, 'Get down you! If
> you want to search for your child get down and let us proceed!'[36]

The story reflects the reality of the frustrations and difficulties
which faced ordinary people who sought government help to
trace abducted women and lost children and to retrieve stolen
goods in the aftermath of Partition. 'Manohar Lal took time
off his work to visit these government offices', the narrator
relates, 'but he was just a nobody and no one took much notice
of him. Month after month passed but he found no lead.'[37] But
the story is not really about bureaucratic corruption and delay,
although this is a favourite theme with the author.[38] It centres
instead around the way in which attachment to religious
shibboleths can stand in the way of concern for the individual.
Pali is a twice victim. A childless Muslim couple take him
into their home after he is separated from his natural parents.
They agree to his conversion to Islam, under the threat of the
local *maulvi*. Pali/Altaf attends the mosque school and grows
up as a pious Muslim. Four years elapse before Manohar Lal
tracks his son down in his erstwhile hometown, but his attempts
to secure his return are thwarted by the *maulvi* who bribes the

petty government functionaries to keep the boy's whereabouts hidden. 'This was not a question of a small bribe nor of returning an adopted child', the narrator retells, 'the matter was taking on a religious slant. By not sending away the child they were doing a service to religion—something which was considered a pious act.'[39]

Three years elapse in an elaborate game of hide and seek, before Shakur Ahmed and his wife, Zenab, are finally forced to produce their adopted son before a magistrate.

> But things seemed to be taking an ugly turn. ... the complexion of the problem was undergoing a change. It had become a Hindu-Muslim question. Questions like 'Whose child is he? Who had brought him up?' seemed to have become extraneous to the situation.[40]

Altaf/Pali eventually recognizes Manohar Lal as his natural father. A heartbroken Zenab agrees to part with him on the condition that he can stay with them every year on the occasion of *Eid*.

Altaf arrives at his new home as confused and unhappy as he had felt many years before at the house of his adoptive parents. He scandalizes the guests who have gathered for his homecoming by offering *namaz*. 'The people around him watched with feelings of disgust ... the *Chaudhri* of the *mohalla* cut Manohar Lal short, 'You must know those people have foisted a Muslim convert on you and yet you have nothing but praise for him.'[41] A frightened and confused Altaf/Pali is forbidden to perform *namaz* by the *Chaudhri*, who ironically remarks that, 'Those Muslas have planted the poison of fanaticism in his mind. And at such a tender age!'[42] A pandit and barber are hurriedly summoned to perform the *mundan* ceremony upon the terrified Pali, who is threatened with having his tongue pulled out if he calls himself Altaf. The story concludes with a tearful Zenab making all sorts of conjectures about when she will see her son again.

Tamas[43] was first published in Hindi in 1974. It has been revised and reprinted in English on a number of occasions since 1981. Considerable controversy was generated by its dramatization for Indian television in 1988. Critics claimed that it distorted history and poisoned communal relations. The state run Doordarshan television network only continued its broadcast after a favourable ruling from the Bombay High Court.[44]

The work in fact bears a strong resemblance to the approach of Urdu 'progressive' writers in that it is informed by a humanism which seeks to portray all communities as equally victims and aggressors in 1947. Sahni does, however, avoid the trap of didacticism more effectively than such authors as Krishan Chander. Such characters as Harnam Singh and his wife, Banto, for example, are not just vehicles for his views. They possess a human warmth and believability which engages the reader's emotions. Even the mass suicide of the Sikh women in the village of Sayyedpur is portrayed realistically and is devoid of melodrama.[45] Indeed, it is only with his depiction of the British Deputy Commissioner, Richard, and his alcoholic wife, Liza, that Sahni loses his sureness of touch.

Tamas begins with the frenzied struggle between Nathu, the tanner, and the black pig which he has lured into his dilapidated dwelling. These opening pages perfectly set the atmosphere of brooding evil which pervades the novel. Nathu's patron, Murad Ali, has in fact duped him into secretly slaughtering the pig, whose carcass is then deposited outside the town's main mosque. Murad Ali's plan works, in that the incident sparks off widespread communal rioting in the town and surrounding countryside. Murad Ali is by no means alone, however, in manipulating communal passions for political ends. Sahni draws an equally sinister picture of Master Devbrat. He turns Ranvir, an innocent fifteen-year-old boy, into a fanatical Hindu youth leader. Ranvir incites a friend to murder an old Muslim perfume seller who wanders into the street in which the boys have built up an arsenal of weapons.[46]

Sahni contrasts the cold-blooded consequences of the boy's action with the romanticized view of violence which Master Devbrat has inculcated in his acolytes.

> The four warriors in the squad were spoiling for action. Stationed on the roof they felt like gallant Rajputs waiting for the Muslim foe down in the Haldi Ghati.
> Being rather short, Ranvir liked to believe he was like that other great short-statured hero Shivaji. ... Sometimes he wished he were wearing a long Rajput coat, a saffron turban on his head and a long sword hanging from a broad cummerbund round his waist. To take part in a fierce fight in loose pyjamas, an ill-fitting shirt and worn out chappals didn't seem right; it was not the dress of a fighting man.[47]

He similarly depicts the embattled Sikhs at Sayyedpur preparing to meet their fate in a ritualized re-anactment of the *khalsa's* past conflicts with the Mughals. Their enemies are not Muslims from neighbouring villages but have been transformed into the 'Turks.' It is in this atmosphere that the mass suicide becomes rationalized, but Sahni ensures, as with the murder of the perfume seller, that realism soon intrudes. The women's heroic sacrifice is quickly brought down to the level of constituting a public health hazard for the British officials. For a 'dough-like flabby' Sikh, it presents a different difficulty: the need to bribe an official so that he can get transport to the village to retrieve his wife's gold bangles.

> They weigh five *tolas* each. And she has a gold chain round her neck. I know she's dead. She must have met the same fate as the other twenty-six women. But how can I forget the bangles and the chain. ... I had (them) made with my hard-earned money. ... We shall take a small chisel along. If it comes to that, we can also take a goldsmith's assistant with us. He can finish the job within minutes. As you know, where there's a will there's a way.[48]

Tamas' strength stems from the fact that while it unequivocally condemns communal hatred and violence, it recognizes the complexity of human character and emotions. Shahnawaz's personal friendship with the trader, Raghunath, is thus depicted as uneasily co-existing with a hatred of Hinduism. While Shahnawaz goes out of his way to protect Raghunath and his property, he violently assaults his hapless servant, Milkhi.

> What had set it off? Was it the sight of Milkhi's centipede-like tuft or was it the thought of the congregation in the mosque? Or was it what he had been seeing and hearing for the past three days finally taking its toll? Taking two steps at a time he kicked Milkhi in the back. Milkhi went crashing down the stairs and struck the wall. His skull cracked open and his back broke. He lay still where he had fallen. … 'You worm', Shahnawaz muttered.[49]

That same night, the narrator tells us, Shahnawaz handed over the jewel box he had retrieved for Raghunath's wife. She 'looked at (him) gratefully. It was almost as though it wasn't a man she was looking at but an angel.'[50]

Tamas concludes with the restoration of order and the convening of a Peace Committee, but Sahni allows only the communist, Devdutt, and the Congress leader, Bakshiji, to approach this devoid of cynicism. Others at the meeting are more concerned with the opportunities for economic and political profit left by the riots. Murad Ali cynically clambers aboard the Peace Bus and leads slogans in favour of communal harmony as it tours the riot-torn areas. The novel ends with the same sense of foreboding with which it began. Bakshiji 'looked sad and pensive, "vultures will fly over the city!" he mumbled to himself. "Many more vultures than you can see now".'[51]

Tamas provides valuable psychological insights for the historian. It reveals not only the complexity of emotions which lay behind communal violence, but their contradictions. Friendship and hate could coexist, as could hope and fear. The abnormal circumstances of riot could call forth bestiality, or the noblest human goodness.

It also points to the need, as do other works, of dehumanizing the victim of violence. Master Devbrat warned his pupil, Ranvir, the narrator tells us, 'Never to size up his adversary. ... if one looked long enough at one's adversary it aroused sympathy for him in one's mind'.[52]

In the story of Iqbal Singh,[53] Sahni humanizes the physical and psychological torment of forced conversion which the historian must otherwise approach only through cold statistics. As in the short story, *Pali*, Sahni leaves the reader with the understanding that excessive zeal for the externalities of religion overrides all its internal truths or feelings for the individual. The issue of abduction is also raised through the minor character of Prakasho. It too is treated with sensitivity, although less powerfully.[54]

Finally, the novel emphasizes the point made earlier by Chaman Nahal that the uprooting violence of 1947 sundered ties to ancestral homes which lay deep in the psyche of all communities. Bhisham Sahni allows the reader to glimpse this in his comment on the village of Sayyedpur.

> It was true that the Sikhs had as much pride in being of the village of Sayyedpur as the Muslims. They were proud of its red soil, of its excellent wheat, its loquat orchards, its extreme winters and icy winds. The Sikhs, like the Muslims of this place, were known for their hospitality, generosity and joviality.[55]

III

Faiz Ahmad Faiz (1911-1984) wrote only occasionally on the theme of Partition, but his work must be included in any study such as this because he was unquestionably the foremost Urdu poet of the second half of this century. His work delighted readers in both Pakistan and India and received international recognition.[56] No poet since his fellow Punjabi, Iqbal,[57] played such a prominent role in public life.[58] Unlike Iqbal, however, he was reviled as well as lauded for this, and indeed was for a time under the threat of execution during the Ayub Khan era, for his alleged role in the Rawalpindi Conspiracy Case.[59]

Faiz's popularity stemmed in part from the range of his poetical skills. He could produce *ghazals*, write in the style of the *qawwali* as well as modern poems on 'progressive' themes. The latter were of course a dominant element in 'progressive' Urdu prose fiction.[60] The poem, *Love, Do Not Ask*, which was published in his 1943 collection, overtly marks a movement from 'love' poetry to 'progressive' concerns.

> Love, do not ask me for that love again.
> Once I thought life, because you lived, a prize—
> The Time's pain nothing, you alone were pain;
> Your beauty kept earth's springtimes from decay,
> My Universe held only your bright eyes—
> If I won you, fate would be at my feet.
>
> It was not true, all this, but only wishing;
> Our world knows other torments than of love,
> And other happiness than a fond embrace.
> Dark curse of countless ages, savagery
> Interwoven with silk and satin and gold lace,
> Men's bodies sold in street and marketplace,
> Bodies that caked grime fouls and thick blood smears
> Flesh issuing from the cauldrons of disease
> With festered sores dripping corruption—these
> Sights haunt me too, and will not be shut out;
> Not be shut out, though your looks ravish still.
>
> This world knows other torments than of love,
> And other happiness than a fond embrace;
> Love, do not ask for my old love again.[61]

Two other poems in this first collection contain a major concern with human suffering and the need for political justice. The whole of *Dogs* is a sustained symbol for the indignity of poverty, whilst *Speak* is a clarion call for 'progressives' to cry out against injustice, come what may. *Speak* possesses a universal quality and is not restricted to any particular situation. In the later work, *Freedom's Dawn*, Faiz, however, directly addresses the situation at the time of Partition. It is worth quoting in full not only because it is one of his best compositions, but, more importantly for the historian, because it provides a powerful insight into the disillusionment felt by many 'progressives' in the aftermath of independence. Prose can help uncover the causes of this alienation, but only poetry such as this can reveal its emotion and pain.

Ye daagh daagh ujaala, ye shab gazida sahar,
Vo intizaar tha jis ka, ye vo sahar to nahin,
Ye vo sahar to nahin jis ki aarzu lekar
Chale the yaar ke mil ja'egi kahin na kahin
Falak ke dasht men taaron ki aakhiri manzil,
Kahin to hoga shab-e-sust mauj ka saahil,
Kahin to ja ke rukega safina-e-gham-e-dil.

Jawaan lahu ki pur asraar shaahraahon se
Chale jo yaar to daaman pe kitne haath pare;
Diyaar-e-husn ki be sabr khwaabgaahon se
Pukaarti rahin baahen, baden bulaate rahe;
Bahut aziz thi lekin rukh-e-sahar ki lagan,
Bahut qarin tha hasinaan-e-nur ka daaman,
Subuk subuk thi tamanna, dabi dabi thi thakan.
Suna hai ho bhi chuka hai firaaq-e-zulmat-o-nur,
Suna hai ho bhi chuka hai visal-e-manzil-o-gaam;
Badal chuka hai bahut ahl-e-dard ka dastur,
Nishaat-e-vasl halaal-o-azaab-e-hijr haraam.

Jigar ki aag, nazar ki umang, dil ki jalan,
Kisi pe chaara-e-hijraan ka kuchh asar hi nahin.
Kahaan se aai nigaar-e-saba, kidhar ko gai?
Abhi charaagh-e-sar-e-raah ko kuchh khabar hi nahin;
Abhi giraani-e-shab men kami nahin aai,
Najaat-e-dida-o-dil ki ghari nahin aai;
Chale chalo ke vo manzil abhi nahin aai.

This stain-covered daybreak, this night-bitten dawn,
This is not that dawn of which there was expectation
This is not that dawn with longing for which

The friends set out, (convinced) that somewhere there would be
met with,
In the desert of the sky, the final destination of the stars,
Somewhere there would be the shore of the sluggish wave of night,
Somewhere would go and halt the boat of the grief of pain.

By the mysterious highroads of youthful blood
When (we) friends set out,
What temptations lay in our way!
From impatient sleeping-chambers of the dwellings of beauty
Arms kept crying out, bodies kept calling;
But very dear was the passion of the face of dawn,
Very close the robe of the sylphs of light;
The longing was very buoyant, the weariness was very slight.
—It is heard that the separation of darkness and light has been
fully completed,
It is heard that the union of goal and step has been fully completed;

The manners of the people of suffering (leaders) have changed
very much,
Joy of union is lawful, anguish for separation forbidden.

The fire of the liver, the tumult of the eye, burning of the heart,—
There is no effect on any of them of (this) cure for separation.
Whence came that darling of a morning breeze, whither has it
gone?
The lamp beside the road has still no knowledge of it;
In the heaviness of night there has still come no lessening,
The hour of the deliverance of eye and heart has not arrived.
Come, come on for that goal has still not arrived.[62]

IV

Urdu novels and short stories contain a rich and largely unmined
vein of material concerning the human dimension of Pakistan's
birth. A number of anthologies have been published, which
further ease the historian's task. One of the best of these is
Mumtaz Shirin's *Zulmat-i-Neem Roze*.[63] This intersperses short

stories with autobiographical accounts. Much of the literature itself is informed by personal experience. Inevitably, quality is variable in such an extensive deposit of material.

We propose to turn, first, to works which, although they are popular or possess literary merit, are of less assistance to the historian because of their didacticism. The novels, *Khak aur Khoon* by Nasim Hijazi, and *Sangam* by Muhammad Ahsan Faruqi, represent Pakistani ideology. Qurat ul-Ain Haider's monumental work, *Aag Ka Darya*, is suffused by Indian nationalist sentiment. While the progressive writers movement's approach to Partition is reflected in the short stories by Krishan Chander contained in the volume, *Ham Wahshi Hain*.

Krishan Chander,[64] like many Urdu writers of this period, was greatly influenced by the Progressive Writers movement.[65] This was launched in London in 1934, before being established at Lucknow in April 1936. Chander was in fact its general secretary for a number of years. His extensive writings on the Partition period are suffused with its ideological beliefs. They included attacks on 'religious obscurantism' and the exploitation of the poor, and condemnation of India's domination by British Imperialism. In the words of a Soviet commentator, the stories in *Ham Wahshi Hain* were designed to awaken in his readers 'disgust at religious obscurantism', and to appeal to their 'reason, their conscience and their feelings of justice'.[66]

Chander sets out to achieve these aims by depicting communal violence in lurid detail, and in a formula which portrays all communities as aggressors. The short story, *Ek Tavaif Ka Khat*, typifies this approach. The heroine, a Bombay prostitute, writes to both Nehru and Jinnah, requesting that they adopt two little girls, one a Hindu, the other a Muslim, whom she has taken in. The story contains graphic details of the fate of the girls' families. It also makes great play of their similar experiences—orphaning and rape at the hands of their tormentors.[67] The author's humanistic/socialist vision is contrasted with the massacre and carnage through the expression of the prostitute's letter:

People in a frenzy have brought shame upon the women who gave
them life, who sang them cradle songs, who bowed their heads
before them in humility, shame and modesty. They have violated
their sisters, brides and mothers. The Hindu religion has lost its
honour. Today all the mantras of the Rig Veda have fallen silent,
today shame has coloured all the *dokhi* of Granth Sahib. Today
each *shlok* of the Gita has been excised. Who today will dare to
speak to me of the Ajanta frescoes, to read the edicts of Ashoka.[68]

Krishan Chander also adopts a studied anti-communalism in
the more famous short story, *Peshawar Express*.[69] When it returns
to Bombay from Peshawar, the train implores that it should no
longer be used to carry 'a cargo of blood and flesh dripping
with hatred', but instead carry 'food-grain to the famine stricken
areas ... coal, oil and iron ore to the mills, and ploughs and
fertilizers to the farms'. It looks forward to the life to come:
'Then there will be no Hindus and no Muslims. They will all
be workers and human beings.'[70]

This is not the setting to discuss whether Krishan Chander's
didacticism detracts from his art.[71] It is obvious, however, that
his stories reveal a progressive understanding of the events they
describe, rather than uncover the complex feelings evoked by
Partition. The characters and their responses are little more
than stereotypes.[72]

Mohammad Ahsan Faruqi has written *Sangam* from an
entirely different intellectual perspective, but his characterization
is equally stylized. The *sangam* in the title is the confluence of
the Ganges and Jumna rivers. It forms the setting for the initial
meeting of the two main characters, Ibn-e-Muslim and Uma
Parvati, who reappear throughout the narrative. The story
commences at the time of Mahmud Ghaznavi's invasions. Ibn-
e-Muslim is a soldier, Uma Parvati a Hindu goddess who has
taken human form. They fall in love, but Ibn-e-Muslim's duty
calls him back to Ghaznavi. They are next brought together
two hundred years later, at the time of Muhammad Ghauri.
On this occasion their love is consummated in marriage, as
Uma Parvati declares before the *qazi* that she has always been a

Muslim in her heart. They are depicted again, he a courtier or companion of a ruler, she a confidante of famous female figures down through the ages of Muslim rule in India. Both characters adopt cultural influences from the other's community with the passage of time.

When Independence arrives, however, Uma Parvati tells Ibn-e-Muslim, now presented as Mr S.M. Muslim, Bar-at-law, that they must part. They return to their original meeting place, where she once again becomes the image of the goddess. S.M. Muslim seeks to become her devoteé, but he is captured by a band of Hindus, who throw him into the Ganges. Whilst floating down it, he passes the confluence with the Jumna and is inspired to think of the greatness of India's Muslim past, before looking with hope to the future. The novel concludes with him living as a penniless refugee in Karachi.[73] The final scene of *Sangam*, like that of *Peshawar Express*, is the setting for the author's credo. S.M. Muslim, upset at the hostility displayed by the local population to the mohajirs, declares that the situation can only be redeemed by securing Islamic unity and solidarity.

> Those who make themselves a nation on the basis of the country are actually Hindus, infidels, even though they have Muslim names. We have to teach the ignorant ones that they too should be Muslims. Instead of being a nation of the land, they have to be a nation of Allah, of Muhammad.[74]

The very strength of the novel's political message means that it must be handled carefully as a source. It also detracts from its literary merits in encouraging unrealistic characterisation.[75] It should be evident even from the foregoing outline of the plot that the outcome of Muslim-Hindu separation is depicted as inevitable.

Sangam was in fact written as a response to Qurat ul-Ain Haider's[76] novel, *Aag ka Darya*, which provoked great controversy when it was published in Pakistan in 1959. Both works take early Indian history as their starting point. They both also use the technique of the reappearance of the main characters in successive periods to raise the question of the Indian Muslims' historical destiny and self-identity. The novels arrive, however, at diametrically opposed conclusions.

Aag Ka Darya opens in the early Buddhist period. The attention is centred upon two students, Gautam Nilamber and Hari Shankar, as they move about Ancient India and through several centuries and rebirths. The female character, Champak, who is to reappear later in the story, is also introduced at this point. The first Muslim protaganist, Abu l'Mansur Kamal ad-Din, a prototype of the modern character, Kamal, appears at the time of Kabir. He is an 'Iraqi' librarian and philosopher who arrives in India on military service. He accepts the validity of both Hinduism and Buddhism, and settles in Bengal where he marries a non-Muslim. He is eventually murdered by Muslim soldiers who accuse him of being a traitor.

The novel continues in early nineteenth century British India with the introduction of a new character, Cyril Ashley, an East India Company servant. The Champak figure reappears as a Lucknow courtesan. Lucknow is also the scene of the early section of the book's finale, which is set in 1939. This examines in depth the experiences of a group of upper class young people. Some critics regard the writer's depiction of the frustrations plaguing this intellectual elite as the most satisfying part of her mammoth work.[77] The group includes the characters, Hari Shankar, and his sisters Laj and Nirmala, his friend Kamal, and his sisters, Talat and Appi, Kamal's step-brother, Amir Raza, and two additional friends, Champa Ahmad and Gautam Nilamber. They all go their separate ways following Partition.

Amir Raza migrates to Pakistan, where he makes a successful career for himself. Kamal stays put in India, even when he is discriminated against. It is only when his family home in Lucknow is declared evacuee property that he leaves for Pakistan. As he leaves Delhi for the last time, he is confronted with the depressing realization that he is cutting himself off from his past. 'In myself', he declares, 'I am the corpse, the gravedigger and the mourner'.[78] Qurat ul-Ain Haider further questions the wisdom of migration to Pakistan through the character Champa. She expresses pride in her Indian heritage by returning to her home town of Benares. The author has her declare, 'I am a resident of *this* country. Where am I going to find another country for myself? The flight-mentality makes no sense to me.'[7] To underscore India's historical unity and continuity, the novel concludes with a repetition of its opening meeting between Gautam Nilamber and Hari Shankar.

The general mood of *Aag Ka Darya* may be summarized as follows: first, that Indian culture is complex and absorptive; secondly, that the Muslims of the subcontinent should approve and affirm this complexity and reject exclusivist religious claims;[80] thirdly, that the creation of Pakistan has cut off many Muslims from their diverse and rich cultural and intellectual inheritance; fourthly, that this dislocation has caused loss of personal identity. The controversy aroused by this message is understandable. It fails to take seriously the genuine ideological motivations of the supporters of the Pakistan movement. It also ignores the significant social dimension of South Asian religious identity, restricting religious commitment to a matter of individual choice.[81] What, then, of the novel's value as a source for the historian? Is it merely a personal testament, even a psychotherapy, as the author struggled to come to terms with her own identity?[82]

I think not. The novel's reception by Indian Muslim readers and critics[83] alike reveals that it has touched a chord. In speaking so powerfully to the many Indian Muslims who did not migrate to Pakistan, it also speaks for them. It as such provides an important counterpoint to the mass of literature on Partition which reflects the mohajir experience.

Khak aur Khoon is as popular with Pakistani readers as is *Aag Ka Darya* with Indian.[84] Like the other books in this section, however, it is highly subjective. The narrative commences with its hero, Saleem, about to enter primary school in his village, which is situated in the Gurdaspur district of the Punjab. It concludes with him as a wounded veteran of the

Pakistan movement and the war with India over Kashmir. The
other main characters are his cousin, Majid, his uncle, Afzal,
and schoolfriend, Daud. Later, Ershad, Akhtar and Altaf are
introduced as college friends, as are Dr Shaukat and two girls,
Ismat and Rahat.

The first part of the novel is the most artistically satisfying. It
realistically portrays such simple scenes from village life as
children swimming in a pool after the onset of the monsoon,
climbing trees to collect birds' eggs and joining in the rough
and tumble of a game of *kabbadi*. Humour shines through in
the episode of Pir Wilayat Shah and the horse which threw
Saleem, and the children inking the face of Mohan Singh's
servant. This authenticity is later lost, when the author interrupts
the narrative to record his comments on the political
developments at the time of the action. The characters also
lose their individuality and lapse into stereotypes.

Saleem is depicted as a college student in Lahore in Part
Two of the novel. He becomes an effective speaker for the
Muslim League cause, when he steps in for his friend, Akhtar,
who falls ill on the eve of an important debate. Saleem trounces
the Muslim nationalist speaker, Altaf, in the meeting. Shortly
afterwards, he is reunited with a secondary school friend, Ershad,
whose family has moved to Amritsar. Saleem joins a propaganda
tour against the Unionist Government of the Punjab. He also
volunteers for the Muslim National Guards after receiving a
letter from a fellow worker which details the atrocities in Bihar.
This section of the book closes with Saleem's arrest during the
civil disobedience campaign against the Unionists early in 1947.

The action next turns to the Partition riots. The author
depicts a Sikh attack on Saleem's village with considerable
conviction and poignancy. Saleem, Daud, and Majid, along with
other survivors, join a large refugee column. Daud is killed just
short of the Pakistan border, but the others make it to safety,
although they are wounded in the fighting. The final section of
the novel has Saleem fighting in Kashmir. Here he encounters
his former debating opponent, Altaf, who is now supporting

the Pakistan cause. Saleem is seriously wounded, but as the novel closes, he is seen to be slowly recovering and resuming his literary career.[85]

The character of Saleem is partly successful as a representation of a common Muslim experience during this period. Many Muslim students in Lahore were at the forefront of the Pakistan movement in the Punjab. But Saleem is a too stereotyped character to be entirely effective. The writer allows too much of his own personality and opinions to intrude, for the work as a whole to move beyond a subjective reality and understanding. We are thus left with a story about the events of Pakistan's birth, which does not get inside them.[86]

We now turn to a very different kind of writer, Saadat Hasan Manto.[87] Manto is one of the most prolific writers on the events of 1947. Like Krishan Chander, he was greatly influenced by the Progressive Writers' movement, although his strong streak of individuality prevented him from becoming wholeheartedly involved with it. This accounts for his less didactic approach than that of Chander and his compatriots. Manto was already a mature writer[88] when he reached Lahore from Bombay in January 1948.[89] Within nine months, he had produced a collection of writings, *Siyah Hashiye*, dealing with the Partition which is noted for its irony and black humour.[90] This was followed in March 1949 by the publication of *Thanda Gosht*.[91] This is the first of a series of short stories which delve into the psychological effects of Partition. Literary critics have acclaimed it as a masterpiece on account of its power, suspense and believability.

Iswar Singh is unable to make love to his equally passionate mistress, Kalwant Kaur, on his return from rioting in the city. She stabs him in a fit of jealousy because she believes he has been seeing another woman. The dying Iswar confesses that after murdering six members of a family, he carried away a young Muslim girl in order to rape her. Whilst engaged in this act, he discovered that she was dead, was cold like ice, as he also is at the end of the tale.

We have here not only a chilling insight into the passions aroused in the miasma of terror and violence. For Iswar's impotence is a compelling symbol of the loss of normal human sensitivities following the spree of looting and murder. Depravity wreaks havoc on the perpetrators as well as the victims of violence. Despite its power, however, *Thanda Gosht* does not provide the universalized vision of the Partition experience which is contained in some of Manto's other short stories.

'The real emotions of real people'[92] caught up in the confusion brought by Partition is most clearly reflected in *Khuda Ki Qasm*.[93] The narrator is a Liaison Officer involved in the recovery of abducted women. He encounters an old Muslim woman looking for her lost daughter, intially in Jullundur, then in Shahranpur and finally in Amritsar. She refuses to accompany him to Pakistan because she is convinced that her daughter is still alive.

> Why?', I asked her.
> Because she is so beautiful—so beautiful that no one will dare to kill her—no one will slap her even', she whispered to me.[94]

At the time of their final meeting in Freed Chowk, Amritsar, the old woman appears so distressed that the Liaison Officer decides to get her admitted to a lunatic asylum in Pakistan. Just at that moment, a sharp-featured young Sikh walks by accompanied by a veiled woman. The Sikh whispers to that 'goddess of beauty', 'Look—your Mother'. The young woman looks for a moment, then averts her eyes and moves away. The old Muslim lady in that brief instant recognizes her daughter and shouts after the officer, 'I have just seen her, just seen her'. He firmly replies, fully aware of what has happened, 'By God, I do not lie. By God she has died'. At this the old woman collapses to the ground.[95]

This touching and powerful ending is not only artistically satisfying, but brings home that Partition involved the death of family ties as well as individuals. The story humanizes the cold statistics of abducted persons which confront the historian. The old woman symbolizes the uncertainties and anxieties of many waiting to hear of loved ones. These emotions overpowered their own relief at safely reaching the goal of their promised land.

The confused and torn identities in 1947 are the subject of Manto's best known short story, *Toba Tek Singh*.[96] Its theme is the exchange of lunatics between India and Pakistan, following Partition. It opens with a series of jibes at the expense of political leaders and national pride on both sides[97], but ends on a note of great poignancy.

The narrative increasingly focuses on an aged Sikh inmate, Bishan Singh, known to everyone as Toba Tek Singh, because of his large landholdings there. He becomes obsessed with the question whether Toba Tek Singh is in India or Pakistan. His insistence so flusters a former Muslim neighbour, Fazal Din, who visits him, that he receives an unclear reply. Bishan Singh only discovers that Toba Tek Singh is in fact in Pakistan whilst he is awaiting evacuation at the border. He then refuses to cross to India and is left standing alone on a spot midway between the boundary lines.

> Just before dawn, an ear-splitting cry issued from Bishan Singh's silent throat. Officials ran from both sides and discovered that the man who had remained upright on his legs for fifteen years was now lying on his face. On one side, behind the barbed wire, was India; Pakistan was behind the wire on the other side. Between them, stretched on the ground of this no-man's land, lay Toba Tek Singh.[9]

Bishan Singh reflects the sense of uprootedness and confusion which faced many refugees in 1947. They were attached to their ancestral villages not out of mere sentimentality, but as the allegory reveals, because it was in them that the core of their identity resided. Finally, the story reflects the bewilderment which many must have felt who awoke to find themselves in a different country to the one in which they had grown up.

Manto wrote a large number of other stories about Partition. They are less valuable as sources, partly because they were produced in order to shock, rather than to explore emotions. This is particularly the case in the well known story, *Khol Do*.[99] In others,[100] Manto's characters are more stereotyped. Consequently, their experiences are neither genuinely moving for the reader, nor are they able to add insights for the historian.

Qudratullah Shahab's short story, *Ya Khuda*,[101] matches Manto's power in uncovering the realities of Partition. It centres around the experiences of a *maulvi's* daughter named Dilshad. Sikhs murder her father and rape her. She arrives penniless in Lahore, where she is treated with indifference and contempt.[102] The writer explores the harsh conditions in the refugee camps and the hypocrisy of many of those involved in charity work through Dilshad's and her friend Zubeida's experiences.[103] The latter has to immodestly uncover herself to keep her son, Mahmood, alive in the bitter cold.[104] The local storekeeper, meanwhile, jealously guards the stock of blankets and sanctimoniously recites Iqbal's poetry.[105]

Dilshad is tricked into going to the house of Mustafa Khan, who claims to know the whereabouts of her beloved, Rahim Khan, who has disappeared during the disturbances. Immediately they reach the house, Mustafa Khan makes sexual advances. This prompts the narrator to ironically comment on the relationship between the refugees and their helpers. It deserves quoting in full:

Lahore, Lahore na tha, Medina tha. Lahore waalay, Lahore waalay na thay. Insaan thay. Naheen, wo to shayid ansaar-i-Medina say bhee kuch darja afzal tar thay. Yahaan, Dilshaad kay liyay har roze ek naya Rahim Khan paida ho jaata tha. Zubaida kay liyay har roze ek naya daada janam leta tha. Baytiyon kay liyay nayae nayae baap thay. Behanon kay liyay nayae nayae bhai, jisam ka rishta jisam say milta tha, khoon ka rishta khoon say.

Lahore was not Lahore, it was Medina, the people of Lahore were not of Lahore, they were the *ansars* of Medina who extended every help to the Holy Prophet and his Companions. They were perhaps better than the *ansars* of Medina. Here, for Dilshad a new Rahim Khan was being born. For Zubeida, a new grandfather was born daily, for daughters new fathers, for sisters new brothers, the relationship of flesh was meeting flesh, and blood with blood.[106]

It is a relief to step back from such emotional intensity to Akhtar Jamal's short story, *Samjhota Express*.[107] The narrative revolves around a Muslim family from Bhopal. The central character, Bi Apa, is portrayed as a dedicated Muslim League worker, who even dressed so that from a distance she looked like a Muslim League banner.[108] She not only made big Muslim League posters, but addressed ladies' rallies in a powerful oratorical style, imitating that of Nawab Bahadur Yar Jung. She marries a fellow graduate from Aligarh who is the commander of the local Muslim National Guards. Disillusionment soon sets in after the marriage. Bi Apa's 'Shaheen' who 'had flown over the rocks of the peaks', had become an 'ox working the village oil mill',[109] giving up his political activities because of work responsibilities.

The tension within the family becomes almost unbearable when Bi Apa's husband insists that they must stay in India at the time of Partition. At one stage she even declares, 'Had I known you would not go to Pakistan, I would not have married you.'[110] She derides her husband as an opportunist, when he insists that the photograph of Jinnah which had decorated their drawing room should be relegated to the *almirah*, and pride of place should now go to a picture of Abul Kalam Azad.

The story can be dismissed too easily as a slight domestic drama. Its artistic strength in fact derives from its lightness of touch. The author carefully avoids sentimentality and displays an apt use of symbols. A valuable insight is provided into the emotional life of the Muslim middle class. The question is raised whether Pakistan was a 'dream' or a 'suicide' for such individuals as Bi Apa and her husband.

The leading Urdu writer, Rajinder Singh Bedi,[111] has set just one short story in the Partition era, but it must be included in any discussion. The work, *Lajwanti*,[112] is a minor literary classic. Firmly rooted in reality, it approaches the subject of the recovery and rehabilitation of abducted women with great sensitivity

and finesse. The action revolves around Sunder Lal and his
wife Lajwanti, who had been abducted during the turmoil which
accompanied Partition. 'Sunder Lal had abandoned all hope of
finding Lajwanti', Bedi tells his readers, 'He had made his loss
a part of the general loss. He had drowned his personal sorrow
by plunging into social service.'[113] This took the form of acting
as secretary for a 'rehabilitation of hearts' committee. Sunder
Lal daily led processions, and publicly debated with those who
refused to take back women who had been abducted.

> People listened to Babu Sunder Lal's exhortations sometimes with
> patience, sometimes with irritation. Women who had no trouble
> in coming across from Pakistan were utterly complacent, like over-
> ripe cauliflowers. Their menfolk were indifferent and grumbled;
> their children treated the songs on rehabilitation like lullabys to
> make them sleep again.[114]

This existence is turned upside down when Lajwanti is
returned to him, following an exchange of abducted women
between India and Pakistan. Sunder Lal 'wanted to run away,
to spread out all the banners and placards he had carried, sit in
their midst and cry to his heart's content', Bedi narrates. But
like other men , all he did was to proceed to the police station
as if nothing untoward had happened'.[115] Lajwanti's Muslim
style of dress and improved appearance displeased Sunder Lal.
Some of the other men who had gathered at the police station
refused to take back their women. But Sunder Lal 'overcame
his revulsion. He had thrown himself body and soul into (the
rehabilitation) movement. And there were his colleagues ...
with their raucous voices yelling slogans over the microphone.'[116]

The story ends on a poignant rather than joyful note. Sunder
Lal refuses to allow Lajwanti to unburden her experiences. He
treats her with an over-exaggerated respect, calling her his *devi*.
The old intimacy is gone. 'She had been rehabilitated but not
accepted. Sunder Lal did not want eyes to see her tears nor ears
to hear her wailing.'[117] Lajwanti is as much a victim in her own
home as she was at the time of her abduction. But Sunder Lal

has also been diminished. Unable to cope with his hurt pride, he denies human emotional contact and instead plunges himself obsessively into the work of the ironically named 'rehabilitation of hearts' committee.

The psychological impact of Partition is given a more extensive treatment than Rajinder Singh Bedi's genre allows, in the full length novel, *Udas Naslen*, by Abdullah Husain.[118] The work has been praised for its subtle characterization, and authentic depiction of rural life in the setting of Raushanpur village. The American critic, John Hanson, has pointed out that, unlike many of the novels of Partition, it represents the views of those who did not go through the upheaval of migration to a new and strange land.[119] It is also of interest to the historian in that it engages with the feelings of working class Muslims through the character of the factory worker, Ali. He is the younger brother of Naim, the novel's main protaganist, but unlike him, Ali is not well-educated and does not aspire to the life of a respectable upper-class Muslim.[120]

The two brothers are caught up in Hindu-Muslim rioting in 1947. Naim, in keeping with his inconsistent and apathetic character, refuses to join Azra in Pakistan, but then apparently aimlessly falls in with a refugee caravan. This includes Ali and his wife, who is killed by marauders. Naim submits to them and is shot without his travelling companions even noticing. This pathetic ending speaks for itself, as does Ali's different fate. He reaches Pakistan alone and befriends and nurses a poor woman named Bano who is searching for a lost child at Lahore railway station. The novel concludes with Ali and Bano's marriage and their attempt to make the best of a new life.[121]

This brief synopsis should not leave the reader with the misapprehension that Abdullah Husain writes with a clear didactic purpose. He in fact claims that history has no plan or order, but is purely accidental.[122] The novel, he has declared, is not about history but about individuals, and his foremost purpose was to make them 'convincing'.[123] Abdullah Husain has undoubtedly succeeded in this respect. It is also true that he is more concerned with the depiction of relationships and individual psychological character than in assessing the meaning of Pakistan's creation for the Muslim community. But he is fully aware of the importance of historical influences on his characters. Through the figure of Ali, he lends insights into the effect of Partition on the common man. While such individuals may not have possessed a clearly-formed philosophical or historical understanding of Pakistan, they actually made it work by picking up the pieces of their shattered lives.

We turn next to the work of Intizar Husain.[124] He has been praised as a unique talent, both by western translators of his stories and by such Pakistani literary critics as Sajjad Baqar Rizvi. They have lauded his narrative style, which is reminiscent of that found in old Urdu *dastans*,[125] and his sensitive creative vision, with its insight into loss of identity and the breakdown of humanistic values.[126]

Whilst Manto addresses the theme of the loss of identity in relation to Partition, Intizar Husain presents it in a way which enables it to be seen as the predicament of the human condition. This universalistic approach to alienation can be read into the timeless *Shahr-e-Afsos*.[127] Another story in the collection of this name, *Sirhiyan*, also focuses on loss of memory and identity, although it is more directly linked to the Partition experience. The main character, Saiyid, has been robbed of his memory. He has also become unable to dream or sleep and subconsciously retrieve his memory in this way. One summer evening he is lying on his *charpoy* alongside three friends, Akhtar, Bashir Bhai and Razi. Bashir Bhai is interpreting a dream Razi has related. It is loaded with past memories of a small town somewhere in the eastern region of UP. When Razi mentions the *imam bara*, a series of past memories and emotions are triggered in Saiyid's mind. He regains his power to dream and, with it, his wholeness and sense of identity, as his past is again part of his present.[128]

This strong feeling for the flow of Indian Muslim history and the sense in which Partition sundered the past is taken up in a number of Intizar Husain's works. The short story, *Akhri Mom Bati*,[129] provides a good example. The narrator returns from Pakistan to visit his aunt in UP. He notices that everything in the village has changed, and that his widowed aunt has suddenly grown old. The house seems silent since the departure of his cousin, Shamina. She has married an Aligarh graduate and gone to live in Karachi. On the eve of *moharram* he remembers how Shamina and aunty used to decorate the *imam bara* and receive the visitors. When he returns from a stroll to the railway station, the *imam bara* is full of light and, to his amazement, Shamina is there. His aunt provides them with food, and laments that this will be the last occasion the *imam bara* is open, as she has no one left to look after it. The narrator lies awake listening to the worship. When he sleeps, he dreams that all the candles have been extinguished, except one through which came the sound of religious songs.[130]

Such works have encouraged critics to accuse Intizar Husain of a reactionary worship of the past. His stories have been dismissed as mere 'elegies of the fading culture of the Muslim nobility of Uttar Pradesh'.[131] Muhammad Umar Memon has, however, pointed out that this misunderstands their true significance and purpose. The past is remembered not to worship it, but to help man understand his present, as for example the character Saiyid in *Sirhiyan*. Only when this has been achieved, can the task of building the future be undertaken. In effect, what Intizar Husain is saying is that a truly Pakistani ethos and sensibility can only emerge after a reassessment has taken place of a past Indian Muslim cultural identity.

Intizar Husain's work brings us back to the creative possibilities of 1947. Much of the literature which we have been examining has omitted this dimension. In order to understand the Partition experience in its totality, we must set alongside the brutality and sense of uprootedness, the enthusiasm which many shared for Pakistan, and the sense of purpose and direction given by the hope of a Muslim homeland. Insights into how ordinary people shared these feelings can be glimpsed in Intizar Husain's short story, *Ek bin likhi razmiyah*.[132] The story is set in the insignificant village of Qadirpur. But even here, Intizar Husain depicts the Muslims as enthusiastically raising Pakistan slogans, despite the hostility of their Jat neighbours. Naim Miyan, the local Muslim League leader, epitomizes the community's sense of pride. He 'would get very irritated if anyone so much as mentioned the Congress. He felt it beneath his dignity to talk to a Hindu.'[133] Pichwa, the wrestler, symbolizes the illiterate Muslims' sense of fulfilment in the Pakistan struggle, even if they were ignorant of its full meaning. He gloried in the opportunities for displaying his skill with the lathi.

> With both authority and excitement, he ordered his band, 'tighten your belts, lads, after a long time dear Almighty God has finally heard us. We're going to have the time of our lives—God be praised!'[134]

Pichwa fought for a personal Pakistan in a small village hundreds of miles in Indian territory. Qadirpur was Pakistan for him, hence he unsuccessfully attempted to fly the Pakistan flag atop the pipal tree which stood beside the *id-gah*. He surely stands for many in his dimly perceived vision that Pakistan afforded the opportunity for 'personal perfection' and was thus worth risking life for against overwhelming odds. Pichwa does not in fact redeem himself in his journey to Pakistan but in his heroic death, on his return home to the newly renamed Jatunagar. But the insight unlocked by Intizar Husain's artistry is that Muslim migration in 1947 could be a redeeming experience. It provided a possibility for the re-enactment of the original *hijrat*.[135]

V

The preceding survey of literary 'representation' of the Partition experience has begun to uncover its human impact. Three themes emerge from the plurality of discourses. The first is that of the searing reality of the agony which the Partition massacres entailed. The emotional losses of Lala Kanshi Ram in *Azadi* and of Shanti in the *Ice-Candy-Man* stand for the experiences of many. It is frequently ignored that significant sections of north Indian society on both sides of the 'great divide' entered the independence era severely traumatized. The long term social and politicial implications of this situation have not been focussed upon.

Secondly, the complexity of human emotions is brought out in the literary texts. Again, Lala Kanshi Ram typifies the many migrants who mixed pride in their new homeland with a severe sense of loss of their ancestral roots. Many of the characterizations point to the conflict between immediate family concerns and the larger complex of political events. Linked with this is the depiction by such writers as Khushwant Singh and Kartar Singh Duggal of external violence breaking in upon locally harmonious relationships.

Finally, there emerges a strong sense of uprootedness brought by migration. The demented character, Toba Tek Singh, represents only an exaggerated case of this malaise. The pain felt at the sundering of historical ties and the sense of identity being linked with the ancestral village is brought out by such varied authors as Manto, Intizar Hussain, Duggal, and Nahal. Historians have not emphasized this aspect of Partition. But it is important not only as a part of the overall story, but because of the way in which such feelings have influenced political and social circumstances in Pakistan and India in the decades that have followed.

Inevitably, there are limitations in the use of literary sources to uncover the emotions, beliefs and experiences of past peoples. In order to explore more fully the human impact of Partition, it is necessary to engage with the personal accounts provided by autobiographies and interviews. This task will be attempted in the two succeeding chapters. Such material will be contextualized, first, by providing an overview of the experience of migration; and secondly, by briefly examining the hastily improvized responses of the Pakistani and Indian governments to the two huge human waves of refugees which swept across their new international boundaries in 1947.

NOTES

[1] For an extended discussion on the problems of treating any fictional works as 'simple documents' or 'realistic reflections of a historical reality', *see*, R. Chartier, (L.G. Cochrane, trans.), *Cultural History: Between Practices and Representations* (Oxford, 1988).

[2] Lucien Goldmann, for example, has maintained that the 'great' writers can express the collective conscience/world vision of their society. Lucien Goldmann, (P. Thody, trans.), *The Hidden God: A Study of Tragic Vision in the 'Pensees' of Pascal and the Tragedies of Racine* (London, 1964). Quoted in ibid., p. 32.

[3] For a succinct introduction to the importance of poetry for Urdu speakers, *see*, Marion Molteno, 'Approaching Urdu Poetry' in, R. Russell, *The Pursuit of Urdu Literature: A Select History* (London, 1992), pp. 5-17.

[4] For a brief introduction to this literature, consult, S. Cowasjee, 'The Partition in Indo-Anglian Literature' in, S. Nandan, *Language and Literature in Multicultural Contexts* (Suva, 1983), pp. 110-120.

[5] In *Azadi*, for example, as the Hindu refugee train passes Kurukshetra, Lala Kanshi Ram admonishes his wife, Prabha Rani, for hating the Muslims.

> 'What I mean is, whatever the Muslims did to us in Pakistan, we're doing it to them here ... every single horror.' ...
> 'But they killed thousands of us without reason, raped our women, drove us out of our homes.'
> 'We're only the same, *exactly* the same.' p. 338.

Muslim characters such as Chaudhri Barkat Ali, Munir and the *hakim* at Narowal are depicted as deploring the violence. Nahal also narrates that Muslim women were paraded naked in Amritsar, just as the Hindu women at Narowal. Nevertheless, Muslim attacks are reported in stark detail, while those by Hindus and Sikhs just receive passing mention. This, together with the reader's natural sympathy for the main protaganists leaves the general impression that the Muslims were the main aggressors. Khushwant Singh is even more sympathetic to Muslim characters. Imam Baksh, for example, is favourably compared with the Sikh priest, Meet Singh. He was known to the villagers of Mano Majra as *chacha* (uncle). He is in fact presented as the only character in the whole novel without a flaw. Like Chaman Nahal, Khushwant Singh does not ignore the fact that Hindus and Sikhs were the aggressors elsewhere. C. Nahal, *Azadi* (London, 1976); K. Singh, *Train to Pakistan* (New York, 1956).

[6] The easy communication between Lala Kanshi Ram and Prabha Rani has been lost following the death of their daughter, Madhi. Arun has been forced to abandon his first love, the Muslim girl, Nurul, in Sialkot. He had

subsequently fallen in love with the servant girl, Chandi, only for her to be abducted.

[7] The novel concludes with the family living in a refugee camp, with Lala Kanshi Ram making fruitless endeavours to secure compensation for the property which they had lost.

[8] Nahal op. cit., p. 130.

[9] Nahal op. cit., pp. 148-9.

[10] Nahal op. cit., p. 368.

[11] For two different literary criticisms of this work, *see*: R.P. Chaddah, 'The Partition in Indo-English Fiction', *Journal of Indian Writing in English*, 5, 11, (1977) p. 53 & ff.; V. A. Shahane, 'Theme, Title and Structure in Khushwant Singh's *Train to Pakistan*', *Literary Criterion* 9, iii (1970), pp. 68-76.

[12] This is neatly conveyed by the description of Ram Lal's house, the mosque and the gurdwara as lying at the centre of the village, 'enclosing a triangular common with a large peepal tree in the middle'.

[13] Singh, op. cit., pp. 170 & 172.

[14] Mumtaz Shah Nawaz, *The Heart Divided*, 2nd ed. (Lahore, 1990).

[15] Ibid., p. 11.

[16] Nawaz op. cit., p. 361.

[17] Nawaz op. cit., p. 361.

[18] Nawaz op. cit., pp. 470-1.

[19] Bapsi Sidhwa, *Ice-Candy-Man* (Delhi, 1989).

[20] This is brought out clearly in the following extract:

> Ice-candy-man visits at last. ... I cannot believe the change in him. Gone is the darkly grieving look that had affected me so deeply the evening he ... almost crashed into us with the grim news of the train-load of dead Muslims.
>
> Ice-candy-man has acquired an unpleasant swagger and a strange way of looking at Hari and Moti. He is full of bravado—and still full of stories.

Sidhwa, op. cit., pp. 154-5.

[21] Sidhwa, op. cit., p. 195.

[22] Sidhwa, op. cit., p. 260.

[23] Sidhwa, op. cit., p. 215.

[24] Sidhwa, op. cit., pp. 195-208.

[25] Sidhwa, op. cit., p. 208.

[26] *See also*, Nanak Singh's work, *Khoon ke sohile* (Amritsar, 1948), which is also set in this region. I am indebted to Darshan Singh Tatla of South Birmingham College for this reference, and for introducing me to Punjabi writings on Partition in general.

[27] K.S. Duggal (J. Ara, trans.), *Twice Born Twice Dead* (New Delhi, 1979), p. 11.

[28] Ibid., pp. 143 & 136.

[29] Duggal, op. cit., p. 130.

[30] Duggal, op. cit., pp. 136-7.

[31] Bhisham Sahni was born in 1915 in Rawalpindi. He came from a devout Arya Samajist middle class family, and was educated at Government College, Lahore. He taught for a time at a local college. At Partition, he settled in Delhi. He has written extensively in Hindi, and translated works from Urdu, Punjabi, Russian, and English into Hindi. In addition to his short stories and novels, including *Tamas*, which has been successfully dramatized for Indian television, he has written a biography of his brother, Balraj Sahni, the famous actor, writer and film producer. He taught for a number of years at a Delhi University college, before working in the Soviet Union as a translator. His short stories set in the Partition period partly reflect his own personal experience of migration. They have stood the test of time and have been critically acclaimed for their literary merit.

[32] The Sahitya Akademi is India's National Academy of Letters which annually awards prizes for works in each of the major Indian languages.

[33] B. Sahni (Jai Ratan, trans.), *We have arrived in Amritsar and Other Stories* (London, 1990).

[34] Ibid., p. 118 & ff.

[35] Sahni, op. cit., p. 119.

[36] Sahni, op. cit., p. 4.

[37] Sahni, op. cit., p. 15.

[38] *See*, for example, the story, *The Theft*, Sahni, op. cit., pp. 66-92.

[39] Sahni, op. cit., p. 17.

[40] Sahni, op. cit., p. 23.

[41] Sahni, op. cit., p. 27.

[42] Sahni, op. cit., p. 28.

[43] B. Sahni (Jal Ratan, trans.), *Tamas*, (New Delhi, 1990).

[44] Ibid., pp. 6-7.

[45] Sahni, *Tamas*, op. cit., p. 198 & ff.

[46] Sahni, *Tamas*, op. cit., p. 141 & ff.

[47] Sahni, *Tamas*, op. cit., p. 137.

[48] Sahni, *Tamas*, op. cit., pp. 218-19.

[49] Sahni, *Tamas*, op. cit., p. 126.

[50] Sahni, *Tamas*, op. cit., p. 127.

[51] Sahni, *Tamas*, op. cit., p. 235.

[52] Sahni, *Tamas*, op. cit., p. 140.

[53] Sahni, *Tamas*, op. cit., p. 187 & ff.

[54] Sahni, *Tamas*, op. cit., p. 223 & ff.

[55] Sahni, *Tamas*, op, cit., p. 196.

[56] Faiz's poems were especially popular in the Soviet Union. He was awarded the Lenin International Peace Prize in 1962.

[57] Both men were born in Sialkot.

[58] Faiz's varied career included wartime service in the Indian Army, editorship of the *Pakistan Times*, and post of Cultural Adviser to Zulfiqar Ali Bhutto.

[59] For further detail on this and other biographical details, *see*, R. Russell, *The Pursuit of Urdu Literature* (London, 1992), pp. 229-248.

[60] See the sections below for an assessment on the Progressive Writer's Movement.

[61] This poem appeared in the Collection, *Naqsh-e-Faryadi*, under the title '*Mujh se pahli si mohabbat, meri mahbub, na maang*'. The version here has been translated by Victor Keirnan in, V. Kiernan (trans.), *Poems by Faiz* (London, n.d.), pp. 65-67.

[62] Ibid., 123-7.

[63] M. Shirin, *Zulmat-i-Neem Roze* (Karachi, 1990).

[64] Krishan Chander, a Punjabi Hindu born in Lahore in 1914, has written extensively in Urdu. His literary talent is internationally recognized. His works have been translated into English, Russian, Chinese, and Polish as well as other Indian languages.

[65] On this movement, *see*, H. Malik, 'The Marxist Literary Movement in India and Pakistan', *Journal of Asian Studies*, XXVI, 4 (August 1967), pp. 649-664; C. Coppola, 'Urdu Poetry, 1935-1970: The Progressive Episode', Chicago, unpublished Ph.D Thesis, 1975, 2 vols; K. H. Ansari, 'The Emergence of Muslim Socialists in India 1917-47', London, unpublished Ph.D Thesis, 1985.

[66] A. S. Sukhochev, *Krishan Chander* (Moscow, 1983), p. 94.

[67] For a summary of the story, consult, Sukhochev, op. cit., p. 94.

[68] Ibid.

[69] This story can be read in English translation in, R . Mathur & M. Kulasrestha (eds.), *Writings on India's Partition* (Calcutta, 1976), p. 69 and ff.

[70] Ibid., p. 77.

[71] Sukhochev praises the fact that Chander does not limit himself 'to the role of an observer on the sidelines, but makes his indictment as a man of advanced views'. But even he is critical of the short story, 'Jackson', in the *Ham Wahshi Hain* collection. Jackson is an Anglo-Indian who wishes to appear as a pure-blooded Englishman. Although he is a police inspector, he sells arms to both Hindus and Muslims and incites them to mutual destruction. His daughter, Rosie, leaves home in disgust at this action. Sukhochev acknowledges that the conclusion of 'Jackson' 'can hardly be considered successful ... and that the psychological motivation ... is not always worked out with the necessary depth'. Sukhochev op. cit., p. 96.

[72] In addition to those characters already discussed, *see*, for example, the Muslim husband in the story *Andhe*, which is set in Lahore.

73 This summary has drawn on, J.A. Hanson, 'Historical Perspectives in the Urdu Novel', in M.U. Memon (ed.), *Studies in the Urdu Gazal and Prose Fiction* (Madison, 1979), pp. 264-5.

74 Muhammad Ahsan Faruqi, *Sangam* (Karachi, 1971), p 258, cited in, M. Rahman, 'Political Novels in Urdu', *Contributions to Asian Studies*, 6 (1975), p. 150.

75 For a discussion of this point, *see*, Hanson, op. cit., pp. 271-2; Rahman op. cit., pp. 150-1.

76 Qurat ul-Ain Haider was born in the Bijnor district of the UP in 1927. Both her parents were prolific writers. She published her first novel in 1947, the year in which she migrated to Pakistan. She worked in England in the 1950s, before returning to India. She was a Visiting Professor in English at Aligarh Muslim University in the 1980s, and in 1989 she became only the second writer in Urdu to win India's coveted Jnanpith literary award.

77 Hanson op. cit., p. 275. For a much fuller assessment of the novel than we have space for here, consult, L.A. Flemming, 'Muslim Self-Identity in Quratulain Hyder's *Aag Ka Darya*, in Memon, op cit., pp. 243-256.

78 Qurat ul-Ain Haider, *Aag Ka Darya* (Lahore, 1968) p. 779. Cited in Flemming, op. cit., p. 253.

79 Ibid., p. 416. Cited in Flemming, op. cit., p. 246.

80 *See*, for example, Champa's criticism of the Wahhabi movement, in a conversation with a Hindu professor. Haider, op. cit., p. 419. Cited in Flemming, op. cit., p. 250.

81 Flemming, op. cit., pp. 255-6.

82 The author initially migrated to Pakistan, but then returned to India.

83 *See*, for example, F. Riaz, *Pakistan Literature and Society* (New Delhi, 1986), p. 22 & ff.

84 The first edition was published on 12 May 1949, the most recent in January 1987. N. Hijazi, *Khak aur Khoon* (Lahore, 1987).

85 This summary draws on an original translation. To my knowledge, there is no published version of the work available in English.

86 The work's conventionality is displayed in such episodes as Altaf's conversion to the Pakistan cause. Saleem's earlier debate with him lacks conviction, because it is too obviously used as a vehicle for the author's own sentiments. Although Saleem is portrayed as an intelligent and sensitive man, the author does not delve into his psychological make up, or explore his response to the misadventures which befall him and his friends.

87 For background on Manto's career and an excellent analysis of his writings, consult, L.A. Flemming, *Another Lonely Voice: The Urdu Short Stories of Saadat Hasan Manto* (Berkeley, 1979).

88 He had written for the weekly *Musawwir* in Bombay, had produced film and radio scripts, and still found time to complete over fifty short stories, in the period 1937-41. Ibid., (60 above), p. 9 & ff.

[89] Although Manto had worked for many years in the Bombay film industry, he originally came from the East Punjab. He gained a reputation for controversy because of the sexual content of such works as *Blauz*, *Hatik*, and *Bu*.

[90] Most of the stories are brief anecdotes. *Karamat* is typical. The miracle of the sweet water in a village well is really to be explained by the fact that a man drowned in it, whilst trying to hide a looted bag of sugar.

[91] This has been translated into English by C.M. Naim and R.L. Schmidt in, *Journal of Asian Literature* 1, (1965), pp. 14-19.

[92] Flemming, *Another Lonely Voice*, op. cit p. 81.

[93] This has been translated into English by Mohammad Ali in, *Pakistan Review*, 13 (April 1965), pp. 33-4.

[94] Ibid., p. 34.

[95] Ali, op. cit., p. 34.

[96] This has been translated into English by R.B. Haldane in, *Journal of South Asian Literature*, 6 (1970), pp. 19-23.

[97] 'One day while bathing, a Muslim shouted the slogan, "Long live Pakistan" so enthusiastically that he slipped down and knocked himself on the floor. ... There was a fat Muslim from Chiniot, formerly an ardent worker for the Muslim league, who took fifteen or sixteen baths a day. He simply quit bathing. As his name was Muhammad Ali, he declared in his ward that he was in fact the Quaid-e-Azam, Muhammad Ali Jinnah himself. Imitating him, a Sikh inmate declared himself to be Master Tara Singh. The ward was spared an almost certain brawl when they were both declared dangerous, and shut away separately.'
Ibid., pp. 19-20.

[98] Haldane, op. cit., p. 23.

[99] For a summary, *see*, Flemming, op. cit., p. 79.

[100] *See*, for example, *Mozel*.

[101] This is contained in the collection edited by Mumtaz Shirin, op. cit., pp. 315-52.

[102] Shirin, op cit., pp. 328-p.

[103] Shirin, op. cit., p 337.

[104] Shirin, op. cit., p. 335.

[105] Shirin, op. cit., pp. 335-6.

[106] Shirin, op. cit., p. 339.

[107] A. Jamal, *Samjhota Express* (Lahore, 1989). For a useful review, *see*, Ariel, 'Samjhota Express: hangover of Partition', *Dawn* (Karachi), 18 May 1990.

[108] Ibid., p. 169.

[109] Jamal, op. cit., p. 173.

[110] Jamal, op. cit., p. 176.

[111] Rajinder Singh Bedi was born into a lower-middle-class Punjabi family. His literary career began in the mid 1930s. Because he wrote about the lives

of ordinary people, he was seen as a member of the Progressive Writers Movement, but he never fully conformed to its ideology and style. For a useful insight into his outlook and career, *see*, 'Mahfil interviews Rajinder Singh Bedi' *Mahfil*, Vol. 8, Nos 2-3 (Summer, Fall, 1972), pp. 139-58

[112] This has been translated by Khushwant Singh in, R. Mathur & M. Kulasrestha (eds.), *Writings on India's Partition* (Calcutta, 1976), pp. 126-35.

[113] Ibid., p. 127.

[114] Bedi, op. cit., p. 128.

[115] Bedi, op. cit., p. 133.

[116] Bedi, op. cit., p. 134.

[117] Bedi, op. cit., p. 135.

[118] Abdullah Husain, *Udas naslen* (Lahore, 1963).

[119] J.A. Hanson, 'Historical Perspectives in the Urdu Novel', in M.U. Memon (ed.), *Studies in the Urdu Ghazal and Prose Fiction* (Madison, 1979), p. 272.

[120] Naim marries Azra, the daughter of Raushan Agha, the leading landowner of Raushanpur village. He works as an activist in the freedom struggle, and is subsequently imprisoned, but after a reconciliation with Azra, he settles down as a government servant. For further details of the plot, *see*, Hanson, op. cit., pp. 265-7.

[121] Hanson, op. cit., p. 267.

[122] Hanson, op. cit., p. 270.

[123] Ibid.

[124] Intizar Husain was born in the Bulandshahr district of the UP. He migrated to Pakistan in August 1947, cutting short his college career in Meerut. For further details of his life and literary criticism of his work, consult the special issue devoted to him in, *Journal of South Asian Literature*, XVIII, 2 (1983), and also M.U. Memon, 'Partition Literature: A Study of Intizar Husain', *Modern Asian Studies*, 14, 3 (1980), pp. 377-410.

[125] These were lengthy romance prose narratives of the Medieval period.

[126] This latter concern is evident in such works as *Akhri Admi* and *Zard Kutta*, in the collection of short stories, *Akhri Admi* (Lahore, 1987).

[127] The work is a record of a conversation between three characters, identified only as the First Man, the Second Man, and the Third Man, who argue inconclusively whether or not they are dead or alive. The First and Third Men relate accounts of rape and other horrors which they could have witnessed in 1947. *See*, F.W. Pritchett, 'Narrative Modes in Intizar Husain's Short stories', *Journal of Asian Literature* XVIII, 2 (1983), p. 193.

[128] This story is summarized in Memon, op. cit., p. 406.

[129] Intizar Husain, 'Akhri Mom Bati', in *Kankary* (Lahore, 1987), pp. 90-104.

[130] This is a summary from an original translation. The story has not yet been rendered into English, to my knowledge.

[131] G.C. Narang, 'Major trends in the Urdu Short Story', *Indian Literature*, 16, nos. 1-2 (1973), p. 132.

[132] This is found in Intizar Husain's first collection of short stories, *Gali Kuche* (Lahore, 1952), pp. 193-224. A summary is found in English in Memon, op. cit., pp. 402-3, and in full translation by L.A. Flemming and M.U. Memon, in *Journal of South Asian Literature*, XVIII, Pt 2 (1983), pp. 6-19.

[133] Flemming and Memon, op. cit., p. 10.

[134] Ibid.

[135] Migration could of course also result in disillusionment. This is expressed in Pichwa's failure to settle in Pakistan, and the loss of creative endeavour by the narrator and would-be author of *Ek bin-likhi razmiya* (An Unwritten Epic).

Chapter 5

Train to Pakistan

Massacres, Migrations and *Mohajirs*

Hundreds of thousands of ordinary men, women and children migrated in 1947 as a result of the larger political circumstances which brought the birth of Pakistan. Their experience has been by no means unique in this, the century of the refugee. The massive social upheavals in Europe caused by the two World Wars have been followed by post-colonial conflicts in Africa, Asia and the Middle East, and post-Cold War conflict in the Balkans, all of which have created large refugee populations. The displacement of people which accompanied India's Partition, however, still remains one of the greatest migrations ever recorded.

Some seven million people were enumerated as of refugee origin in Pakistan's 1951 census.[1] They constituted one in ten of the total population. Most refugees had entered Pakistan between August and November 1947; at the same time, an almost equal number of Hindus and Sikhs had departed for India. The migrations had been accompanied by horrific massacres which, at the most conservative estimate, claimed two hundred thousand lives. In the confusion, families had been split up, their womenfolk kidnapped and disgraced. Many lost all their possessions, and stumbled exhausted and dying into their new homeland.

Despite the immense social impact of the upheavals of 1947, comparatively little[2] has been written about this aspect of Pakistan's emergence. There is no equivalent of the recollections of the East Punjab Rehabilitation Commissioner, M. S.

Randhawa.[3] In particular, there have been no serious attempts
to understand the refugee experience 'from beneath'. We have
already seen in the previous chapter that literary sources throw
an important light on popular responses to, and experiences
of, Pakistan's birth. The present chapter will begin to explore
the theme still further through the study of autobiographical
accounts. These will restore a human dimension to the historical
discourse on Partition. Before hearing these voices, it is
necessary, however, to fill in much of the missing detail
concerning refugee origins, migration patterns and
arrangements for evacuation and resettlement of refugees. This
helps both to set individual accounts in a context, and illustrates
that there was no uniformity in the refugee experience. Our
point of embarkation, however, must be a consideration of the
term refugee, and its Urdu equivalent, *mohajir*, as there is a
significant distinction between them, although authors tend to
regard them as interchangeable.

I

There are a variety of definitions of a refugee. According to the
United Nations Convention of 1951, refugees are people who
have been forced to leave their country because of a 'well-
founded fear of being persecuted for reasons of race, religion,
nationality, membership of a particular social group, or political
opinion'.[4] The 1951 Census of Pakistan defined a refugee as 'a
person who had moved into Pakistan as a result of partition or
for fear of disturbances connected therewith'.[5] The term *mohajir*
has a much narrower meaning than either of these definitions,
and does not share with them a connotation of involuntary
flight. It can only be understood in the Islamic context of
religious flight. Such flight (*hijra*) is central to Islam. The
beginning of the Muslim calendar is of course dated from the
Prophet's flight from Mecca to Medina in AD 622. The term
mohajir was applied to the faithful who accompanied him. It
has always since been used for Muslims who have fled to preserve

their religious freedom. The Koran encourages such action: 'He who emigrates in the path of God', it records, 'will find frequent refuge and abundance'.[6] The western stigma attached to being a refugee, thus, is absent in the Islamic world. On the contrary, it is a matter of pride to be a *mohajir*, and such a status is expected to command respect. In the true meaning of the word, a *mohajir* is not an involuntary refugee who is a victim of circumstance, but is rather an individual who has made a sacrifice for his faith.

II

Political science literature on refugees draws a distinction between what is termed anticipatory, and acute, migration. The former is a planned response to a perceived, albeit future, threat. The latter is flight from immediate physical danger. The historical example of anticipatory migration most frequently cited is the emigration of Jewish intellectuals from Germany in the early 1930s. There was very little anticipatory Muslim migration before August 1947, although Jinnah did encourage some 'nation-building' enterprises to establish themselves in the Pakistan areas. Anticipatory migration was partly discouraged by the uncertainty of the actual boundary demarcation until Independence. It was of course expected that Pakistan would contain a large non-Muslim population. The Muslim League offered no encouragement to migration from India immediately prior to Partition. None of the politicians foresaw the violence which transformed the trickle of refugees into a flood. There had been in fact, earlier warning signs of the impact of communal conflict on population movement.

Forty thousand Sikhs had taken refuge in hurriedly established camps before being transported to the safety of Amritsar, following disturbances in the Multan, Mianwali, Jhelum, Attock and Rawalpindi districts of the West Punjab in March 1947.[7] The Hindu attacks on Muslims in Bihar, which started in Patna on 26 October 1946 and then spread throughout the Monghyr district, had within a month created a refugee problem which involved over one hundred thousand people.[8] Despite British efforts, many refugees refused to return to their villages from the camps in which they were housed. By the end of November, more than four hundred Muslims were daily crossing the provincial boundary to the safety of Bengal.[9]

During the final days before the publication of the Radcliffe Boundary Award, Sikh raiding parties launched heavy attacks on Muslim villages in disputed 'border' areas of the Punjab.[10] From May onwards, there had been a widespread collection of funds, manufacture and import of arms, and enlistment of Sikhs in private armies such as the Akal Fauj and *Shahidi jathas* in these areas. An organization of 'dictators', 'company commanders' and village 'cells' had been established, in which ex-INA and military men played a leading role. Many sought employment in the Amritsar gurdwaras at this time.[11] Shortly before Partition, five thousand Muslim refugees reached Lahore from the disturbed Amritsar district. They arrived at an over-whelmingly Muslim city. Its large Hindu and Sikh population had already packed its bags, following weeks of communal disturbances.

The Sikh attacks in the East Punjab increased in ferocity following the British departure. The publication of the Boundary Award added desperation to the desire for revenge for the March violence, for it involved the loss to Pakistan of the rich Sikh farmlands of Lyallpur[12] and the shrine of Nankana Sahib.[13] There was much evidence of the dangerous mood of the community during the weeks between the agreement of the 3 June Partition Plan and the announcement of the Boundary Award. Amar Singh Dosanjh, acting President of the Shiromani Akali Dal, produced Gurmukhi posters which declared that Pakistan was death for the Sikhs, and that the community's minimum demand was for a sovereign state from the Chenab to the Jamna. The All-India Sikh Student Federation also issued posters advocating a strong confederacy of Sikh districts and States. Mohan Singh of the INA preached Hindu-Sikh inseparability, and asserted that the two communities could together defeat the Muslims;

while the Akali leader, Master Tara Singh, called for funds 'for the forthcoming struggle'. He particularly emphasized that territory full of Sikh religious places and properties should not be included in Pakistan at any cost, and that Sikhs should enlist in *Shahidi jathas*.[14]

The Sikh *jathas* not only attacked Muslim villages in the Jullundur and Amritsar districts, but the packed refugee trains heading for Pakistan. One incident alone, an attack on a train just outside Khalsa College, Amritsar, resulted in the massacre of over a thousand Muslims.[15] Many of the *jathas* operated from the safety of the neighbouring Sikh Princely States. The situation became so chaotic that the Sikh Akali leader, Master Tara Singh, was forced to admit to India's first Chief of General Staff that he could not guarantee Muslim refugees safe passage through Amritsar.[16]

The collapse of the civil administration in the East Punjab rendered the violence uncontrollable. The British Governor of the West Punjab wrote to Jinnah on 23 September 1947, that 'the East Punjab government has lost all control of the situation and that in fact it has ceased to exist as a government'.[17] The rot had set in during the closing months of British rule, which had seen a communalization of the police, disintegration of the intelligence service, and declining morale and discipline amongst officials.[18] Moreover, Partition had stripped the East Punjab of thirteen thousand Muslim policemen. In such districts as Jullundur, power consequently lay, not with the Deputy Commissioner, but with Sikh Committees of Action. In these circumstances, Muslims fell prey to the wiles of such Sikh landlords as Raja Bachan Singh. He initially promised protection for the twelve hundred Muslims of village Rorka Kalan, but subsequently ordered them to demolish their mosque and convert to Sikhism. Amir Abdullah Khan Rokri, in his autobiography, *Mayn aur mera Pakistan*,[19] maintains that between thirty and forty per cent of East Punjabi Muslims were forced to abandon their faith. But this seems to be an exaggeration.

The police lost all discipline in the East Punjab. They raped, looted and killed on numerous occasions, according to eye-witness accounts. On 3 September, for example, a Police Sub-Inspector, Sampuran Singh, led a party which butchered about 300 Muslims from Hansi in the Hissar District.[20] Sita Ram, the Deputy Superintendent of Police, Ambala, supervised attacks on Muslims, including an assault on a refugee train on 1 September which claimed a thousand lives.[21] The Sikh Assistant Sub-Inspector of Police invited a raid of Qadian, and participated in the assault on the Muslim *mohalla* of Darul Anwar. This was undertaken by Sikhs, aided by Hindu troops and non-Muslim policemen.[22] Sardar Bishen Singh, a Sub-Inspector of Police from Soofian, shot Muslim refugees during the ambush of a column at Gorala, *tehsil* Ajnala, Amritsar District. Before the attack had commenced, the *Tehsildar* had tried to persuade the refugees to save themselves by embracing Sikhism.[23] The Sub-Inspector of Police, Police Station Sarhali, extorted Rs 10,000 from the villagers of Kot Muhammad Khan as the price for a military escort.[24] The police received even richer pickings when they relieved refugees of their cash and jewellery. Those who resisted were shot at. They looted trains to such an extent that the Governor, Sir Chandulal Trivedi, exclaimed at a conference on 17 September that 'He would not be sorry if the army shot ... those (police) who exist ... including their officers'.[25]

Those Muslims who made it to the safety of transit camps received short shrift from Indian officials, many of whom had been displaced themselves from the West Punjab. According to one British observor, a 'very real dislike of Pakistan pervaded (their) ranks'.[26] Muslims travelling on foot to Pakistan faced appalling conditions in the transit camps. The smell emanating from one of the biggest of these just outside Ludhiana was so bad, 'that it continued for almost a mile down the road'.[27] Diseases such as cholera spread rapidly amongst the refugees. According to K.C. Neogy, the Indian Minister for Relief and Rehabilitation, there were between 100 and 250 deaths from cholera in one foot convoy from Rohtak alone, besides another 200 serious cases.[28] When the Pakistan government complained about the lack of sanitation and low rations in such camps,

Nehru was forced to privately concede that these criticisms were justified.[29] British observers also commented upon the fact that the refugees fleeing from Jullundur and Ludhiana experienced, 'far worse treatment than anything … in Montgomery and Lahore'.[30]

There were immediate calls for revenge when Muslim survivors straggled into Lahore from the East Punjab. The *Zemindar* published in verse the overwhelming Muslim feeling.

> Strange are the ways of the justice of
>> the government of the Hindus
> The mosques have become desolate while
>> the Gurdwaras stand intact
> May the Almighty keep us from this
>> time of trial!
> Lo, our chests are exposed to their bullets,
> The hour has arrived for the extinction
>> of the new civilization
> About to fall are the stars from the skies,
> Destruction must befall the Sikhs and
>> their allies![31]

Muslims launched reprisals against Hindus and Sikhs who were still living in the West Punjab, and also attacked those who were travelling to India. The worst violence was in Sheikhupura,[32] where looting, killing and burning lasted for twenty-four hours on 25–26 August. Two wells in the Namdhari Gurdwara were filled with the bodies of Hindu and Sikh women who had committed suicide to save themselves from assault.[33] Elsewhere in the district, Sangla Hill and Sharakpur suffered much loss of life and physical destruction. Wazirabad, Narowal and Raiwind were notorious for the large number of attacks on refugee trains. The railway track between Sialkot and Amritsar was strewn with the dead bodies of Sikhs.[34]

The mounting disturbances sparked a mass exodus of Muslims from the East Punjab and reverse migrations of Hindus and Sikhs to India. Within just ten days of Partition, an estimated twenty-five thousand Muslims were each day streaming into

Pakistan from the East Punjab.[35] On 5 September alone, fifty thousand Muslim refugees arrived in Kasur on foot from the Ferozepore district and the neighbouring Sikh States.[36] Three weeks later, eighty thousand Muslims reached Wagah safely from Amritsar.[37] Such caravans were visible from miles away because of the clouds of dust rising from the thousands of bullock carts. At best they might cover twenty miles in a day. In the evenings their camp fires pierced the darkness. They were thus easily recognizable targets for their assailants. Many caravans had no protection. Eye witness accounts recall the bodies heaped either side of the road from Amritsar to Lahore, converting the whole area into a massive graveyard.

> *Lahawr say Amritsar ki paintees meel lambi*
> *sarak kay dono kinaaron par jaa bajaa laashon kay*
> *dher thay. Yun lagta tha kay saara ilaaqa ek taveel-o-arz*
> *qabristaan mein tabdeel ho gaya hay.*[38]

On both sides of the 35-mile-long road between Amritsar and Lahore, there were heaps of corpses. It appeared as if the entire territory had been converted into an extensive graveyard.

Death could come quickly and brutally. An old man, for example, left the main refugee column to chase after a nanny goat, the sole possession he had been able to bring with him. All of a sudden, an eyewitness recalls, 'a Sikh came out of the sugarcane field carrying a drawn sword, cut off the old man's head, picked up the goat, and disappeared into the field.'[39]

During the first week of November, half a million Muslims swept over the border from India.[40] This was, however, the final surge as, by the end of the month, the flood of refugees was reduced to a trickle. In the three and a half months since Independence, 4.6 million Muslims had been evacuated from the East Punjab.[41]

The tide of humanity had swept with equal force in the opposite direction. More than a million and a quarter Hindus and Sikhs crossed into India by train alone from August to November 1947.[42] There were also large foot columns from the Lyallpur, Montgomery and Sheikhupura districts. Over eight hundred thousand people, with hundreds of bullock carts and cattle, crossed over to India in this way between 18 September and 29 October 1947.⁴³ The arrival of Hindu and Sikh refugees led to violence in Delhi and the western UP, which sparked a second great Muslim migration.

Widespread rioting broke out in Ajmer in late November, following the arrival of large numbers of Hindu refugees from Sindh. Many Muslims fled almost immediately to Pakistan, despite the efforts of a local Congress leader, Kanahiya Lal Khadiwal, to persuade them to stay.⁴⁴ Events followed a similar course, although on a much larger scale, in Delhi. Trouble began in and around the capital early in September, following the advent of the first fugitives from Pakistan. They instigated attacks on Muslim localities and in some instances forcibly seized property. Muslims were driven to barricade their streets, then to seek sanctuary in refugee camps, before beginning the trek to Pakistan. This began in earnest in the middle of October, but there were still twenty-eight thousand Muslims housed in the largest refugee camp as late as January 1948.⁴⁵

The migration from Delhi and the UP was, however, by no means the final chapter in the Muslim refugee history. The Indian 'police action' in the Princely State of Hyderabad in September 1948 led to a further influx of refugees to Pakistan. According to the 1951 Census, there were ninety-five thousand Hyderabadi refugees.⁴⁶ Riots in Karachi in January 1948 led to a belated departure of over eleven thousand Hindus from the city. The violence again centred around refugees who initially attacked Sikhs who had been transported from the interior of Sindh, before turning their attention to the indigenous Hindu population. This episode marked the final non-Muslim migration from Pakistan, but Muslims have continued to leave India at times of communal tension, and particularly in the wake of the wars of 1965 and 1971.

The dark side of humanity is bleakly exposed in the cruelty, shame and horror of many of the events of August 1947. The better side also, however, revealed itself. At considerable risk to themselves, Hindu, Muslim and Sikh villagers sheltered friends from other communities. The three quotations which follow are taken from interviews with Hindu Jat refugees from the Multan district, but evidence could be equally included of Hindus and Sikhs saving Muslims amidst the chaos caused by their co-religionists.

The Muslims of our area were the ones who warned us to leave or we would be slaughtered. They were Rajputs before, who had become Muslims in the old times, and they had a certain amount of sympathy for us.

A lot of people came to our village and I saw this happen—killings and murders with my own eyes. Actually, many of the big landholding Muslims were very helpful. They gave us shelter, and tried to protect us from the others, from the small Muslims, like have-nots who wanted to push us out … kill us off and take our land. These big, big landlords protected us.

The five fingers are not the same. Some people want to trouble you and others want to help you. The Muslims were like that too. … There was a Muslim man. … He said, no matter what happens, I will let nothing happen to these people. He was an officer on the Pakistani side. He made 'sure that we left safely. … There were others who helped us. Like in our own village, there were people who extended hands of help to us and wouldn't let any harm come to us.[47]

Another striking feature which emerges from the collection of oral histories is that even when neighbours did not give shelter, they refrained from joining in incidents of violence and looting. Whilst aggressors might well seek to blame all the trouble on outsiders to absolve themselves, this evidence from survivors is difficult to refute. 'There was trouble in the village', Sona Devi, a sixty-year-old Jat recalled, 'But generally it was not the people who lived in our village—those Muslims who tried to attack us, but it was the Muslims who came from outside. They are the ones who caused the trouble and tried to kill us'.[48]

There was considerable variation in the conditions which greeted the refugees on their arrival in Pakistan. Many of the local people were true *ansars*, eagerly waiting to help them, as Amir Abdullah Khan Rokri records for the Mianwali district ('because they knew that these people were being driven out of India simply because they were Muslims').[49] The author moved his entire family to one small room to accommodate refugees, and paid for their needs out of his own pocket. He records, however, that some landowners and bureaucrats saw the refugee situation as an opportunity to feather their own nests. They acquired the lion's share of the property left behind by the Hindus and Sikhs. He even recalls one incident in the main Muslim transit camp in Pathankot in which Muslim officers, in connivance with local Muslim and Hindu businessmen, sold on to the black market rationed goods which had been provided by the Indians for the refugees.[50]

Not all refugees were helpless victims of the chaotic situation. Some seized the opportunity to occupy abandoned property. In the Sindhi city of Hyderabad, even tonga drivers were found residing in the houses of former Hindu businessmen. They took advantage of the spacious accommodation to stable their animals inside. At Thatta, Muslim refugees took over almost all the shops in the bazaar. The *Statesman's* correspondent reported, 'the trend of social mobility appears to be upwards. The former itinerant tailor now runs a cloth shop, a former tinker a hardware shop.'[51] The first arrivals in the rich canal colony lands in the West Punjab found the fields almost ready for harvesting, millet and rice crops provided them with food, while cotton could be sold for cash.

Many refugees, however, did not fare so well. Even in February 1948, three quarters of a million still languished in the West Punjab's refugee camps. A further nine months were to elapse before they were finally settled. Insufficient records, both of the property abandoned by Hindus and Sikhs and that left behind in India by Muslim refugees, complicated resettlement in its early stages. It was not in fact until October 1948 that the governments of East and West Punjab exchanged their revenue records.[52] Rokri even claims that some refugees brought fake papers which exaggerated their claims for compensation, 'while good and righteous people got nothing'.[53]

While most refugees went to West Pakistan, the influx into the eastern wing should not be forgotten. At the time of the 1951 Census, some seven hundred thousand refugees were reported as residing in East Bengal.[54] Two-thirds of these had originated in West Bengal and Assam. The remainder were Urdu speaking migrants from Bihar and the UP. This displacement of population, unlike that in the East Punjab, was not the result of acute migration. Bengal was relatively peaceful in the aftermath of Partition. Large minority populations remained in its Indian and Pakistani territories. Even such prominent Muslim politicians as Husain Shaheed Suhrawardy continued to reside in Calcutta until 1949. The refugees from Bihar and the UP, on the other hand, had fled communal violence. Their attachment to North Indian culture led to increasing conflict with the indigenous Bengali elite. Those who were able, embarked on the second migration of their life in 1971.

Even in West Pakistan, the ease with which refugees settled depended to a certain extent on their place of origin. It is important, therefore, to identify both the regional and class composition of the *mohajir* population. Around three quarters of all *mohajirs* were Punjabis (4.7 million). A high percentage of these (63 per cent) were agriculturalists.[55] Large numbers were attracted to the Canal Colony areas abandoned by Sikh Jat cultivators. The Lyallpur district's population rose by over forty per cent, Multan's, Montgomery's and Sheikhupura's by twenty per cent.[56] In the Jaranwala tehsil of the Lyallpur district, the ratio of refugees to former landholders was 3:1[57] At the same time as the Punjabi refugees squeezed themselves into lands and houses vacated by Hindus and Sikhs east of the Chenab, to its west the population actually fell. The land here was less fertile, as well as being further from the refugees' ancestral homes. Many of the non-Muslim evacuees from this region had been traders and moneylenders, occupations which held no attraction for East Punjabi farmers. The urban population of the Mianwali district fell by thirty per cent; even in the countryside it was down ten per cent.

There was little cultural difference between the West and East Punjab. Muslim migrants from the East did not, therefore, have to make the linguistic and social adjustments which usually confront refugees. They spoke Punjabi and Urdu along with the locals and entered a landscape which climatically and economically resembled their home villages. Few refugees were forced to abandon farming. Nor was there the levelling of landholdings amongst displaced persons which occurred in the East Punjab. There, a scheme of graded cuts had to be introduced because of the gap which existed in the amount of land abandoned in West Pakistan and which was available to refugees.[58] Not suprisingly, Punjabi Muslim migrants were easily assimilated, and rapidly abandoned the *mohajir* label.

Khoja and Memon refugees from Bombay and the Kathiawar coast who settled in Karachi made a similarly smooth transition. They numbered around one hundred and sixty thousand.[59] Like the Punjabis, they were able to relocate in a culturally similar region and to continue their traditional occupations. Karachi formed part of the Gujarati speaking western India coastal belt, as a result of its attachment to Bombay province until 1935. Khojas and Memons set up trading activities in the port before Partition. Bombay-based businesses also established subsidiaries in Karachi. Some of these refugees had therefore already established a foothold in Karachi before their permanent re-location there. Moreover, they were able to step into the shoes of the departed Hindu business class, for the indigenous Sindhi population lacked the necessary capital and expertise to do so. Many businesses in 1948 in fact changed hands from Gujarati speaking Hindus to Gujarati speaking Muslims.[60]

Mohajirs from North India did not share the advantages of Punjabis and Gujaratis. There was no cultural region in the Pakistan areas similar to their home. Around sixty per cent of the four hundred and sixty-four thousand *mohajirs* from the UP[61] resettled in Sindh. The greatest concentration was in Karachi and Hyderabad, but a small proportion was dispersed in the towns of the interior. Several reasons lay behind this migration to Sindh rather than to the Punjab, the region of Pakistan nearest to their homes. Some stayed in Karachi simply because they had been routed there by rail. On a less mundane note, Karachi was seen as an attractive destination because it was Pakistan's leading commercial centre and the initial headquarters of the Pakistan government. It thus afforded better employment prospects for the mainly middle class North Indian *mohajirs* than the rural West Punjab. Finally, it is possible that the *mohajirs* were discouraged from settling in such Punjabi cities as Lahore and Multan because of their domination by the traditional landed elites. Whatever the motives, the North India refugees who came to settle in Sindh almost four decades ago have impacted dramatically on the 'local' culture, whilst retaining their own strong cultural distinctions. The transformation of Karachi and Hyderabad into Urdu speaking enclaves within Sindh has created acute tensions.

Muslim migrants from South India formed the smallest refugee community. They came mainly from Madras, and numbered around eighteen thousand in 1951.[62] Two-thirds of them settled in Karachi, where they could continue their traditional trading activities. Like the refugees from the Kathiawar coast, some of them were 'returnees' who possessed family connections in Karachi which predated Partition. Unlike the Punjabis, they were not acute migrants, as there was little violence in South India during the period of the British departure.

It is now possible to pull together some general observations concerning the origins and patterns of resettlement of Pakistan's refugee population. The most important distinction is between the Punjabis and the other communities. The former settled almost exclusively in the West Punjab, where a much higher proportion than in other groups relocated in the countryside. Because they were not separated from the indigenous population by social or cultural differences, the large East Punjabi refugee community was easily assimilated. Non-Punjabi *mohajirs* settled largely in the towns and cities of Sindh. They transformed

Karachi and Hyderabad, in particular, into Urdu centres which
were socially and culturally divorced from their Sindhi
surroundings. *Mohajirs* from northern India experienced much
greater difficulty in adapting to their new environment than
Muslims from the western Indian trading communities. Like
their 'Bihari' counterparts in East Pakistan, they were to
continue to bear the hallmarks of an uprooted community,
clinging to their language, traditions and lifestyle.

III

The Governments of India and Pakistan had to hurriedly
improvise administrative structures to cope with the refugee
situation. They rapidly assumed responsibility for evacuating
refugees from riot torn areas, receiving them in temporary
camps, resettling and rehabilitating them and managing evacuee
property. Concerns about the provincial governments' handling
of the refugee problem led the centre to intervene, the main
difference being, in the Indian case, that Nehru insisted on the
linking of rehabilitation with development through the
formation of a Development and Rehabilitation Board.[63]

The task of evacuating refugees was thrust upon the Indian
and Pakistani governments by the failure of the Punjab
Boundary Force. This force of fifty-five thousand men drawn
from the future Indian and Pakistani armies had a British
Commander, Major General T.W. Rees.[64] It was, however,
woefully inadequate to maintain order in the 37,500 square
mile area which it patrolled.[65] The disintegration of the Punjab's
police force and the deliberate efforts to subvert its men[66] made
an already hopeless task impossible. When it was not standing
by helplessly, it actually added to the carnage.[67] Senior Pakistani
and Indian officials as a result demanded that it be wound up.
Despite Mountbatten's misgivings, this was agreed at a Joint
Defence Council meeting at Lahore on 29 August. The Punjab
Boundary Force was replaced by Indian and Pakistani Military
Evacuation Organizations. Their task was to provide rail and

road transport, organize foot convoys and supply troops to escort the columns of refugees across the frontiers between the two States. The last Indian troops involved in this operation did not return home until July 1948.[68]

A former Commander-in-Chief of the Pakistan Army, General Musa, who was the Principal Staff Officer in Lahore in 1947, has given a vivid first hand account of the work of the Military Evacuation Organization. He describes the escort of a refugee caravan from Amritsar which comprised of a hundred thousand people and four-and-a-half thousand bullock carts. The column was so long that its head had reached the Pakistan border at Wagah when the stragglers were still in Amritsar.[69] Despite Indian objections, the Pakistan Air Force flew sorties over the column to ensure its safety.

Aur qaafla sahi salaamat sarhad paar kar kay Pakistan mein damhal ho gaya, tab ham ne itminaan ka saans lia. Fawji jawaan bahut thak gai thay, voh din bhar bari tezi say sarak par phirtey rahtey thay. Taham, voh baray mutma'in thay kay unhon nay mahaajiron ko hifaazat kay saath unkay nai vatan pohncha dia tha. Mujhe is kaarnamey par intihaai fakhr mahsus hua.

And the caravan crossed the border and entered Pakistan safely. Only then, we felt relieved. The soldiers were very tired, they had been marching on the roads and throughout the day and doing their jobs. However, they were very satisfied that they had brought these immigrants to their homeland. I was very proud of doing this job well.[70]

The Pakistan and Indian Military Evacuation Organizations set up headquarters on both sides of the new international boundary. They organized road transportation in army trucks and requisitioned civilian vehicles. Officials of the East and West Punjab Railways were similarly stationed in each others' headquarters to increase the efficiency of the evacuation process. A joint civilian machinery was also established consisting of Liaison Officers. The two Chief Liaison Officers held the status of Deputy High Commissioners. The Pakistani holder of this position was Chaudhri Muhammad Hasan, who was himself an East Punjabi and led the bloc of Muslim Assembly Members from this region. Their attempt to concentrate their kinsmen and clients in resettlement in the West Punjab in order to maximize their political influence was to result in increasing political controversy in the summer of 1948.[71] Beneath the two Chief Liaison Officers, there were the district officials. They were provided with funds, escorts, and scarce supplies of petrol to facilitate their work on behalf of the refugees.

The prevailing atmosphere of hatred and mistrust undermined the cooperation between the Pakistani and Indian Liaison Officers. The collapse of the East Punjab administration, of which we have already made mention, presented another major stumbling block. Sir Francis Mudie despatched a series of increasingly exasperated letters to his East Punjabi counterpart. 'I hesitate to make a suggestion regarding another province and I understand your difficulties', he wrote in typical fashion on 17 September, 'but ... I do suggest that the first duty of your government with if necessary the help of the government of India is to suppress the turbulence and arrogance of the Sikhs and to ensure that they remain no longer in a position to prevent the carrying out of agreements ... loyally carried out by us. Very regrettable things have happened in the West Punjab. ... But they are isolated incidents. ... Although in many cases Sikhs have been driven from their homes ... their exodus from Montgomery and Lyallpur was voluntary and planned. ... In East Punjab the case is different. The Sikhs are carrying out a well organized plan to exterminate the Muslims and drive them from the Province.'[72]

The West Punjab government established a network of reception camps in the border areas. The largest permanent camps were in Multan and Lahore. Three hundred thousand refugees were housed in camps in the latter city, a third of this number in the former. The largest camp for Hindu and Sikh refugees in the East Punjab, at Kurukshetra, had a capacity of two hundred thousand. Camps were also set up in the important railway destinations of Ambala, Rohtak, Hissar and Gurgaon.

The Deputy Commissioner was responsible for furnishing each camp within his jurisdiction with medical, food and sanitary requirements. In reality, administrative oversight lay with the District Refugee and Evacuee Officer. Each camp had its own commandant, who was ordered to keep a strict account of numbers, purdah considerations notwithstanding. The District Medical Health Officer made periodic visits, but basic health care was provided by volunteers. Indeed, they undertook much of the various camps' work.[73]

Local volunteers were drawn from Muslim Students' Federations and from the Zenana branches of the Muslim League. Many doctors came from abroad, especially Britain and America. They were frequently connected with missionary organizations. Some retired ICS officials found their way into the camps, as did a redoubtable lady of seventy who answered a call for volunteers carried in the personal column of *The Times*.[74] The prominent Punjabi author, Kartar Singh Duggal, has recorded in his autobiography, *Kis pahe khola Ganthri*,[75] how his Muslim wife, Ayesha, worked among the refugee camps in Jullundur. Her actions, however, raised suspicions and the 'Muslim factor' was to cause Duggal problems as he later sought promotion in All-India Radio's expansive bureaucracy.[76]

The provincial governments met the cost of feeding the camp residents.[77] Charitable organizations partly alleviated the cost. Money, from the Quaid-e-Azam Fund, for example, was used to purchase cloth which was then made up into clothing by the West Punjab branch of the Pakistan Red Cross. Quilts, which had been provided by charities, were distributed at night, literally being thrown over sleeping refugees who awoke to find themselves covered. Most camps broadcast devotional readings and music over their loudspeakers. Much time was also spent relaying information about missing persons in an endeavour to reunite families.

Considerable efforts were made to counteract the demoralizing effects of prolonged stay in the camps.[78] Although 1.5 million displaced persons had been settled in towns and 2.9 million in the countryside by February 1948, there was still a permanent camp population of over seven hundred thousand.[79] Refugees were encouraged to cook their own food. Instructors were brought in to organize drills and physical exercises for the men. Games and some schooling were provided for the children. Workshops were set up in Sindhi camps to provide training in various crafts. Labour exchanges operated in many West Punjab camps. They directed skilled workers to towns where they could find appropriate employment. Woollen handloom weavers were, for example, directed to Jhang, carpet weavers to Gujarat.[80]

Many of the refugees had left everything behind them in the chaotic two-way flight.[81] The following figures illustrate the scale of this problem: Hindu and Sikh refugees vacated 9.6 million acres of land in Pakistan, abandoned 1,798 urban factories and around 400,000 houses;[82] Muslims left behind 5.5 million acres of land in India.[83] According to Indian sources, the total value of Hindu and Sikh evacuee property in Pakistan was 38.1 billion rupees, while that of Muslim property abondoned in India amounted to 3.8 billion.[84] This claim is, however, highly controversial, and was even questioned at the time by the Indian Minister of Rehabilitation.[85] The failure to agree an evaluation did in fact constitute a major stumbling block to inter-governmental attempts to come to terms with the question of evacuee property.

The Governments of East and West Punjab initially agreed on a common response to the problem of abandoned property early in September 1947. They refused to recognize the illegal seizure of property, and appointed custodians to oversee evacuees' possessions. They reversed their positions, however, when it became apparent that the massive transfer of population was permanent. They introduced ordinances to limit the evacuees' rights to transfer or repossess their property, in order to ease the rehabilitation of refugees. The evacuees' hope of compensation, moreover, receded as the governments squabbled over its terms. Pakistan was reluctant to accept the Indian valuation of evacuee property as this would have resulted in the payment of a large sum to New Delhi in any mutual transfer of respective liabilities. It also challenged the Indian decision to extend evacuee legislation to all areas except Assam and West Bengal. This both discouraged refugees from returning to areas which had not been seriously disturbed, and created insecurity amongst those who remained. For they feared the seizure of their property. This anxiety was greatly increased in October 1949 when the Indian government created the category of 'intending evacuees.' Progress on the issue of evacuee property was therefore limited to the category of moveable property. An arrangement was secured regarding this, whereby evacuees were permitted to apply for its recovery and to sell or export it.

Inter-Dominion cooperation was more successful when it came to the recovery of abducted women and children. Recovery Offices and transit camps were established in both countries, following agreement in November 1948. Counselling services were also provided for the victims. By October 1952, just over eight thousand women and children had been rehabilitated from Pakistan. Twice this number of Muslim women and children had been recovered from India.[86] The human misery and physical and psychological scars created by abduction is of course hidden by such bald statistics. Such Urdu novelists as Rajinder Singh Bedi[87] and Saadat Hasan Manto[88] have brilliantly portrayed the horror and pathos arising from abduction. Amrita Pritam, through the character Pooro-Hamida in her novel, *Pinjer*,[89] has achieved a similar result through the medium of Punjabi. In English, we of course have the account of the sufferings of Lenny's *ayah* in Bapsi Sidhwa's novel, *Ice-Candy-Man*.[90]

While the recovery of women was the most dramatic aspect of rehabilitation, governments more routinely faced the problem of finding shelter and employment for refugees. Agriculturalist Muslim refugees were rehabilitated on Crown Land in the Canal Colonies, as well as on land vacated by Hindus and Sikhs. In the West Punjab, refugees received eight acres,[91] in Sindh, where land was less fertile, nearly double this amount. The land was supposed to be allotted in cultivatory, rather than proprietory right, but in the Montgomery district, many refugees without authorization took ownership rights and squeezed what rent they could out of fellow refugee cultivators. Such irregularities reflected a situation which the Governor of the West Punjab admitted, was 'so obscure that anything might be taking place.'[92]

Responsibility for the settlement of refugees on the land theoretically lay with the overworked Deputy Commissioners and Tehsildars who acted as Assistant Rehabilitation Commissioners for the areas under their jurisdiction. From the beginning of 1948, however, a competing agency was introduced in the West Punjab. This was an Allotment Revising Committee. It had been established by the Premier, the wealthy Nawab of Mamdot. This Committee continued to function even after Jinnah, acting as Governor-General, had withheld assent to the Bill giving it statutory powers. This action had followed the hostility of the Pakistan and West Punjab Joint Refugees and Rehabilitation Council to Mamdot's creation. There was in fact growing disquiet concerning Mamdot's personal supervision of the allotment of abandoned cars and houses in Lahore and his arrangements for the former tenants of his East Punjab estate.[93]

Refugees who were allotted land received grants to buy agricultural equipment and seed. In Sindh, each family was given up to five hundred rupees in cash or in kind, as well as agricultural implements.[94] Muslim refugees who settled on land east of the River Chenab received a monthly subsistence allowance of five rupees a head for a three month period, beginning in July 1948. Those who were allotted land in the less fertile region west of the Chenab received slightly more. Free timber for house construction was also provided.[95]

The East Punjab government made similar arrangements. It endeavoured to resettle Sikh Jat farmers from the Canal Colonies in their ancestral districts.[96] Loans were made available for the purchase of agricultural implements. The government also improved the rural infrastructure of the East Punjab, which lagged behind the Canal Colonies of the West. Urban Hindu and Sikh refugees, however, received less encouragement. Their sense of relative deprivation was to possess important political consequences.[97]

In one important respect, the rural resettlement policies differed considerably between the two Punjabs. The governments of the East Punjab and PEPSU (Patiala and East Punjab States Union) rapidly introduced tenancy reforms and redistributed land.[98] The opportunity was, however, passed over by the West Punjab government. Despite the fact that progressive politicians such as Mian Iftikhar-ud-Din pressed for such policies as the breakup of large estates to distribute land to refugees,[99] this met with the immediate disapproval of the unreconstructed landowning Premier. Mamdot ensured that plenty of water was poured into Mian Iftikhar-ud-Din's heady brew. Seeing that his ideas were going nowhere, the latter sensationally resigned. His departure brought the organizational and ministerial wings of the Punjab Muslim League virtually to blows. The different policies pursued by the East and West Punjab governments accentuated the variations in landholding structure which had already been a marked feature of the colonial period. While landlordism continued to hold sway in the West Punjab, affluent peasant proprietors dominated the scene in the East.

IV

Bare historical accounts of the riots, massacres and migrations of 1947 cannot convey the full impact of what was both a brutalizing experience and also one which, for many Muslims, contained a spiritual element which redeemed their terrible physical deprivations. We have already encountered the ability of such literary masters as Intizar Husain to represent the welter of emotions engendered amongst Muslims by Partition. We shall listen now to the voices of those who were eye-witnesses. These have gone unheard in standard accounts of Pakistan's birth. Yet they contribute a human dimension which has been sorely missed. Most of the material will be drawn from autobiographical Urdu sources, partly because such works are far more representative of this type of literature; but in the main because they have been totally neglected in standard texts. Before concentrating on the more well-known Urdu sources, however, we shall turn first to Khwaja Ahmad Abbas's autobiographical account, *I am not an island*.[100] It is interesting not only for its personal insights, but for the way it reveals that for some writers, art came to mirror reality.

Khwaja Ahmad Abbas came from a Panipat family whose ancestors had migrated to India from Afghanistan during the thirteenth century AD. Like his father before him, he was educated at Aligarh. Whilst at the College, he had brought out the first University Students' Weekly in India, called *Aligarh Opinion*. The Vice-Chancellor eventually banned it because of its anti-British sentiments.[101] Thereafter, as might be expected, Khwaja Ahmad Abbas embarked on a journalistic career, working first for *The National Call* and later for the *Bombay Chronicle*. He added work as a film critic and scriptwriter as strings to his bow. He was drawn in, as so many other intellectuals were, to the Progressive Writers' Movement. This radical political stance colours his views of the events of 1947, as does his friendship with Nehru. The Indian Premier personally ensured that Abbas's mother and sisters were safely transported from Panipat to Delhi.

Khwaja Ahmad Abbas vividly describes the communal tension in Bombay on the eve of Independence. He recalls how his witnessing a communal murder near the Harkissandas Hospital inspired him to write the novel, *Main Kaun Hoon?* The affray was especially bizarre as the victim was mistaken by a Hindu assailant as a Muslim. When the murderer tugged at the corpse's pyjama cord and saw that he was not circumcized, he uttered the phrase which continually haunted Abbas, 'Mishtake hogaya'.[102] Another actual event similarly inspired a story, a Sikh Sardar's protection of Abbas's cousin from RSS gangs in Delhi leading to the writing of *Sardarji*.[103]

Abbas relates the division of Bombay into Muslim and Hindu no-go areas. His family were virtually the only Muslims left in the Shivaji Park sea-front area, which was given over to RSS parades and drills.[104] The creation of self-defence organizations for localities, and the tension and fear which stalked the streets at night, are powerfully recalled. On one occasion when walking home, he fears that he is being shadowed by a would be assailant, only to be relieved to discover that it is his neighbour, who is equally afraid, 'the two brothers stalking each other in the forest that is curfew-bound Bombay.'[105]

The author also provides glimpses of the disruptions his family faced in Panipat, and their misconception concerning the emergence of Pakistan. His mother had to discard the burqa for the first time in her life, to carry her belongings the two miles from her house to the military lorry which was to transport her to Delhi. His cousins rebuffed Hindu would be purchasers of their attractive property because they regarded Pakistan as a new kind of province, 'with favourable employment chances for Muslims where one could go' and then return to India. *'Aur jab naukri chhore kay',* my cousin remonstrated, *'pension lay kay aaengay, to ham kahaan rahengay?'* (And where shall we stay after being pensioned off?)[106]

The experience of Abbas's family was however atypical of that of most East Punjabi Muslims. The account given in Mashkur Hassan's Urdu autobiography, *Aazaadi ke charaagh,*[107] is far more representative. They lived in a predominantly Hindu neighbourhood in Hissar. Mashkur Hassan's moving account of what befell them during the communal violence of August 1947 forms the focus for his autobiography. The harrowing work seems to have touched a universal chord, for it has proved enormously popular with Pakistani readers and has gone through three editions.

The writer recalls that the Hindus began to attack their home on 29 August. When the police were called, they joined in the assault. Mashkur Hassan graphically describes the death of his cousins, his wife, Khadija, and youngest daughter, Masoor. His anguish was worsened by the fact that he was lying paralysed, assumed dead, at the time, and their slaughter was in full view. Parched by the heat of the fire elsewhere in the building, he licked the blood which was flowing from the victims' wounds. Twelve hours elapsed before he was finally able to stagger from the shattered remains of the building. He was reunited with his father, who took him to a hospital in the Police Lines. The remainder of the book is taken up with memories of other family members and servants who were slain.[108]

The work is not just a catalogue of horrors, but provides glimpses of the link between Pakistan's birth and personal renewal, which is explored so profoundly in the fiction of Intizar Husain. The writer records the exact time, 4 o'clock on the morning of 2 November, when he entered the 'country of our new dreams'. He goes on to declare that he felt born again, that his real date of birth was 2 November 1947.

While Khwaja Ahmad Abbas remained in India in 1947, another of the luminaries of the Progressive Writers' Movement, Shahid Ahmad, migrated to Pakistan. His account of the violence which engulfed Delhi and his subsequent journey to Pakistan, is contained in the valuable Urdu autobiographical source, *Dilhi ki Bipta*.

Shahid Ahmad came from a wealthy Delhi family which owned land in the Raichur district. In the light of both his father's and grandfather's literary interests,[109] it was not surprising that he opened a publishing house at the conclusion of his studies. This brought out the works of such progressives as Manto and Chughtai. Shahid Ahmad also founded the monthly, *Saqi*, in 1930 to popularize the work of promising radical authors. In addition, he established the periodical, *Shahjahan*, as the mouthpiece for the Delhi branch of the Progressive Writers' Movement. Ahmad played a very active role in its early years, although ideological differences with the leadership led him to eventually fade from the scene.[110]

Dilhi ki Bipta contains a vivid first hand account of the violence in Delhi in September 1947, and of the conditions which faced those Muslims who were forced out of their homes. Shahid Ahmad describes how Muslim houses in such suburbs as Karol Bagh were marked so that they could be identified by assailants. He also details the defence systems of gates on streets, guard groups, and coloured lights—red if riots threatened, green as an all clear signal—which the Muslims designed for their protection. When they had been evacuated, Muslims were herded into camps in such places as Purana Qila and Humayan's Tomb. The latter camp was bulging with over 30,000 refugees by December 1947.[111] Shahid Ahmad details the desperate conditions which prevailed, as a result of lack of shelter and sanitation.[112]

The most gripping part of the account is formed by his narration of the train journey from Delhi to Pakistan. Evidence of the overcrowding is found in the fact that it took the writer half an hour to force his way into a compartment. It was intended for thirty-two people, but he counted one hundred and twenty-five occupants.[113] This was by no means unusual. The Chief Commissioner of the Indian Railways noted, for example, in his report, that a single train left Saharanpur on 11 November with 6,550 refugees and government servants who had opted for Pakistan.[114] Before such trains departed, all the passengers were ordered to surrender their weapons, and were warned not to drink water at any of the stops, in case the wells had been poisoned. Ahmad recalls how tempers became increasingly frayed in the suffocating September heat. At Muzaffarnagar Station, boys on the platform gave them water and roasted nuts. They were dressed as Congressmen, but were in fact local Muslim League people. There was great relief and joy when the train safely crossed the Pakistan border and a large crowd laden down with food greeted them at Jallo Station.

Aadhay ghantay kay baad yahan say gaari rawaana hui to jasyi murdon mayn jaan par gai. Pakistan Zindabad aur Quaid-e-Azam Zindabad kay naaray lagnay shuru ho gaye. Maaloom hua kay ham Pakistan ki sarhad mayn daakhil ho chukay hain. Thori der kay baad Pakistan ka pehla station Jallo aa gaya. Yahaan sainkron aadmi rail kay intezaar mayn kharay thay. Rail kay ruktay hi har dabay par kayi kayi aadmi aa gayay aur sab ko rotian, daal, aur achaar taqseem karnay lagay. Do din kay bhookay in rotion par iss tarha giray jaysay kabhi roti daykhi hi na thhee. Aik aik aadmi das das rotian hokay mayn dabaa kay bayth gia. Aurtein aur bachay, jo dusri taraf thhay, maangtay he rah gayay. Woh to kahiye kay khanany ka intizaam iss qadar wafir thha kay sab ko hisa mil gaya.

After half an hour the train started as if the dead have had new life. 'Pakistan Zindabad' and 'Quaid-e-Azam Zindabad' slogans started to be raised. We understood that we have now entered the borders of Pakistan. After a little while we reached Jallo, the first station of Pakistan. Here hundreds of people were waiting for the train. As the train stopped, many people came to each compartment and started distributing bread, lentils and pickles. Hunger-stricken for two days, they fell on the food as if they had never seen anything to eat. Each man took tens of chappaties in greed and sat down. Women and children, who were on the other side, kept on begging. Fortunately, the food was so plentiful that everyone got their share.[115]

The refugees were, however, greeted rather differently at Lahore. They had hardly alighted before they were assailed with questions concerning their sufferings, so that revenge attacks could be planned, and the entire debt 'repaid with interest'.[116] The locals, rather than acting as *ansars*, attempted to fleece them of the little money which remained. Shahid Ahmad recalls that:

Lahore kay station par quli bari mushkil say milay aur munh maangay daam lay kar unhon nay taangay tak hamayn puhnchaaya. Ab tangon-waalon-ki- baari thee—kay jo jee chahay ham say talab kar layn. Urdu suntay hee un kay kaan kharay ho jaatay aur rayt chaugnay ho jaatay. Baahar haal issay aakhri manzil samajh kar inn ka mutaaliba bhee pura kiya.

At Lahore Station, it was very difficult to find coolies. Whatever rate they demanded, they got, to take our luggage to the tongas. Now it was the turn of the tonga drivers. They asked whatever they wanted; as soon as they heard us speaking Urdu, their ears would prick up and the rates would go up fourfold. However, considering this as the last of the hurdles, we agreed to their demand.[117]

Shahid Ahmad returned to his native Delhi seven months after his flight to Pakistan. He was at first struck by the physical changes which had resulted from the refugee influx from the West Punjab: the congested streets and markets, the pavements crammed with migrants selling their wares on trays.[118] In the midst of all this bustle, he became aware of a deeper feeling of loss, of a sundering of links with the past.

Mein apni maan ki goad may dil-e-shakista lay kar aaya thaa. Aur dil-e-murda lay kar wapis aya. Maan ka randapa dekha, beevi kay aansu deykhey. Shahjehaani masjid ko milguji chaandni mayn dekha to samjha kay maan kay donon haath dua kay liye aasmaan ki taraf utthey huay hain. Aur Mariam ki tarah isskay dil may sholay bhharak rahay hain. Yeh tasawwar kuch aisa bandha kay bhulaaye nahin bhoolta, aur baar baar dil mayn yeh sawaal paida hota hai: 'Maan! kya tera suhaag hamesha key liye ujar gaya?'

I came to my mother's lap with a broken heart and returned with a dead heart. I saw a mother's widowhood, and witnessed a wife's tears. I saw the Shah Jehan mosque in beautiful moonlight and felt as if mother had lifted her hands towards the heavens in prayer, and, like Mary, her heart is aflame. This vision has been engraved (in my memory) in such a manner that I can never forget it. And repeatedly the question arises in my mind, 'Mother, has the bliss of marriage forsaken you for ever?'[119]

For Shahid Ahmad, Delhi has been lost to the Muslims. It has been widowed, as earlier were Cordova and Granada. Like them, it will continue to haunt the Muslims as a memorial to their vanished glory. A sense of loss could be felt, however, not only for a great Muslim city like Delhi, but, as Intizar Husain reminds us, in the remembrance of a local imam bara in a quiet UP village. The elegiac quality of his fiction is captured in the autobigraphical passages set out below from the pen of an Amritsar refugee, A. Hameed.

Baat yeh hay, keh Amritsar meiray liay bichhra hua yarosalam hay,
aur mein uski divaar-e-giria hoon. Amritsar to meirey Khun mein
gardish kar raha hay. Amritsar ko dekh kar sota hoon, aur subha
uthh kar sab say pahlay usi ko dekhta hoon. Chalta hoon, to kampni
baagh meiray saath hota hay, baythta hoon, to saktari baagh ke
darakht mujh par saaya kiay hotey hein. Bolta hoon, to mujhe
Amritsar ki masjidon ki azaanain sunaai deti hein, khamosh hota
hoon, to Amritsar ki nahron ka paani meiray kaanon say sargoshiaan
kartey huey guzarta hay. Apnay ek haath ko dekhta hoon, to us par
sard raton mein apnay mohallay ki galiaan khaabeeda dikhai deiteen
hein.

In fact Amritsar for me is a Jerusalem separated from me, and I am
her 'wailing wall'. Amritsar is circulating in my body, with my
blood. I see Amritsar before I go to sleep, and the first thing I see
when I get up in the morning is Amritsar. When I walk, Company
Garden accompanies me. When I sit, the trees of Saktari Garden
give me shade. When I speak, I hear the call for prayer from the
mosques, and when I am silent, I hear the flowing water in the
canals of Amritsar whisper in my ears. When I cast a glance at the
palm of my hand, on it I see, in the cold of night, the sleeping
lanes and pathways of my familiar neighbourhood.[120]

Hameed recalls 'the stars which illuminated the heaven of
Amritsar', such people whom he knew as Saadat Hasan Manto,
Saif-ud-din Saif, Sufi Ghulam Mohammad Butt, and Sufi
Ghulam Mustafa Tabassum. But along with such luminaries,
he also has fond memories of Shahaba the ice cream seller.[121] In
his imagination, he visits such places as Hal Bazar, Chawk Farid,
Katra Safaid, and Company Garden, but finds them sad and
desolate.

Vahaan musalmaanon kay kalchar aur saqaafat kay naqsh-e-paa
bhi nahin thay. Masjideyn marsia khaan theen, kashmirion ki
baythakon mein Hindu aurtein gobar ka lip kar rahi theen.

Even the footprints (ruins) of Muslim culture were not visible.
The mosques seemed to be reciting elegies. Hindu women were

plastering with cow dung the walls of rooms which once formed the rendezvous for Kashmiris.[122]

He remembers the martyrs 'whose fragrance we find in the roses of Pakistan, and whose light we can see in the rising sun of Pakistan'.

Yey woh loag thay jo aik undaikhay vatan ki khaatir shaheed hogaye, Amritsar ki gali kuchon mein.

These were the people who were martyred for an unseen homeland in the lanes of Amritsar.[123]

Nations which forget such martyrs, he warns, are forgotten themselves. Like Shahid Ahmad, he compares the loss of Muslim India to Spain, where the call to prayer is similarly stilled.

Uski masjidon ki khaak mein merey aabaa-o-ajdaad kay sajdon kay nishaan posheeda hayn, aur uskey gali koochon mein shaheedon kay khoon ki laali bikhri hui hay.

> *Haspaania, too khoon-e-musalmaan ka ameen hay*
> *Maanind-e-haram-e-paak hay too meri nazar mein*
> *Posheeda tiri khak mein sajdon kay nishaan hain*
> *Khamosh azaanain teri baad-e-sahr mein.*

In the dust of its (Amritsar's) mosques, are hidden the imprints of the prostrations of my ancestors, and its lanes are red with the blood of the martyrs.

> O Spain! You are the trustee of the blood of Muslims.
> In my eyes you are as sacred as the pure *Haram*.
> In your dust are concealed the imprints of the prostrations,
> And silent calls to prayer can be heard in your morning breeze.[124]

Spain is a popular symbol for Muslim writers concerned with past Islamic glories, but what we have here is something more than mere literary convention. Both Hameed and Shahid Ahmad provide glimpses of a haunting loss which is almost too deep for words. This lies at the heart of the Partition experience for many South Asian Muslims. It is part of a wider emotional current in Muslim society which Akbar Ahmed has termed the Andalus syndrome. He sees its existence wherever a great Muslim civilization has been lost and its descendants face an uncertain future. His personal view is that it creates an unhealthy neurosis in which there is a permanent perplexity and trauma.[125]

Hameed's remembrances are contained in the foreword to Khwaja Iftikhar's book, *Jab Amritsar jal raha tha*. This work has been enormously popular in Pakistan and has run to nine editions in the space of a decade. The author has been awarded the gold medal of the Pakistan movement and has earned the epithet, *Musavvir-e-Haqiqat* (The painter of realities). Its power has stemmed not only from the author's personal recollections, but his extensive use of eye-witness accounts which are supported by photographic material. He has pieced together a gripping narrative from the first day of the riots in Amritsar on 3 March 1947 until the final Muslim exodus in August.

Western historians have, however, surprisingly neglected what is an invaluable source for exploring the human dimension of Pakistan's emergence. The sacrifices of individual Muslims are starkly depicted, as are the actions of unsung heroes: such as the personal bravery of Zahur Ahmad, a young railway employee whose bravery and resourcefulness matched any fictional Jugga Singh in thwarting an attack on a refugee train.[126] The poignancy of such short stories as *Lajwanti*, *Khuda ki qasm*, and *Khol do*, dealing with the subject of abduction, is similarly fleshed out in the eye-witness account of seventeen year old Zenab's purchase by the aged Sikh, Boota Singh, for fifteen hundred rupees.[127]

Zenab was just one of the thousands of female victims of the brutalities of 1947. Despite the fiction of Chughtai, Mumtaz Shah Nawaz and others, and the autobiographical account of Begum Ikramullah,[128] women's voices are silent in the history of Pakistan's birth. They are generally invisible in standard historical accounts. Their experiences have not been recorded and recognized, although they constitute half of humanity. Until this neglect has been put right, the full truth of the emergence of Pakistan will be obscured. This major task is beyond the scope of this present work. It is, nevertheless, appropriate to conclude this section by drawing on the account of Dr Zahida Amjad Ali's train journey from the Old Fort in Delhi to Pakistan.

> All passengers were forced into compartments like sheep and goats, because of which the heat and suffocating atmosphere was intensified, and it was very hard to breathe. In the ladies' compartment, women and children were in a very bad condition. Because of panic and distress, they were extremely restless and nervous. But in this suffocating atmosphere, with an air of unknown and mysterious fear, they tried in vain to calm down and comfort their children. … If you looked out of the window, you could see dead bodies lying in the distance. Human skulls without flesh were an obvious proof that there had been a brutal massacre. At many places, you could see corpses lying on one another and no one seemed to have any concern. And on some roads and walls you could see the signs of *Holi* played with human blood. At one place, we saw the dead bodies of innocent children, in such condition that even the most stone-hearted person would stop breathing for a moment if he saw them. By looking at a newly born baby, I could immediately see that his body was torn apart by pulling the legs. These were the scenes that made your heart bleed, and everybody around loudly repented their sins and recited verses to ask for God's forgiveness. Fear showed on everyone's face, their red and white faces had turned pale, although nothing extraordinary had happened yet. Even so, every moment seemed to be most terrifying and agonizing.[129]

Zahida's narration builds to a horrifying climax.[130] The refugee train, like so many others, is attacked by Sikhs in a pre-planned operation. The Dogra troops which had been detailed to protect it, stand by and do nothing. The refugees were defenceless, all their weapons had been confiscated at the beginning of the journey, down to the smallest pocket knife. The attackers broke their way into the barricaded compartments and threw women and children outside. The author's six months old sister, Mobina, was clinging to her mother's breast. Unaware of the mayhem outside, she started to move her legs and hands playfully. This caused her *pazeb* (ankle ornaments) to tinkle. '*Maan nay koshish ki keh uskay paaon pakar lay takeh pazeb ki aawaaz band ho jai.*' (The mother tried to hold still the girl's legs to stop the pazeb from jingling.) But the ensuing struggle alerted the attackers outside.

> He came running fast and pierced through her chest and the mother's ribs with the same powerful blow of his spear. Down came another blow on the child, and she died instantly.[131]

V

This brief examination of personal experiences of Partition-related violence and migration has attempted to restore a human dimension to the historical discourse of Pakistan's birth. This has been lost sight of in the literature's emphasis on elite conflict, politics and the role of colonial policy. The presence of such a human dimension is necessary, however, not only in the interests of justice, but also of truth. The recollections of such eye-witnesses as Shahid Ahmad and A. Hameed harmonize with the elegies of Intizar Husain. While Indian Muslims thrilled at the birth of Pakistan, which had been created according to the dictates of their faith, they also mourned the loss of ancestral homes: the graveyards which would remain unattended; the mosques which would no longer resound with the call to prayer; the empty places—*havelis*, palaces and monuments which would stand as memorials to a vanished glory; finally there was the loss of familiar sights and sounds, the city walls, the fields which surrounded it, the whispering of water in the canals.

The reverse side of the coin of Pakistan's birth was, however, a renewed sense of pride and Muslim community which redeemed this sense of loss. The complex attitudes and motivations of ordinary Muslims will be further explored in the next chapter through the story of one ordinary Muslim woman who journeyed to Pakistan in 1947.

NOTES

[1] Cited in, K.R. Sipe, 'Karachi's Refugee Crisis: The Political, Economic and Social Consequences of Partition-Related Migration'. Duke University, unpublished Ph.D Thesis, 1976, p. 73.

[2] A notable exception is Chapter 13 of C.M. Ali, *The Emergence of Pakistan* (New York, 1967).

[3] M. S. Randhawa, *Out of the Ashes* (Jullundur, 1954).

[4] Sipe, op. cit., p. 10.

[5] Sipe op. cit., p. 14.

[6] Surah 4, Women, cited in A.S. Ahmed, *Discovering Islam: Making Sense of Muslim History and Society* (London, 1988), p.108.

[7] See, I. Talbot, *Punjab and the Raj 1849-1947* (New Delhi, 1988), p. 228.

[8] H. Dow to Wavell, 22 November 1946, L/P&J/5/181, IOR.

[9] *The Statesman* (Calcutta), 27 December 1946.

[10] Punjab FR 30 July 1947; 13 August 1947. L/P&J/5/250, IOR.

[11] Pakistan Government, *Note on the Sikh Plan* (Lahore, 1948), pp. 17-29.

[12] Sikhs had acquired lands in its Canal Colonies which they had helped develop. On 13 September 1947, a convoy of forty thousand Sikhs left the Lyallpur Colony taking with them all they could load on bullock carts. *Civil and Military Gazette* (Lahore), 19 September 1947.

[13] This was the birthplace of the founder of Sikhism, Guru Nanak. The village of Nankana Sahib lies some forty miles west-south-west of Lahore.

[14] *The Sikh Plan*, op. cit., pp. 26-7.

[15] *Civil and Military Gazette* (Lahore), 19 September 1947.

[16] H.V. Hodson, *The Great Divide. Britain-India-Pakistan* (London, 1969), p. 411.

[17] Mudie to Jinnah, 23 September 1947, Mudie Papers, Mss. Eur. F 164/15, IOR.

[18] See, for example, Punjab FR 14 March 1997; 13 August 1947, L/P&J/5/250, IOR.

[19] Amir Abdullah Khan Rokri, *Mayn awr mera Pakistan*, 2nd edition (Lahore, 1989), p. 75.

[20] Pakistan Government, *The Sikhs in Action* (Lahore, 1948) p. 34.

[21] *The Sikhs in Action*, op. cit., p. 29.

[22] *The Sikhs in Action*, op. cit., p. 33.

[23] *The Sikhs in Action*, op. cit., p. 31.

[24] *The Sikhs in Action*, op. cit., pp. 31-2.

[25] Report of Colonel Sher Khan. Administrative Headquarters. Military Evacuation Organization, Amritsar. 24 September 1947. Mudie Papers, Mss. Eur. F 164/15, IOR.

[26] Report of Mr. Hadow's Tour of Jullundur, Hoshiarpur, Ludhiana and Ferozepore districts. 7 January 1948. East Punjab Affairs 1947-50. G 2275/80 Do. 35 3181, Dominions Office and Commonwealth Relations Office PRO.

[27] Ibid.

[28] Extract Minutes, 27th Meeting, Emergency Cabinet Committee, MB1/D276, Mountbatten Papers, University of Southampton.

[29] Indian High Commissioner to Commonwealth Relations Office, Cypher 27 October 1947, East Punjab Affairs 1947-8, Weekly Reports G 2275/14 Do. 35 3159, Dominions and Commonwealth Relations Office, PRO.

[30] Report of Mr Hadow's Tour, op. cit. This view was endorsed by Lady Mountbatten during a three day tour of the West Punjab in late October. Her main impression

> was that , so far as resources permitted, every effort was being made to safeguard and cater for the minorities and to arrange for the safe evacuation of refugees. The food supply was generally satisfactory, sufficient was available either on purchase or issue. Accommodation arrangements for the Hindus and Sikhs were good. Health conditions were reasonably good, but there was an overall shortage, which applied to hospitals and Muslim refugees as well as to non-Muslim refugees, of medical facilities and supplies.

Emergency Committee 25th Meeting, held 31 October 1947, MB/1 D278, Mountbatten Papers, University of Southampton.

[31] *Zemindar* (Lahore), 13 September 1947. R/3/1/174, IOR.

[32] Non-Muslims formed around a third of the population of the Sheikhupura district. The Sikhs had played an important role in its agricultural development. The district of course contained the Nankana Sahib birthplace of Guru Nanak. The resistance put up by the Hindu and Sikh villagers of Bhullair has been commemorated in folk song and story. Randhawa, op. cit., p. 15.

[33] G. S. Talib, *Muslim League Attacks on Sikhs and Hindus in the Punjab 1947* (Amritsar, 1950), p. 170.

[34] Ibid., p. 191.

[35] *Eastern Times* (Lahore), 26 August 1947.

[36] *Eastern Times* (Lahore), 9 September 1947.

[37] *Eastern Times* (Lahore), 2 October 1947.

[38] Khwaja Iftikhar, *Jab Amritsar jal raha thaa*, 9th edition (Lahore, 1991), p. 252.

[39] Iftikhar, op. cit., pp. 252-3.

[40] *Eastern Times* (Lahore), 13 November 1947.

[41] The exact figure given by Brigadier F.H. Stevens, Commander of the Pakistan Military Evacuation Organization, had been, 4,680,000. Quoted in *Eastern Times* (Lahore), 25 December 1947.

[42] *The Statesman* (Calcutta), 16 November 1947.

[43] Randhawa, op. cit., p. 27.

[44] Ajmer FR, 2nd Half of December 1947. L/P&J/5/287, IOR.

[45] Indian High Commissioner to Commonwealth Relations Office, Cypher 10 January 1948. East Punjab Affairs 1947-8. Weekly Reports G 2275/14 Do. 35 3159, Dominions and Commonwealth Relations Office, PRO.

[46] Sipe, op. cit., p. 109 & ff.

[47] Miriam Sharma & Urmila Vanjani, 'Remembrances of Things Past. Partition Experiences of Punjabi Villagers in Rajasthan', *Economic and Political Weekly*, 4 August 1990, p. 1731.

[48] Ibid., (46) above, p. 1730.

[49] Rokri, op. cit., p. 72.

[50] Rokri, op. cit., p. 76.

[51] *The Statesman* (Calcutta), 5 May 1948.

[52] Randhawa, op. cit., pp. 77-8.

[53] Rokri, op. cit., p.73.

[54] T. P. Wright, 'Indian Muslim Refugees in the Politics of Pakistan', *Journal of Commonwealth & Comparative Politics* XII (1975), p. 194.

[55] Sipe, op. cit., p. 86.

[56] Summary of the Migrations of 1947-8, n.d., Mudie Papers, Mss. Eur. F. 164/47, IOR.

[57] Ibid. (40) above.

[58] For details, consult, Randhawa, op. cit., p. 93 & ff.

[59] Sipe, op. cit., p. 90.

[60] Sipe, op. cit., p. 205.

[61] Sipe, op. cit., p. 75

[62] Sipe, op. cit., p. 109.

[63] For details of this, consult, MB1/D278 Mountbatten Papers, University of Southampton.

[64] The Partition Council had decided upon the formation of the force on 22 July 1947. Rees was responsible to the Supreme Commander, General Sir Claude Auchinleck, and through him, after Independence, to the two successor governments. The senior Indian Officer attached to the Boundary Force was Brigadier Dhigambir Singh, his Pakistani counterpart was Brigadier Mohammad Ayub Khan.

[65] This included seventeen towns, nearly seventeen thousand villages, and a population of 14.5 million in the twelve districts of the central Punjab.

[66] G. Auchinleck, Note on the situation in the Punjab Boundary Force Area for the Joint Defence Council, 15 August 1997. R/3/1/171, IOR.

[67] M.K. Sinha, Report of the Deputy Director, Intelligence Bureau, n.d., R/3/1/173, IOR.

[68] *The Statesman* (Calcutta), 12 July 1948.

[69] Iftikhar, op. cit., p. 256.

[70] Iftikhar, op. cit., pp. 256-7.

[71] *See*, for example, Deputy High Commissioner, Lahore to Acting High Commissioner, Karachi, 22 August 1948, L/P&J/5/332; Mudie to Jinnah, 5 August 1948, Mudie Papers, Mss. Eur. F. 164/15, IOR.

[72] Mudie to Trivedi, 17 September 1947, Mudie Papers, Mss. Eur. F. 164/15, IOR.

[73] The writer, H.S. Gill, provides a cynical view on the motivations of some of the East Punjab volunteers.

> Each day the social service workers went about rendering good deeds to all and sundry. One couldn't blame them because they had to muster up an impressive tally of services rendered at the end of their duty in the camp, before Punjab University would grant them their social service degrees. There were a lot of genuine do-gooders but the majority were opportunists who had earlier failed their examinations and were endeavouring to get their degrees in this way.

H.S. Gill, *Ashes and Petals* (New Delhi, 1978), p. 15.

[74] Summary of the Migrations of 1947-8, n.d., Mudie Papers, Mss. Eur. F 164/47, IOR.

[75] K.S. Duggal, *Kis pahe khola Ganthri* (New Delhi, 1985), pp. 424-440.

[76] I am indebted to Darshan Singh Tatla of South Birmingham College for this and the above reference.

[77] Mian Mumtaz Daultana, the Punjab Finance Minister, reported that his government had spent 370,000,000 rupees on feeding refugees and 1.5 crore rupees on incidentals.

78 The growing discontent amongst refugees both in India and Pakistan finds fictional representation in Kartar Singh Duggal's novel, *Twice Born Twice Dead*.

> No one was happy. The village folk found the villages here so different, the townspeople found the cities so small. Even those who had been allotted houses were unhappy. ... Those who had no shelter were positively hostile, everyone blamed the government. ... The furniture of the camp office was smashed, the officers beaten up and the glass panes of the doors, windows and skylights of the main office were broken to pieces.

K.S. Duggal, *Twice Born Twice Dead* (New Delhi, 1979), pp. 145 & 149.

[79] H.S. Stephenson, Deputy High Commissioner, Lahore to the British High Commissioner, Karachi, 1 February 1948, L/P&J/5/332, IOR.

[80] *Eastern Times* (Lahore), 16 September 1947.

[81] Kartar Singh Duggal graphically depicts, for example, the reduced circumstances of many Sikh refugees.

They came having lost whole families. ... People were in rags, high ranking chaudhries were without turbans, their hair dishevelled and matted with tons of dust. Brides came barefooted.

K.S. Duggal, *Twice Born Twice Dead* (New Delhi, 1979), p. 50.

[82] Ali, op. cit., p. 269.

[83] J.B. Schechtman, 'Evacuee Property in India and Pakistan', *Pacific Affairs*, 24,(1951), pp. 411-12.

[84] Schechtman, op. cit., p. 407.

[85] Schechtman, op. cit., p. 407.

[86] Ali, op. cit., p. 274.

[87] For a discussion of Rajinder Singh Bedi's famous story, *Lajwanti*, on this subject, *see*, Mumtaz Shirin (ed.), Zulmat-e-Neem Roze (Karachi, 1990), p. 29 & ff.

[88] Manto tackles this theme in such short stories as *Khuda ki qasm* and *Khol do*.

[89] The narrative centres around the abduction of Pooro, the daughter of a West Punjabi Hindu moneylender, by a young Muslim farmer who is avenging his own dishonour. The novel, which was published in Punjabi in 1950, has been translated by Khushwant Singh. K. Singh, *The Skeleton* (Delhi, 1973).

[90] Bapsi Sidhwa, *Ice-Candy-Man* (New Delhi, 1989).

[91] Mudie to Jinnah, 19 April 1948, Mudie Papers, Mss. Eur. F 164/15, IOR.

[92] Ibid.

[93] Mudie to Jinnah, 23 February 1948, Mudie Papers, Mss. Eur. F 164/15, IOR.

[94] Mudie to Jinnah, 26 March 1948, Mudie Papers, Mss. Eur. F 164/15, IOR.

[95] Deputy High Commissioner, Lahore to British High Commissioner, Karachi, 4 July 1948, L/P&J/5/333, IOR.

[96] M. Robinson, 'Religion, Class and Faction. The Politics of Communalism in Twentieth Century Punjab', University of Sussex, unpublished D.Phil Thesis 1988, p. 174.

[97] Robinson, op. cit., p. 184.

[98] Robinson, op. cit., p. 182.

[99] He advocated a ceiling on estates of fifty acres. He also called for the nationalization of basic industries, the provision of a dole of five rupees a month, and the exchange of refugee property through officially appointed trustees. *Eastern Times* (Lahore), 29 September 1947.

[100] Khwaja Ahmad Abbas, *I am not an Island: An Experiment in Autobiography* (New Delhi, 1977).

[101] K.H. Ansari, 'The Emergence of Muslim Socialists in India 1917-47', London, unpublished Ph.D Thesis 1985, p. 440.

[102] Abbas, op. cit., p. 277.

[103] Abbas, op. cit., p. 283.

[104] Abbas, op. cit., p. 278.

[105] Abbas, op. cit., p. 279.

[106] Abbas, op. cit., p. 295.

[107] M. Hassan, *Azadi ke charagh*, 3rd edition (Lahore, 1986).

[108] As, for example, Husna, his cousin's sister, and his cousin Asfar. He tells the touching story of his cousin, Intizar Hassan, who as a child used to proudly carry the Pakistan flag at Muslim League rallies and who died on 29 August and lay slumped on the floor with the Pakistan flag as his pillow.

[109] His grandfather, Nazir Ahmad, wrote some of the earliest novels in Urdu. His father, Bashir al-Din, authored a three volume history of Delhi. The pioneering journalists, Saiyid Mumtaz Ali, who edited *Tehzib-e-Niswan*, and Mahbub Alam, who edited *Paisa Akhbar*, were also close relatives. Ansari, op. cit., pp. 476-7.

[110] Ansari, op. cit., p. 477.

[111] Report of A.S. Bhatnagar, Secretary to the Chief Commissioner, Delhi, 4 December 1947. MB1/D276, Mountbatten Papers, University of Southampton.

[112] *Dilhi ki Bipta* is contained in the Collection edited by M. Shirin, *Zulmat-e-Neem Roze* (Karachi, 1990). *See*, pp. 145-7.

[113] Shirin, op. cit., pp. 148-9.

[114] Report of Chief Commissioner, Indian Railways, 13 November 1947, MB1/D276, Mountbatten Papers, University of Southampton.

[115] Shirin, op. cit., pp. 154-5.

[116] Shirin, op. cit., p. 155.

[117] Shirin, op.cit., p. 157.

[118] Shirin, op. cit., pp. 164-5.

[119] Shirin, op. cit., p. 169.

[120] A. Hameed, Foreword in Khwaja Iftikhar, *Jab Amritsar jal raha tha*, 9th edition, (Lahore, 1991), p. 35.

[121] Iftikhar, op. cit., p. 41.

[122] Ibid., above.

[123] Iftikhar, op. cit., p. 42.

[124] Iftikhar, op. cit., p 43.

[125] A.S. Ahmed, *Discovering Islam. Making Sense of Muslim Society and History* (London, 1988), pp. 159-60.

[126] Iftikhar, op. cit., pp. 247-8.

[127] Iftikhar, op. cit., p. 254.

[128] Begum Shaista S. Ikramullah, *From Purdah to Parliament* (London, 1963)

[129] Iftikhar, op. cit., pp. 259-61.

[130] Zahida's real life experience may be compared with the fictional account provided by H.S. Gill of the Muslim attack on a Sikh refugee train, in his work, *Ashes and Petals.*

> Shots rang out into the night, and confused dialogues between friends and foes ensued. Some children could be heard crying and their shouts were only drowned by the fearsome wailing of their mothers.
>
> The agonizing cry of a young girl rent the air. 'Hai hai, they are carrying me off. Hai Wahe guru save me. Mother save me', she cried out in panic.

In this atmosphere, one of the book's leading characters, Santa Singh, shoots his fourteen-year-old granddaughter, Baljeeto, rather than let her fall into the marauders' hands. 'In other parts of the train', the author declares, 'the same ghoulish scene was being repeated by others in a similar predicament'. Gill, op. cit., pp. 8-9.

[131] Iftikhar, op. cit., p. 264

Chapter 6

Hurmat Bibi's Story

The challenge for the historian is to seek to introduce a human element into the discourse on Pakistan's birth. There has been very little writing on this, as we have had cause to note on numerous occasions during this work. It is not simply a case of approaching Partition from a different angle for the sake of it. Rather, it is integral to an understanding of this great event and its legacy at the profoundest level. The logic of the argument we have been pursuing about the humanizing of the historical record demands that the impact of Partition be examined through the eyes of a single individual.

There are naturally problems involved in so shrinking our angle of vision. We are left perhaps with conjecture, with dimly remembered stories distorted by the received wisdom of then and now. Claustrophobia creeps in. It is one reason why historians are happier in dealing with more orthodox sources. Yet this approach need not lead to a dead end. It can provide excitingly fresh insights which can be tested and contextualized. This final chapter aims to illustrate the possibilities offered by shifting the angle of vision to the invidual. It looks at the Pakistan movement and Partition through the story of Hurmat Bibi. Her own words, translated from Urdu, form the basis of the text. Her account is at once both intensely personal and representative of the experiences and attitudes of the many Muslims who migrated to Pakistan in 1947.

Hurmat Bibi was living in dignified retirement in Lahore when she retold her story to the researcher, Tahmina Farhi Manazar. This was subsequently included in the collection,

Azadi kay mujahid (Crusaders of Freedom), which was published in 1989 under the auspices of the Information and Culture Department of the Punjab Government. At the time of Partition, Hurmat Bibi lived with her extended family in their home in Nikodar in the East Punjab. She evidently came from a prosperous background, as she records that:

hamaaray baray makaan mein khula aangan aur baraamaday mein ek dusray say mutassil kamray thay.

In our big house there was a spacious terrace and rooms attached to it along the veranda.[1]

In addition to this urban property, her father also owned a house in their ancestral village. Hurmat Bibi's separatist beliefs come across clearly in such remarks as: 'Hindus and Sikhs had different kinds of pots and pans than those of the Muslims. Their food was also very different from ours. ... The Muslims slaughtered cows in an Islamic way and ate the meat, but Hindus worshipped the mother-cow.'[2] Episodes which point to the real pain of the Muslim minority in Nikodar lie alongside these conventional expressions of difference. Reminiscing about the town's commercial life, Hurmat Bibi recalls:

Hindus and Sikhs dominated the business markets of the city. If a Muslim ever attempted to run a shop to do some business, the Hindus plotted against him to throw him out of the business. That is why Muslims had no business of any significance in Nikodar. Only a few Muslims worked as brokers in the market.'[3]

The Muslims were also treated as socially inferior, especially by the Brahmins, who would consider themselves unclean if they passed a Muslim in the street, and would immediately go home and wash themselves. Hurmat Bibi makes a point of recalling her own experiences of the aloofness of Hindu women:

Hindu aurtein bhi hamaaray gharon mein bahut kam aati theen, aur jab aateen to do gaz kay faaslay par bayth kar baat karteen.

Meiray ghar mein eik isaai aurat kaam karti thi. Us nay mujhey bataaya: ay yeh Hindu aurtein jab aap kay ghar say vaapas jaati hain, to do baar ganga kay paani say nahaa kar apnay aap ko paak karti hain.

Hindu women rarely visited our homes. If they came at all, they sat two yards away from us. A Christian woman worked in my house as a maidservant. She told me that 'Hindu women, after visiting you, wash themselves twice with Ganges river water'.[4]

Hurmat Bibi and her relatives were enthusiatic supporters of the Muslim League. She recalls approvingly that the Pakistan demand became a main topic of conversation in their home, 'as in other Muslim homes in Nikodar'. Her father and brother joined the League, while she attended the Zenana Muslim League meetings with female relatives. She delights in remembering that the enthusiasm for the freedom struggle was so great that 'the word "Pakistan" would make people's faces light up, and they would forget if they were physically tired'. The family arranged a recitation of the Koran in thanksgiving when the 3 June Plan was announced. On independence day, Muslim houses in Nikodar were decorated, and slogans of 'Pakistan zindabad', 'Muslim League zindabad' and 'Qaid-e-Azam zindabad' rent the air.

From the moment that the Partition Plan was agreed, communal relations in Nikodar rapidly deteriorated. Hurmat Bibi gives us details of the incident that sparked off the clashes which were to martyr most of her family.

Ek chota saa juloos sabz jhandian uthaai ek baazaar mein sey guzar rahaa tha. Achaanak eik Hindu halvaai ney khaulta hua ghee Musalmaanon par pheink diaa. Do Musalmaan vaheen shaheed ho gaey. Hindu aur Sikh baalam aur talvaarein, kirpaan aur banduqein lay kar Musalmaanon par toot paray.

A quite small procession of Muslims was passing through a bazaar, when all of a sudden a Hindu sweet merchant threw boiling *ghee* (clarified butter) over the Muslims, two of whom were martyred on the spot. Hindus and Sikhs armed with spears and swords, daggers and guns, fell upon the Muslims.[5]

The communalization of the police in Nikodar, as in other parts of the Punjab, meant that the Muslims were largely defenceless. Hurmat Bibi states that the non-Muslim policemen and servicemen joined in the subsequent attacks and looting. Documentary evidence to which we have referred earlier, substantiates these allegations. Hurmat Bibi graphically describes an attack on a school in which many Muslims who were taking refuge were killed. She has this to say about the sense of hopelessness which prevailed:

Kuch samajh mein na aata tha keh Pakistan kaysey pauncha jaaey. Abhi baqaaida mahajir camp nahin banay thhey.

No one knew how to get to Pakistan. There were as yet no proper refugee camps.[6]

Hurmat Bibi's family was more fortunate than many others in that they could retreat to their old house in the village. They also possessed firearms. The women armed themselves with kitchen knives. They took food, including cereals, with them, so that they could bake bread. Hurmat Bibi's father and brother took turns to stand guard at night on the roof of their house. On the second night of their arrival, however, Hindus and Sikhs launched a murderous attack:

We heard ear-splitting sounds of Hindu and Sikh war slogans: '*sat sari akal*' and '*har har mahadev*'. My father and brother were on the roof top. My father addressed the ladies from above and said heathens are coming to attack, as long as we (the men) are alive, we will not let any one come near you. We, the women and children, stood speechless. Hindus and Sikhs started to shoot as they came close to our house. My father and brothers also fired at them. A frightening and ear-splitting noise filled the surroundings. We bolted the doors from inside, we were extremely terrified, and horror and hopelessness took hold of us. We had small harmless kitchen knives which were nothing as compared to swords and guns. Despite this fact, we had made a decision to sacrifice our lives for Pakistan, before someone attempted to rape us. For about ten to fifteen minutes the Sikhs and Hindus kept on shooting. Our firing kept them from advancing. We could hear the screams from the houses of Muslims who lived nearby in the village, and then my father and brothers came downstairs. They told us they had run out of ammunition, 'but we shall fight to the last', they said. But how could they face guns, rifles and swords with empty rifles? Then the Hindus and Sikhs set fire to the doors of the house, they entered the house shouting war slogans as the door collapsed. The next moments were like hell. Swords and spears were being used in the darkness, amid screams and shouts. My father and brothers were killed with swords right in front of my eyes. In a few moments, the broken and bloody corpses of my sisters and sisters-in-law were lying on the veranda. My husband, my five sons and three daughters were also martyred. I was lying between corpses. … In the meantime, my youngest son, Ali Raza, who was badly wounded, asked for water. Having heard his cry, a Sikh shouted 'He is still alive'. As he said this, he chopped his body in two with one blow of his sword. I felt as if he had stabbed my heart. I wanted to scream, but my voice stuck in my throat. The horror paralysed my strength to scream. Hindus and Sikhs, waving their swords in the air and laughing, went out of the house. There were about forty corpses lying on the veranda. There was blood everywhere. I heard the cries of a baby nearby. I removed the dead bodies of my brothers and sister-in-law, and saw that my younger sister was lying there with her baby in her arms, wide-eyed with terror.[7]

We have already encountered all too similar accounts of the mayhem which accompanied Partition in August 1947. Hurmat Bibi's graphic descriptions are not intended to invoke hatred or revenge, but are offered as a memorial to those who died. They are also presented, as are the other recollections in *Azadi kay Mujahid*, to remind the coming generations of the 'sacrifice of blood and honour' to 'get this piece of land' (p. 5). The remainder of Hurmat Bibi's recollection is taken up with her dramatic flight to Pakistan. This reads in parts like an adventure story, but the events it describes were by no means an uncommon experience.

May nein apni bahn ka baazu pakar kar usey uthaaya aur kaha Khuda ko yuheen manzur tha. Pakistan par ham nay sab kuch qurbaan kar dia hay, ab hamein kisi tara Pakistan pahuchna hay. Khuda hamaari madad karega.

I held my sister's hand and lifted her up. 'This is the will of God', I said. 'We have sacrificed everything for Pakistan. Now we have got to reach Pakistan somehow. God will help us.'[8]

Hurmat Bibi recalls the deathlike silence as she and her sister picked their way through the ruined village. They walked across fields littered with bodies, as they headed in the direction of the Grand Trunk Road. Hurmat Bibi was able to find her way through the darkness, as she had come this way many times before with her husband, after alighting from the bus while going to Bhatinda from Nikodar. The blackness and silence so unnerved her sister that she pleaded for them to return to the village. She hid behind a tree when a lorry approached from the direction of Bhatinda, but Hurmat Bibi screwed up her last ounce of courage and stood in the middle of the road in the hope that it was transporting Muslims to Pakistan. The lorry turned out to be an army truck which, fortunately for the sisters, contained Muslim soldiers from the Baluch Regiment. They transported them to the refugee camp in Jullundur. 'There we saw countless numbers of Muslims in desperate conditions'.

Teesrey din camp mein mujhey mera bara larka (Ali Ahmad) mil gaya, magar loot maar, aatish zani aur musalmaanon kay qatl-e-aam ko dekh kar uska zehni tawaazan bigar chuka tha.

On the third day, I found my eldest boy (Ali Ahmad), but after witnessing the plunder, looting, arson and ruthless massacre of Muslims, his mental equilibrium had been disturbed.[9]

After what seemed an interminable stay in the refugee camp, Hurmat Bibi and her surviving relatives set out for Pakistan. She recalls what to us is now a familiar story of a huge caravan of men, women, children and bullock-carts slowly wending its way westwards, harried by Sikh attacks during both day and night. Hurmat Bibi describes the emotion which greeted their arrival in Pakistan:

> At last, somehow or other, after crossing the sea of fire and blood, we stopped on the lovely land of Pakistan. The slogans 'Long live Pakistan', 'Long live Islam', echoed from every corner.[10]

She interjects at this point in the narrative to recount her own personal feelings. These reveal how deeply touching the arrival in Pakistan was for those who had journeyed to freedom.

> I had lost everything, forty people of our (extended) family were martyred, but the happiness I found when I saw the Pakistani flag flying at the Pakistan border, is still living in every cell of my body.[11]

Hurmat Bibi's story ends with her affirming that the sacrifice of so many for the achievement of Pakistan was not in vain. 'Thanks be to God', she declares, 'that we found our country in the form of Pakistan, and freedom from the slavery of the Hindus'. She writes:

> *Ham log rookhi sookhi kha kar apna pait paaltay hayn; mayn iss umr mein bhi silaai kaarhi kay kaam karti hoon. Mujhey fakhr hay keh mein Pakistan ki baasi hoon aur Islam ka naam aazaadi say ley sakti hoon.*

> We survive by eating very simple and ordinary food. Even at this age I sew clothes for people and do embroidery work to earn a living, but I am proud that I am a citizen of Pakistan and can speak the word 'Islam' without any fear.[12]

It is difficult for the historian standing outside the events which Hurmat Bibi describes not to dismiss her account as conventional and stereotypical. Cynicism should not be allowed, however, to obscure the clues which she provides concerning the feelings which many Muslims shared in 1947. Hurmat Bibi typifies those whose experiences of Hindu domination in the minority areas committed them to the ideology of Muslim separatism. Pakistan was duly attained as a result of Jinnah's inspired leadership and the greatest Muslim mass mobilization in the first half of the twentieth century.

But there was a price to pay. Even today, the exact number of those who died is unknown. Hurmat Bibi herself provides a graphic account of the horrors which accompanied Partition. Like many other survivors, she was able to redeem the terrors of murder, looting and arson by reaffirming her faith through the experience of migration. The long silences of her contemporaries now needs to be broken so that we can fully hear the various experiences that made up the great human event of Partition.

NOTES

[1] Tahmina Farhi Manazar, 'Raushan Chiraagh', in, M.M. Mirza and S. Bakht (eds.) *Azadi Kay Mujahid* (Lahore, 1989) p. 11.

[2] Ibid.

[3] Manazar, op. cit., p. 11.

[4] Manazar, op. cit., p. 11.

[5] Manazar, op. cit., p. 12.

[6] Manazar, op. cit., p. 12.

[7] Manazar, op. cit., pp.13-14.

[8] Manazar, op. cit., p. 14.

[9] Manazar, op. cit., p. 16.

[10] Manazar, op. cit., p. 16.

[11] Manazar, op. cit., p. 16.

[12] Manazar, op. cit., p. 16.

Conclusion

This study undermines the portrayal of the Muslim League as being unable 'to sustain a mass movement in the face of official repression'.[1] Its direct action campaigns in the Punjab and Frontier early in 1947 mobilized large numbers of Muslims, despite police firings and massive arrests. The law and order agencies in both provinces were not easy targets, but possessed a justified reputation for toughness, as Khaksars and Red Shirts alike had found to their earlier cost. The civil disobedience movements were prolonged campaigns which severely undermined governments hostile to the League in key 'Pakistan' areas.

Pressures from 'beneath' had already seriously weakened the Unionist Party's grip on power in the Punjab. In the key constituencies in the Rawalpindi division, the elite factional realignment which preceded the 1946 elections had been largely prompted by them. The Unionist Party was never able to recover from the loss of such key Rajput supporters as Major Farman Ali Khan and Raja Fateh Khan.[2] Many of the Muslims who flocked to hear Jinnah speak at, for example, the 1944 Muslim League Conference at Sialkot, or garlanded him on his triumphant motorcade to Lahore that July, could not of course vote, but the popular enthusiasm for the Pakistan demand undoubtedly influenced those who were able to do so. The politics of *biraderi* and local power were by no means destroyed in 1946, but they had to compete, often unsuccessfully, with the Muslim League's ideological appeals. This explains the huge majorities which the latter's candidates piled up in such former citadels of Unionist power as the Gujrat, Jhang, Jhelum, and Rawalpindi constituencies.[3] Significantly, the League's best performances were in the major recruiting areas of Jhelum and

Rawalpindi, where popular pressures against the Unionist Ministry were the strongest.

Punjabi Muslims responded to the Muslim League's appeals for a variety of reasons. Idealism was of much greater significance than the Cambridge School allows, although it was tempered with material interests. The role of the *pirs* in mobilizing rural support for the freedom struggle has been rightly highlighted. Students of course vied with the former in taking the Pakistan message to the villages and creating a millenarian atmosphere there. As a frustrated Zamindara League worker exclaimed, 'Wherever I went, everyone kept saying, *bhai*, if we do not vote for the League, we would have become kafir.'[4]

The identification of support for Pakistan with individual commitment to Islam was first established in the urban milieu of North India. It arose out of the nineteenth century Islamic reform, which was reworked and popularized by Iqbal. He took up the idea of individual Islamic transformation, but made the important linkage between this and the need for Muslim political authority. The Muslim National Guards were the physical embodiments of this philosophy. They were 'representatives' of Muslim activism at the same time as providing the symbolic trappings of a nascent Muslim state which could alone enable Muslims to find their true Islamic worth. The emotional impact of the the Guards' ceremonial for urban Muslims has been gravely overlooked by historians. They have also not fully explored the symbolic significance of Jinnah's leadership.

Literary sources amplify individuals' sacrifices for the establishment of Pakistan. The physical hardships which faced Muslims as they journeyed to their new home is a constant theme in the novels of Partition. Intizar Husain, however, looks beyond the physical effect of migration and thereby provides the illuminating insight that the journey to Pakistan was, for many Muslims, a true *hijrat*. The self-awareness and renewal which it brought, transcended the sufferings. This does not mean, however, that Partition did not also bring in its wake a sense of uprootedness. Intizar Husain's own haunted picture of the deserted *imam bara* captures this perfectly.

The most poignant account of the confused identities brought by Partition is provided in Manto's brilliant piece, *Toba Tek Singh,* but the theme of divided loyalties to birthplace, country, and faith run throughout many novels. Qurat ul-Ain Haider most forcefully and therefore most controversially reflects in her work the feeling that Partition interrupted the even flow of Muslim history in India.

Manto and Chander in their different styles point to the existence, side by side in 1947, of hope and despair, humanity and depravity. Their sometimes heart-rending accounts clearly attest to what was both the best and worst of times. For those interested more widely in the Partition experience, interesting parallels could be drawn between the cathartic element in their and other Urdu authors' work and that of such Punjabi writers as Kartar Singh Duggal, Nanak Singh, Sohan Singh and Naranjan Tasneem.[5]

A word of caution should, however, be interjected here concerning the use of Urdu literary and autobiographical sources in order to uncover the human dimension of Partition. These invariably emphasise the *mohajir* experience, but it was not only Muslims from the minority areas who sacrificed for the achievement of Pakistan. This is apparent even from autobiographies written in the medium of Urdu. Pirzada Mohammad Anwar Chishti's *Matri ki Mohabbat*, for example, has revealed the difficulties his family experienced at the hands of local officials because of their opposition to the Unionists. They eventually had to leave their native Pakpattan for Arifwala, and were indeed, to paraphrase the great eighteenth century Urdu poet, Mir, foreign travellers in their own land.[6] Materials in Punjabi, Bengali and Pushtu would certainly reinforce that this kind of sacrifice was not uncommon amongst the 'Pakistan' area populations.

Exploration of the Partition experience is not the only way in which Pakistan's emergence can be approached from the perspective of the 'new' history. Work could also be done on such areas as the relationship between Bombay workers' organizations and the Muslim League, or on the Kisan movement and the League in the Punjab. The political economy of the Muslim press awaits exploration, as does a theoretically sound analysis of the role of women in the freedom struggle. Whichever areas attract scholarly attention, they will require innovative use of sources, coupled with an inter-disciplinary approach, if they are to be tackled effectively.

Increased attention to popular politics and consciousness during the freedom struggle are likely to further undermine those explanations which see it solely in terms of a bid for power by self-interested groups. The theme of self-sacrifice as epitomized by the Muslim National Guards' movement, and the belief that the migrations of 1947 were a true *hijra*, emerge strongly from this study. The view that Pakistan's birth afforded opportunities for individual and community renewal is dissonant with Paul Brass's understanding of elite 'fancy free' manipulation of Islamic symbols. Yet such 'idealism' runs not only through personal reflections, but also official speeches and resolutions which talked of making Pakistan a laboratory for Islam and of 'levelling up the general standard of living amongst the masses'.[7] It was also present in the view that the establishment of a Muslim homeland in the Indian subcontinent was significant for the Islamic world at large.

In this wider context, Pakistan's emergence can be seen as completing one phase of mass Muslim opposition to colonial rule in Asia, which dated back to the end of the nineteenth century. At the same time it also encouraged those still struggling, physically and spiritually, against the hegemony of the West in the arc of Muslim territory which stretched from Palestine to Indonesia.

NOTES

[1] S. Sarkar, *Modern India, 1885-1947* (London, 1989), p. 427.
[2] The Muslim League candidate captured nearly 85 per cent of the total vote in the Rawalpindi East former constituency of Raja Fateh Khan. The result was even more impressive in the Gujar Khan seat, once held by Farman Ali Khan. Raja Said Akbar Khan, who stood on the Muslim League ticket,

won 91 per cent of the votes cast. Calculated from, *Return Showing the Results of the Elections to the Central Legislative Assembly and the Provincial Legislatures 1945-6* (Delhi, 1948).

³ Ibid.

⁴ Report by Ch. Shahwali of Ghumman, Zamindara League worker, Jhelum, 20 February 1946. Cited in D. Gilmartin, *Empire and Islam. Punjab and the Making of Pakistan* (Berkeley, 1988), p. 218.

⁵ In all, there are about a dozen novels, a hundred short stories, and fifty poems in Punjabi on the theme of Partition. I am indebted to Darshan Singh Tatla of South Birmingham College for this reference.

⁶ Pirzada Mohammad Anwar Chishti, 'Matri ki Mohabbat' in, M.M. Mirza and S. Bakht (eds.), *Azadi key Mujahid* (Lahore, 1989), p. 43 & ff. The water channel to the family's canal was blocked and they were socially boycotted.

⁷ The Muslim League is of course always depicted as being both politically and economically conservative. The activities of its Economic Planning Committee, which was established in September 1943, display none of the supposedly uncritical acceptance of private enterprise. Jinnah, in a speech to the Committee in November 1944, supported this attitude.

Speech of Jinnah to the All-India Muslim League Economic Planning Committee, 5 November 1944, All-India Muslim League Economic Planning Committee 95 (1), SHC.

APPENDICES

Appendix A

Provincial, District and City Commanders of the Muslim National Guards

1. Khwaja Nur-ul-Din
2. Aziz Laljee
3. Habib Ullah
4. Hashim Ali Inamdar
5. Mohammad Suleman Jan
6. Col. I.A.S. Dara
7. Sayyed Amir Hussain Shah
8. Mohammad Haroon
9. Jamal Mohi-ul-Din
10. Khan Faiz Mohammad Khan
11. Abdul Jalil
12. Manzur-ul-Haque
13. Dr Bashir-ul-Huq
14. S.A. Qadvi
15. Khan Sahab Mazhar Imam
16. Nawabzada Walayat Ali Khan
17. I.A. Mahajar
18. Zaheer-ul-Din (ex MNA)
19. Mohd. Sadrala Nam Khan
20. Mohammad Azam
21. Imam Ali
22. F. Rabi
23. Abdul Munim Khan
24. Maulana Noor-uz-Zaman
25. Muzaffar Ahmad Shah (ex MNA)
26. Khairat Hussain
27. Hassan Raza
28. Abdul Karim
29. M.A. Yamni
30. Adam Minhar
31. Abdul Hamid
32. Qazi Mohammad Akbar
33. Qasim Hoot Sahab
34. Sayyad Haroon
35. S. Abdul Razzaq Hussaini
36. Ismail Tabish
37. Taj Ali Khan
38. Fida Mohammad Babuzi
39. Sayyed Badrul Hassan
40. Mohammad Ayub Khan
41. Abdul Samad
42. Abdul Waheed
43. Mohammad Qasim
44. Abdul Alim
45. Maulana Asad–ul–Qadri
46. Shamsher Khan

Source: Siddique Ali Khan, *Be Tegh Sipahi* (Lahore, 1971), pp. 232-3.

Appendix B

Rehabilitation of Refugees
in Urban Areas of West Punjab

[Urban Population, Figures in thousands, + increase/– decrease]

District & Tehsil Towns	Hindu & Sikh evacuees	Refugees rehab.	x/–
Lahore Division			
Lahore District	266.1	277.9	+ 11.3
Lahore Tehsil	234.7	250.3	+ 15.6
Lahore Munip.	210.6	235.4	+ 24.8
Lahore Cantt.	24.1	14.9	– 9.2
Chunian Tehsil	16.9	13.5	– 3.9
Chunian	5.3	3.7	– 1.6
Mandi Pattoki	9.1	5.6	– 3.5
Khudian	2.5	4.2	+ 1.7
Kasur Tehsil	14.5	13.6	– 0.9
Kasur	14.5	13.6	– 0.9
Sialkot District	58.2	57.5	– 0.7
Sialkot Tehsil	41.8	30.2	– 11.6
Sialkot	35.1	27.4	– 5.9
Sialkot Cantt.	8.7	2.8	– 5.9
Pasrur Tehsil	4.3	4.7	+ 0.4
Pasrur	2.3	4.7	+ 2.4
Chawinda	2.0	0.0	– 2.0
Narowal Tehsil	4.6	6.9	+ 2.3
Narowal	4.6	6.9	+ 2.3
Daska Tehsil	7.5	15.7	+ 8.2
Daska	6.0	15.7	+ 9.7
Sambrial	1.5	0.0	– 1.5
Gujranwala District	75.4	93.7	+ 18.3
Gujranwala Tehsil	51.1	67.7	+ 16.6
Gujranwala	38.9	52.7	+ 13.8
Kamoke	8.4	7.6	– 0.8
Aminabad	2.0	4.4	+ 2.4
Qita Singh Didar	1.8	3.0	+ 1.2
Wazirabad Tehsil	14.3	11.7	– 2.6
Wazirabad	7.8	4.4	– 3.4
Ramnagar	1.3	1.4	+ 0.1
Akalqarh	3.2	3.3	+ 0.1

District & Tehsil Towns	Hindu & Sikh evacuees	Refugees rehab.	x/−
Sodhra	0.8	0.8	0.0
Gakhar	1.2	1.8	+ 0.6
Hafizabad Tehsil	10.0	14.3	+ 4.3
Hafizabad	7.4	11.7	+ 4.3
Pindi Bhattian	2.6	2.6	0.0
Sheikhupura District	32.2	71.9	+ 39.7
Sheikhupura Tehsil	20.8	37.3	+ 16.5
Sheikhupura	11.8	24.9	+ 13.1
Sangla	4.5	6.2	+ 1.7
Kano Mandi	4.5	6.2	+ 1.7
Nankana Tehsil	10.7	33.5	+ 22.8
Nankana	10.7	33.5	+ 22.8
Shahdara Tehsil	0.7	1.1	+ 0.4
Shahdara	0.7	1.1	+ 0.4
Total Lahore Division	431.9	500.5	+ 68.6
Rawalpindi Division			
Gujrat District	38.0	28.7	− 9.3
Gujrat Tehsil	12.5	13.3	+ 0.8
Gujrat	6.2	7.3	+ 1.1
Jalalpar Jattan	4.1	3.9	− 0.2
Kunjal	2.2	2.1	− 0.1
Kharian Tehsil	10.2	7.2	− 3.0
Dinga	4.3	0.0	− 4.3
Lalamusa	5.9	7.2	+ 1.3
Phalia Tehsil	15.3	8.2	− 7.1
Malakwal	3.9	0.0	− 3.9
Mandi Baha-ud-Din	11.4	8.2	− 3.2
Shahpur District	64.0	80.1	+ 16.1
Shahpur Tehsil	7.8	5.7	− 2.1
Shahpur Cantt.	1.2	0.8	− 0.4
Shahpur Shahr	2.1	2.0	− 0.1
Sahiwal	3.2	2.9	− 0.3
Jhawarian	1.3	0.0	− 1.3
Khushab Tehsil	9.5	8.5	− 1.0
Khushab	3.9	8.5	+ 4.6
Mithawala	2.3	0.0	− 2.3
Nurpur	2.5	0.0	− 2.5
Hidoli	0.8	0.0	− 0.8
Bhalwal Tehsil	18.0	18.5	+ 0.5
Bhalwal	4.1	4.9	+ 0.8

District & Tehsil Towns	Hindu & Sikh evacuees	Refugees rehab.	x/−
Bhera	5.2	9.1	+ 3.9
Miani	2.9	4.5	+ 1.6
Kot Momin	1.7	0.0	− 1.7
Phularwan	4.1	0.0	− 4.1
Sargodha Tehsil	28.7	47.4	+ 18.7
Sargodha	25.6	40.4	+ 14.8
Sillanwali	3.1	7.0	+ 3.9
Jhelum District	26.1	14.5	− 11.6
Jhelum Tehsil	14.2	9.4	− 4.8
Jhelum	14.2	9.4	− 4.8
Pind Dadan Khan Tehsil	4.0	4.0	0.0
Pind Dadan Khan	4.0	4.0	0.0
Chakwal Tehsil	7.9	1.1	− 6.8
Chakwal	5.6	1.1	− 4.5
Bhun	2.3	0.0	− 2.3
Rawalpindi District	104.6	65.3	− 39.3
Rawalpindi Tehsil	103.9	64.1	− 39.8
Rawalpindi	71.4	64.1	− 7.3
Rawalpindi Cantt.	27.8	0.0	− 27.8
Chaklala Cantt.	4.7	0.0	− 4.7
Murree Tehsil	0.7	1.2	+ 0.5
Murree	0.6	1.2	+ 0.6
Murree Cantt.	0.1	0.0	− 0.1
Attock District	34.4	8.0	− 26.4
Attock Tehsil	22.7	5.8	− 16.9
Attock Fort	0.2	0.0	− 0.2
Campbellpur	6.8	4.0	− 2.8
Military Camp	8.2	0.0	− 8.2
Hazro	4.2	0.9	− 3.3
Hasan Abdal	3.3	0.9	− 2.4
Pindigheb Tehsil	5.9	0.8	− 5.1
Pindigheb	4.3	0.8	− 3.5
Jund	1.6	0.0	− 1.6
Talagang Tehsil	3.5	0.6	− 2.9
Talagang	3.5	0.6	− 2.9
Fatehjung Tehsil	2.3	0.8	− 1.5
Fatehjung	2.3	0.8	− 1.5
Mianwali District	22.9	3.0	− 19.9
Mianwali Tehsil	14.6	1.2	− 13.4
Mianwali	14.6	1.2	− 13.4

District & Tehsil Towns	Hindu & Sikh evacuees	Refugees rehab.	x/−
Bhakkar Tehsil	5.4	1.1	− 4.3
Bhakkar	1.4	1.1	− 0.3
Kallarkot	4.0	0.0	− 4.0
Isakhel Tehsil	2.9	0.7	− 2.2
Isakhel	1.6	0.3	− 1.3
Kala Bagh	1.3	0.4	− 0.9
Total Rawalpindi Division	290.9	199.6	− 90.4
Multan Division			
Montgomery District	59.5	70.3	+ 10.8
Montgomery Tehsil	30.4	29.8	− 0.6
Montgomery	24.4	24.2	− 0.2
Chichawanti	6.0	5.6	− 0.4
Okara Tehsil	14.5	21.1	+ 6.6
Okara	14.5	21.1	+ 6.6
Pakpattan Tehsil	14.6	19.4	+ 4.8
Pakpattan	9.1	12.7	+ 3.6
Arifwala	5.5	6.7	+ 1.2
Shujabad Tehsil	8.0	18.6	+ 10.6
Shujabad Pirwala	5.4	14.1	+ 8.7
Jalalpur	2.6	4.5	+ 1.9
Lodhran Tehsil	1.4	8.4	+ 7.0
Lodhran	1.4	8.4	+ 7.0
Mailsi Tehsil	10.5	16.7	+ 6.2
Mailsi	5.0	6.4	+ 1.4
Burewala	5.5	10.3	+ 4.8
Khanewal Tehsil	21.0	44.2	+ 23.2
Khanewal	12.0	44.2	+ 32.2
Telamba	3.4	0.0	− 3.4
Mian Channu	5.6	0.0	− 5.6
Muzaffargarh District	25.0	24.8	− 0.2
Muzaffargarh Tehsil	7.7	6.2	− 1.5
Muzaffargarh	4.7	6.2	+ 1.5
Khangarh	3.0	0.0	− 3.0
Alipore Tehsil	3.4	5.1	+ 1.7
Alipore	3.4	5.1	+ 1.7
Kot Adu Tehsil	4.6	7.9	+ 3.3
Kot Adu	4.6	7.9	+ 3.3
Leiah Tehsil	9.3	5.6	− 3.7
Leiah	6.3	3.8	− 2.5
Karor	3.0	1.8	− 1.2

District & Tehsil Towns	Hindu & Sikh evacuees	Refugees rehab.	x/−
Dera Ghazi Khan District	32.8	14.3	− 18.5
Dera Ghazi Khan Tehsil	16.1	8.0	− 8.1
Dera Ghazi Khan	14.4	6.6	− 7.8
Kot Chuta	1.7	1.4	− 0.3
Sangarh Tehsil	3.2	0.6	− 2.6
Vehoa	1.4	0.4	− 1.0
Taunsa Sharif	1.8	0.2	− 1.6
Rajanpur Tehsil	6.2	4.5	− 1.7
Rajanpur	2.1	1.4	− 0.7
Mithankot	1.7	2.2	+ 0.5
Rajhan	2.4	0.9	− 1.5
Jampur Tehsil	7.3	1.2	− 6.1
Jampur	4.3	1.2	− 3.1
Dajal	3.0	0.0	− 3.0
Total Multan Division	361.4	462.5	+

Source: M. Hassan, Secretary, Board Economic Inquiry, West Punjab
     Government, *A Statistical Review of the Distribution of Refugees in
     West Punjab* (Lahore, n.d.), Mudie Papers, Mss Eur. F/164/147,
     IOR.

Appendix C

Rehabilitation of Refugees in Rural Areas of West Punjab

[Rural Population,   Figures in thousands,   + increase/– decrease]

District & Tehsil		Hindu & Sikh evacuees	Refugees rehab.	x/–	
Lahore Division					
Lahore		303.3	368.0	+	64.7
	Lahore	93.2	132.6	+	39.4
	Chunian	137.3	168.4	+	31.1
	Kasur	72.8	67.0	–	5.8
Sialkot		490.2	363.8	–	126.4
	Sialkot	100.3	69.2	–	31.1
	Pasrur	72.8	55.0	–	17.8
	Narowal	106.5	79.3	–	27.2
	Daska	69.7	66.2	–	3.5
	Shakargarh	140.9	94.1	–	47.8
Gujranwala		153.9	218.6	+	64.7
	Gujranwala	98.2	156.7	+	58.5
	Wazirabad	25.3	28.1	+	2.8
	Hafizabad	30.4	32.8	+	2.4
Sheikhupura		242.8	360.7	+	117.9
	Sheikhupura	134.0	229.9	+	95.9
	Nankana Sahib	48.9	79.3	+	30.4
	Shahdara	59.9	51.5	–	8.4
Rawalpindi Division					
Gujrat		132.2	111.2	–	21.0
	Gujrat	40.4	24.1	–	16.3
	Kharian	26.8	38.2	+	11.4
	Phalia	65.0	48.9	–	16.1
Shahpur		101.2	102.7	+	1.5
	Shahpur	16.4	6.7	–	9.7
	Khushab	16.0	3.7	–	12.3
	Bhalwal	24.0	24.4	+	0.4
	Sargodha	44.8	67.9	+	23.1

District & Tehsil		Hindu & Sikh evacuees	Refugees rehab.	x/–
Jhelum		46.2	18.5	– 27.7
	Jhelum	12.4	10.8	– 1.6
	Pind Dadan Khan	15.6	4.9	– 10.7
	Chakwal	18.2	2.8	– 15.4
Rawalpindi		57.9	14.4	– 43.5
	Rawalpindi	17.0	2.7	– 14.3
	Gujar Khan	24.8	19.5	– .5.3
	Murree	1.5	0.0	– 1.5
	Kahuta	14.6	2.2	– 12.4
Attock		35.7	3.0	– 32.7
	Attock	5.5	0.8	– 4.7
	Pindi Gheb	12.3	1.0	– 11.3
	Talagang	8.6	1.1	– 7.5
	Fatehjung	9.3	0.1	– 9.2
Mianwali		53.4	4.8	– 48.6
	Mianwali	19.6	1.4	– 18.2
	Bhakkar	30.9	3.2	– 27.7
	Isakhel	2.9	0.2	– 2.7
Multan Division				
Montgomery		364.9	639.9	+ 275.0
	Montgomery	108.5	202.6	+ 94.1
	Okara	74.2	138.9	+ 64.7
	Dipalpur	70.1	85.5	+ 15.4
	Pakpattan	112.1	212.9	+ 100.8
Lyallpur		424.8	875.5	+ 450.7
	Lyallpur	128.2	266.1	+ 137.9
	Samundri	75.4	146.9	+ 71.5
	Toba Tek Singh	96.6	213.8	+ 117.2
	Jaranwala	134.6	248.7	+ 114.1
Jhang		106.3	77.2	– 29.1
	Jhang	44.0	29.1	– 14.9
	Chiniot	30.1	26.2	– 3.9
	Shorkot	32.2	21.9	– 10.3
Multan		235.9	426.1	+ 190.2
	Multan	27.9	44.0	+ 16.1
	Shujabad	19.5	27.8	+ 8.3
	Lodhran	33.0	58.4	+ 25.4
	Mailsi	66.5	142.2	+ 75.7
	Khanewal	51.9	99.9	+ 48.0
	Kabirwala	38.0	53.8	+ 15.8

District & Tehsil	Hindu & Sikh evacuees	Refugees rehab.	x/−	
Muzaffargarh	81.0	83.1	+	2.1
Muzaffargarh	23.8	30.7	+	6.9
Alipore	27.9	31.0	+	3.1
Kot Adu	13.5	11.6	−	1.9
Leiah	15.8	9.8	−	6.0
Dera Ghazi Khan	42.4	13.7	−	28.7
Dera Ghazi Khan	18.4	5.7	−	12.7
Sangarh	9.8	0.1	−	9.7
Rajanpur	8.5	6.1	−	2.4
Janpur	5.7	1.9	−	3.8

Source: M. Hassan, Secretary, Board Economic Inquiry, West Punjab Government, *A Statistical Review of the Distribution of Refugees in West Punjab* (Lahore, n.d.), Mudie Papers, Mss Eur. F/164/147, IOR.

Appendix D

Profession of Refugees housed in West Punjab Camps
1947

Key: Culti. = Cultivator (including owners)
     Bus.   = Businessmen (including shopkeepers)
     Ind.   = Industrialists (including technicians)
     Art.   = Artisans
     Lab.   = Labourers (including those employed in services)

[Figures in thousands]

District Camp	Culti	Bus	Ind	Art	Lab	Total
Lahore						
Kasur	2.3	0.3	0.1	0.1	0.2	3.0
Lahore	319.6	12.4	8.8	17.4	13.1	371.4
Total	321.9	12.7	8.9	17.5	13.3	374.4
Sialkot						
Sialkot	0.9	0.0	0.0	0.0	0.0	0.9
Total	0.9	0.0	0.0	0.0	0.0	0.9
Gujranwala						
Wazirabad	3.7	1.6	0.4	0.9	1.8	8.4
Gujranwala	10.3	0.3	0.0	0.2	0.8	11.6
Total	14.0	1.9	0.4	1.2	2.6	20.0
Sheikhupura						
Chuharkana	0.9	0.0	0.8	0.0	0.0	1.7
Sheikhupura	4.6	0.1	0.1	0.1	0.3	5.2
Mandla	0.7	3.0	0.0	0.0	0.0	3.7
Sangla	3.1	0.5	0.0	0.0	0.0	3.6
Total	9.3	3.6	0.9	0.1	0.3	14.2
Gujrat						
Gujrat	3.7	0.2	0.3	0.1	0.2	4.6
Total	3.7	0.2	0.3	0.1	0.2	4.6
Shahpur						
Shahpur	0.1	0.0	0.0	0.0	0.0	0.1
Sargodha	8.9	0.5	0.1	0.2	0.4	10.1
Total	9.0	0.5	0.1	0.2	0.4	10.2

District Camp	Culti	Bus	Ind	Art	Lab	Total
Jhelum						
Kala	0.5	0.0	0.0	0.0	0.0	0.5
Chakwal	0.4	0.0	0.0	0.0	0.0	0.4
Total	0.9	0.0	0.0	0.0	0.0	0.9
Rawalpindi						
Wah	8.0	0.0	0.0	0.0	0.3	8.3
Total	8.0	0.0	0.0	0.0	0.3	8.3
Attock						
Mansehra	0.3	0.0	0.0	0.0	0.0	0.3
Total	0.3	0.0	0.0	0.0	0.0	0.3
Mianwali						
Mianwali	8.0	0.6	0.3	0.3	0.7	9.9
Waniphawani	1.5	0.0	0.0	0.0	0.2	1.7
Pilani	3.7	0.0	0.0	0.1	0.2	4.0
Khudani	2.2	0.0	0.0	0.0	0.0	2.2
Bhakkar	12.5	0.0	0.0	0.3	0.5	13.3
Daryakhan	0.9	0.5	0.0	0.9	0.4	2.7
Kallurkot	9.1	0.1	0.1	0.1	0.2	9.6
Harloni	2.0	0.2	0.0	0.7	0.1	3.0
Total	39.9	1.4	0.4	2.4	2.3	46.4
Montgomery						
Montgomery (urban)	6.1	0.0	0.0	0.0	0.0	6.1
Montgomery (rural)	13.2	0.0	0.0	0.0	0.3	13.5
Okara	11.5	0.0	0.0	0.2	0.0	11.7
Total	30.8	0.0	0.0	0.2	0.3	31.3
Lyallpur						
Khalsa Coll	14.5	0.0	0.5	1.0	1.2	17.2
Arya School	5.4	0.2	4.6	0.4	0.2	10.8
Total	19.9	0.2	5.1	1.4	1.4	28.0
Jhang						
Chiniot	2.6	0.6	0.0	0.3	0.4	3.9
Jhang Maghiana	1.2	0.1	0.0	0.5	0.2	2.0
Shorkot	0.0	0.0	0.0	0.1	0.0	0.1
Total	3.8	0.7	0.0	0.9	0.6	6.0
Multan						
Central Jail (Multan)	17.8	0.4	0.3	0.0	0.5	19.0
Multan Cantt.	38.7	2.0	0.3	0.9	3.2	45.1
Multan Fort	17.5	0.2	0.5	0.3	0.1	18.6
Khanewal	7.0	0.3	0.5	0.0	0.2	8.0
Total	81.0	2.9	1.6	1.2	3.5	90.7

District Camp	Culti	Bus	Ind	Art	Lab	Total
Muzaffargarh						
Muzaffargarh	0.8	0.0	0.0	0.0	0.0	0.8
Total	0.8	0.0	0.0	0.0	0.0	0.8
Dera Ghazi Khan						
Rajanpur	0.6	0.0	0.0	0.0	0.0	0.6
Dera Ghazi Khan	1.0	0.4	0.0	0.0	0.2	1.6
Total	1.6	0.4	0.0	0.0	0.2	2.2
West Punjab Total	545.8	24.5	17.9	25.2	25.4	639.2

Source: M. Hassan, Secretary, Board Economic Inquiry, West Punjab Government, *A Statistical Review of the Distribution of Refugees in West Punjab* (Lahore, n.d.), Mudie Papers, Mss Eur. F/164/147, IOR.

Appendix E

Film and Partition
M.S. Sathyu's *Garm Hawa*

The 'representation' of Partition through the medium of film is uncharted territory for the historian, despite the renowned impact of film on South Asian society and the pioneering work of such scholars as Robert Hardgrave on politics and film in Tamilnadu.[1] This reflects, however, not just a conservatism in historians, but the ambivalence with which the Indian film industry itself has viewed the subject matter. The controversy surrounding the dramatization of *Tamas* for television has already been referred to. Many producers have been chary of risking the wrath of the censor on the grounds that their portrayal of Partition might damage 'national integration'.

A young Hindu film maker from Karnataka, M.S. Sathyu, however, actually launched his career in 1973 with an adaptation of Ismat Chughtai's story, *Garm Hawa* (Scorching Wind). This centres around the experiences of a Muslim family from Agra in the aftermath of Partition. Sathyu successfully lobbied for the censor board's ban on the production to be lifted.[2] The Hindi medium film played to large audiences and secured an award for its fledgling producer. This was a due reward not only for the film's artistic merit, illuminated by the masterful performance of Balraj Sahni as Salim Mirza in his last role, but for Sathyu's courage in tackling a taboo area. He had to overcome not only the threat of censorship, but harassment from bystanders when filming on location in Agra. He ingeniously diverted unwanted attention by establishing a fake 'second unit'.

The film faithfully reflects Ismat Chughtai's frankness in dealing with female sexuality and her probing of the Indian Muslim identity. There is no hint of communal bias. The opportunism of Salim Mirza's relatives in switching their allegiance from the Muslim League to the Congress after independence is in fact unfavourably contrasted with the Hindu character, Mr Ajmani. Despite losing his home and business in Karachi, he shows no bitterness, but rather stands alone beside Mirza as his business and personal world crashes around him.

The strength of attachment to the ancestral home which we have already commented upon emerges strongly from the film. Salim sees no reason to run off to Pakistan because of the changes brought by Partition. 'At my age', he declares, 'you don't leave a country, you leave this world'. His mother, who only dimly grasps the significance of Partition, is even less ready to sunder her ties with the past. She is heart-broken when they have to move house after it has been declared evacuee property, following Salim Mirza's departure for Pakistan. When Salim's eldest son, Baqar, also departs, she laments, 'They all left without waiting for my funeral'.

The film brings out powerfully the fact that Partition weakened family ties. A recurrent image is of Salim going by tonga to the station to see off relatives to Pakistan. When he is finally about to retrace their steps, the driver remarks that he knew all along Salim would also depart. As with much of the literature on Partition, personal tragedy symbolizes the wider upheaval, as well as being created by it. Amina, Salim's daughter, is initially separated from her beloved Kazim, when he moves with his family to Pakistan. She treasures his letters and rebuffs the advances of another suitor, her cousin Shamshad. Kazim secretly returns to India to marry her to circumvent an arranged marriage with the daughter of a Pakistani official who has secured him a scholarship to Canada. The Indian authorities catch up with him, however, and he is deported four days before their wedding.

Amina's sister-in-law arranges a visit to Salim Chishti's shrine in the hope that Shamshad will win his way into her affections, now that Kazim has departed. The match-making works, and on her return from Fatehpur Sikri, Amina tears up the old love letters. The two become lovers, and disport in a boat moored within view of that great monument to love, the Taj Mahal. But Shamshad, like Kazim before him, has to accompany his family to Pakistan. Tragedy strikes when Shamshad's mother, Akhtar, pays them a return visit. Both Amina and her parents think that she has come to make marriage arrangements, but in reality she is only concerned with securing money owed to her. The wedding clothes Amina helps her purchase are intended for Shamshad's Pakistani bride. Amina, in a moment of intense poignancy, locks herself in her room where she commits suicide, wearing the bridal garments which now become her death-shroud.

Amina's death completes a Job-like sequence of misfortunes for Salim. He has lost his house, his shoe making business has foundered, and his eldest son, Baqar, has gone, following a disagreement. When he naively sends plans of the old family house to his relatives in Karachi, the Indian authorities arrest him on a charge of espionage. All that is left of the extended family is his wife, Jamila, and his youngest son, Sikander, who is unemployed.

Salim finally reluctantly agrees to take the train to Pakistan himself. On the way to the station, they come across a red flag demonstration. Salim allows Sikander to join it, declaring, 'How long can one live in isolation?' The film concludes with him also alighting from the tonga and slowly following in the wake of the crowd.

The film derives its greatest immediate impact from the tragedy of the 'star-crossed lover', Amina. But the real power and tragedy lies in the gradual disintegration of Salim Mirza's hopes. His growing disillusionment, apathy and resignation is beautifully portrayed in a series of telling episodes. Balraj Sahni draws on his years of acting experience to produce a finely-crafted characterization. This is true not only to Ismat Chughtai's story, but to the reality of thousands of Muslims who stayed on in India in 1947.

The preceding brief analysis of a single film points to the ways in which fresh perspectives on Partition can be gleaned from this medium. Such study will require examination of the 'reception' of films as 'texts' as well as their contents. It will also be necessary to consider the pygmy Pakistani film industry as well as its giant Indian neighbour. This approach to Partition still awaits its historian.

Appendix F

Suggestions for Further Reading

Reference Works

Cohn, Bernard S., *India: The Social Anthropology of a Civilization*, Englewood Cliffs, New Jersey: Prentice–Hall, 1971.

de Bary, W.T., *Sources of Indian Tradition*, New York: Columbia University Press, 1958.

Mansergh, N; Lumby, E.W.R.; Moon, P, (eds.), *Constitutional Relations between Britain and India: The Transfer of Power 1942–7*, 11 vols., London, 1970–82.

Moon, P. (ed.), Wavell: *The Viceroy's Journal*, London: Oxford University Press, 1973.

Muthiah, S. (ed.), *A Social and Economic Atlas of India*, Delhi: Oxford University Press, 1987.

Pandey, B.D., *The Indian Nationalist Movement, 1885–1947, Select Documents*, London, 1979.

Philips, C.H. & Wainwright, M (eds.), *The Partition of India: Policies and Perspectives 1935–1947*, London, 1970.

Robinson, Francis (ed.), *The Cambridge Encyclopedia of India, Pakistan, Bangladesh, Sri Lanka, Nepal, Bhutan, and the Maldives*, Cambridge: Cambridge University Press, 1989.

Muslim League Sources

Afzal, M. Rafique, (ed.), *Speeches and Statements of Quaid–i–Azam Mohammad Ali Jinnah 1911–34 & 1947–8*, Lahore, 1966.

Ahmad, Jamil–ud–Din (ed.), *Historic Documents of the Muslim Freedom Movement*, Lahore, 1970.

Ahmad, Jamil–ud–Din (ed.), Speeches and Writings of Mr Jinnah, 2 vols., Lahore, 1960 & 1964.

Ahmad, Waheed (ed.), *Quaid–i–Azam Mohammad Ali Jinnah: The Nation's Voice. Speeches and Statements*, 2 vols., Lahore, 1992–3.

Jinnah, M.A., *Quaid–i–Azam Mohammad Ali Jinnah. Speeches and Statements 1947–8*, Lahore, New Edition 1989.

Mujahid, Sharif Al, *Quaid–i–Azam and his Times. A Compendium*, 2 vols., Lahore, 1990 & 1992.

Pirzada, Syed Sharifuddin (ed.), *Foundations of Pakistan. All–India Muslim League Documents 1906–47*, 2 vols., Karachi, 1969–70.

Sherwani, L.A., (ed.), *Speeches, Writings and Statements of Iqbal*, Lahore, 1977.

—— (ed.), *Pakistan Resolution to Pakistan. 1940–47: A Selection of Documents Presenting the Case for Pakistan*, Karachi, 1969.

British Imperialism and Muslim India

Gallagher, J. et al. (eds.); *Locality,. Province and Nation: Essays on Indian Politics, 1870–1947*, Cambridge: Cambridge University Press, 1973.

Hardy, P., *The Muslims of British India*, Cambridge: Cambridge University Press, 1972.

Hodson, H.V., *The Great Divide. Britain–India–Pakistan*, London: Hutchinson, 1969.

Hutchins, F.G., *The Illusion of Permanence: British Imperialism in India*, Princeton: Princeton University Press, 1967.

Jalal, Ayesha, *The Sole Spokesman. Jinnah, the Muslim League and the Demand for Pakistan*, Cambridge: Cambridge University Press, 1988.

Moon, P., *Divide and Quit*, London: Chatto and Windus, 1962.

Moore, R.J., *The Crisis of Indian Unity, 1917–40*, Oxford: Clarendon Press, 1974.

Moore, R.J., *Churchill, Cripps and India 1939–45*, Oxford: Clarendon Press, 1979.

Page, D., *Prelude to Partition: The Indian Muslims and the Imperial System of Control 1920–1933*, Delhi: Oxford University Press, 1982.

Rizvi, G., *Linlithgow and India: A Study of British Policy and the Political Impasse in India 1936–43*, London, 1978.

Robinson, Francis, *Separatism Among Indian Muslims: The Politics of the United Provinces' Muslims 1860–1923*, Cambridge: Cambridge University Press, 1974.

Seal, Anil, *The Emergence of Indian Nationalism*, Cambridge: Cambridge University Press, 1971.

Singh, Anita Inder, *The Origins of the Partition of India 1936–1947*, Delhi: Oxford University Press, 1987.

Tomlinson, B.R., *The Indian National Congress and the Raj 1929–1942, The Penultimate Phase*, London: Macmillan, 1979.

Islam, Politics and the Pakistan Movement

Ahmad, Aziz, *Islamic Modernism in India and Pakistan 1857–1964*, Oxford: Oxford University Press, 1967.

Ahmad, Imtiaz (ed.), *Modernization and Social Change among Muslims in India*, Delhi: Manohar, 1983.

Brass, Paul, *Language. Religion and Politics in North India*, Cambridge: Cambridge University Press, 1974.

Faruqi, Ziaul Hasan, *The Deoband School and the Demand for Pakistan*, Bombay: Asia Publishing House, 1963.

Gilmartin, David, *Empire and Islam. Punjab and the Making of Pakistan*, Berkeley: University of California Press, 1988.

Gopal, Ram, *Indian Muslims. A Political History, 1858–1947*, London: Asia Publishing House, 1959.

Hasan, Khalid Shamsul, *Sindh's Fight For Pakistan*, Karachi: Royal Book Company, 1992.

Hasan, Mushir-ul, *Nationalism and Communal Politics in India, 1916–1928*, Delhi: Manohar, 1979.

Ikram, M.S., *Modern Muslim India and the Birth of Pakistan*, Lahore: Shaikh Muhammad Ashraf, 1970.

Jansson, Erland, *India, Pakistan or Pakhtunistan? The Nationalist Movements in the North-West Frontier Province, 1937–47*, Uppsala: Acta Universitatis Upsaliensis. Studia Historica Upsaliensia 119, 1981.

Jones, Kenneth W., *The New Cambridge History of India: Socio–Religious Reform Movements in British India*, Cambridge: Cambridge University Press, 1990.

Lelyveld, David, *Aligarh's First Generation: Muslim Solidarity in British India*, Princeton: Princeton University Press, 1978.

Low, D.A. (ed.), *The Political Inheritance of Pakistan*, London: Macmillan, 1991.

Malik, Hafeez, *Moslem Nationalism in India and Pakistan*, Washington: Public Affairs Press, 1963.

Malik, Hafeez, *Sir Sayyid Ahmad Khan and Muslim Modernization in India and Pakistan*, New York: Columbia University Press, 1980.

Malik, Iftikhar Haider, *Sikander Hayat Khan. A Political Biography*, Islamabad: National Institute of Historical and Cultural Research, 1985.

Metcalf, Barbara. D., *Islamic Revival in British India: Deoband 1860–1900*, Princeton: Princeton University Press, 1982.

Minault, Gail, *The Khilafat Movement: Religious Symbolism and Political Mobilization in India*, New York: Columbia University Press, 1982.

Mujeeb, Muhammad, *The Indian Muslims*, London: George Allen & Unwin, 1967.

Naim, C.M (ed.), Iqbal, *Jinnah and Pakistan*, Delhi: Jinnah Publishing House, 1982.

Qureshi, I.H., *The Muslim Community of the Indo–Pakistan Subcontinent*, The Hague: E.J. Brill, 1962.

Qureshi, I.H., *The Struggle for Pakistan*, Karachi: University of Karachi Publications, 1965.

Saiyid, M.H., *Mohammad Ali Jinnah: A Political Study*, Lahore: Shaikh Muhammad Ashraf, 1962.

Sayeed, Khalid bin, *Pakistan: The Formative Phase. 1857–1948*, London: Oxford University Press, 1968.

Schimmel, Anne-Marie, *Islam in the Indian Subcontinent*, Leiden–Koln: E.J. Brill, 1980.

Shaikh, Farzana, *Community and Consensus in Islam. Muslim Representation in Colonial India 1860–1947*, Cambridge: Cambridge University Press, 1989.

Smith, Wilfred Cantwell, *Modern Islam in India*, Lahore: Shaikh Muhammad Ashraf, 1969.

Talbot, Ian, *Provincial Politics and the Pakistan Movement. The Growth of the Muslim League in North-West and North-East India 1937-47*, Karachi: Oxford University Press, 1988.

Wolpert, Stanley, *Jinnah of Pakistan*, New York: Oxford University Press, 1984.

Zakaria, Rafiq, *Rise of Muslims in Indian Politics: An Analysis of Developments from 1885 to 1906*, Bombay: Somaiya Publications, 1970.

Partition, Migration and Refugees

Bourke–White, M., *Halfway to Freedom*, Bombay: Asia Publishing House, 1950.

Keller, S.L., *Uprooting and Social Change: The Role of Refugees In Development*, New Delhi: Manohar, 1975.

Khosla, G.D., *Stern Reckoning*, New Delhi: Bhawani and Sons, 1952.

Kosinski, L.A. & Elahi, K.M. (eds.), *Population Redistribution and Development in South Asia*, Reidel: Dordrecht, 1985.

Nanda, J., *Punjab Uprooted*, Bombay: Hind Kitabs, 1948.

Schechtman, J.B., *Population Transfer in Asia*, New York: Hallsby, 1949.

Sondhi, K., *Uprooted*, New Delhi: Arnold-Heinemann, 1977.

Novels and Short Stories*

Ansari, Hayatullah, *Lahu ke Phul*, Lucknow: Kitabdan, n.d.

Chander, Krishan, *Ghaddar*, Delhi: Asia Books, 1967.

Cooper, Parr, *Time is so Short*, London: Peter Davies, 1949.

Haidar, Qurat ul–Ain, 'Housing Society' in, *Pat-jhar ki Awaz*, New Delhi: Maktaba-i-Jami'a, 1965.

Husain, Abdullah, *Udas Naslen*, Lahore: Naya Idara, 1963.

Malgonkar, Manohar, *A bend in the Ganges*, London: Hamish Hamilton, 1964.

Malgonkar, Manohar, *Distant Drum*, London: Asia Publishing House, 1960.

Nahal, C. L, *The Weird Dance*, New Delhi: Arya Book Depot, 1965.

Saghal, Nayantara Sahgal, *Storm in Chandigarh*, New York: Norton, 1969.

Savi, Ethel Winnifred, *The Human Heart*, London: Hurst and Blackett, 1948.

*I would like to acknowledge the suggestion of these titles by Darshan Singh Tatla.

Abbreviations

The following abbreviations are used in the notes to the text:

FMA	Freedom Movement Archives
IOL	India Office Library
IOR	India Office Records
FR	Fortnightly Report
SHC	Shamsul Hasan Collection
QIAP	Quaid-i-Azam-Papers
NAI	National Archives of India
NAP	National Archives of Pakistan

Select Bibliography

Unpublished Sources

Private Papers

Linlithgow Papers, India Office Library, London, Mss., EUR F125.
Mian Fazl-i-Husain Papers, India Office Library, London, Mss., Eur E325.
Mountbatten Papers, University of Southampton.
Mudie Papers, India Office Library, London, Mss., Eur. F164.
Quaid-i-Azam Papers, National Archives of Pakistan, Islamabad.
Syed Shamsul Hasan Collection, Karachi, Pakistan.
Unionist Party Papers, University of Southampton.

Government Records

India Office Library, London.
National Archives of India, New Delhi.
Public Record Office, Kew.

Records of the Political and Secret Department, 1928-47, L/P&S/10; L/P&S/12; L/P&S/20.
Records of the Public and Judicial Department, 1929-47, L/P&J/5; L/P&J/6; L/P&J/7; L/P&J/9.
Records of the Military Department, 1940-2, L/Mil/14.
Records of the Home Department (Political) of the Government of India, 1927-45.
East Punjab Affairs 1947-50. Do.35, Dominions Office and Commonwealth Relations Office.

All-India Muslim League Records.

All-India Muslim League Committee of Action meetings 1944-7.
All-India Muslim League Working Committee Meetings 1932-7.
The Balochistan Muslim League.
The Bengal Provincial Muslim League.
The North-West Frontier Province Muslim League.
The Punjab Muslim League.
The Sindh Provincial Muslim League.

Theses

Ansari, K.H., 'The Emergence of Muslim Socialists in India 1917-47', Ph.D. thesis, London University, 1985.

Coppola, C., 'Urdu Poetry, 1935-1970: The Progressive Episode', Ph.D. thesis, Chicago University, 1975.

Jones, A.K., 'Muslim Politics and the Growth of the Muslim League in Sind, 1935-41', Ph.D. thesis, Duke University, 1977.

Rittenberg, S.A., 'The Independence Movement in India's North-West Frontier Province, 1901-47', Ph.D. thesis, Columbia University, 1977.

Robinson, M., 'Religion, Class and Faction. The Politics of Communalism in Twentieth Century Punjab', D.Phil. thesis, Sussex University, 1988.

Sipe, K.R., 'Karachi's Refugee Crisis. The Political, Economic and Social Consequences of Partition-Related Migration', Ph.D. thesis, Duke University' 1976.

Published Sources

Official Publications

Government of India, *Census of India, 1941* (Delhi, 1943), *Return Showing the results of Elections to the Central Legislative and the Provincial Legislatures 1945-6* (New Delhi, 1948).

Government of Pakistan, *Note on the Sikh Plan* (Lahore, 1948); *The Sikhs in Action* (Lahore, 1948).

Newspapers

Civil and Military Gazette, Lahore, 1936-47.
Dawn, Delhi, 1943-6.
Eastern Times, Lahore, 1943-6.
Nawa-i-Waqt, Lahore, 1945-6.
Star of India, Calcutta, 1943-6.
Tribune, Ambala, 1936-44; 1944-6.

Annuals

The Indian Annual Register, Mitra, N.N. (ed.), 1944-7, Calcutta.

Printed Secondary Works

Abbas, Khwaja Ahmad, *I Am Not An Island. An Experiment in Autobiography*, (New Delhi, 1977).

Ahmad, Waheed (ed.), *Quaid-i-Azam Mohammad Ali Jinnah: The Nation's Voice Towards Consolidation. Speeches and Statements, March 1935–March 1940*, (Karachi, 1992).

Ahmed, Akbar S., *Discovering Islam: Making Sense of Muslim History*, (London, 1988).

Ali, Chaudhri Muhammad, *The Emergence of Pakistan* (New York, 1967).

Anderson, W.K., 'The Rashtriya Swayam Sevak Sangh', *Economic and Political Weekly* 7,(1972), i-iv, pp. 589-97.

Ata, A., *Kutch Shikasta Dastanein, Kutch Pareshan Tazkarey*, (Lahore, 1966).

Azad, Abul Kalam, *India Wins Freedom*, (Bombay, 1959).

Aziz, K.K., *The Making of Pakistan. A Study in Nationalism*, (London, 1967).

Bhattacharya, S., 'History from Below', *Social Scientist* 119, (April, 1983), pp. 3-20.

Bolitho, H., *Jinnah* (London, 1954).

Bon, G. Le, *The Crowd* (London, 1952).

Bose, Sugata., 'The roots of "communal violence" in rural Bengal. A Study of the Kishoreganj Riots 1930', *Modern Asian Studies* 16,3 (1982), pp. 463-91.

Brass, P., *Language, Religion and Politics in North India*, (Cambridge, 1974).

Brown, J., Modern India. *The Origins of an Asian Democracy*, (Oxford, 1985).

Burki, S. J., 'Migration, Urbanization and Politics Pakistan', in, W.H. Wriggins & J.F. Guyot (eds.), *Population, Politics and the Future of South Asia*, (New York, 1973).

Cashman, R.L., *The Myth of Lokamanya: Tilak and Mass Politics in Maharashtra*, (Berkeley, 1975).

Canetti, E., (C. Stewart, trans.), *Crowds and Power* (Harmondsworth, 1981).

Chaddah, R. P., 'The Partition in Indo-English Fiction', *Journal of Indian Writing in English* 5, 11 (1977) pp. 52-58.

Chandavarkar, R., 'Worker's politics and the mill districts in Bombay between the wars', *Modern Asian Studies*, 15, 3 (1981), pp. 603-647.

Chander, Krishan, *Ham Wahshi Hain*, (Bombay, 1947).

Chander, Krishan, *The Peshawar Express*, in, R. Mathur & M. Kulasrestha (eds.), *Writings on India's Partition*, (Calcutta, 1976), pp. 69-77.

Chartier, R., (L.G. Cochrane, trans.), *Cultural History: Between Practices and Representations*, (Oxford, 1988).

Coppola, C., 'Iqbal and the Progressive Movement', *Journal of South Asian and Middle Eastern Studies*, 1, 2 (December, 1977), pp. 49-57.

Cowasjee, S., 'The Partition in Indo-Anglian Fiction', in, Nandan, S., (ed.), *Language and Literature in Multicultural Contexts*, (Suva, 1983), pp. 110-120.

Das, Suranjan, *Communal Riots in Bengal 1905-47*, (Oxford, 1991).

Das, Veena, (ed.), *Mirrors of Violence. Communities, Riots and Survivors in South Asia*, (Delhi, 1990).

Davis, N. Z., The rites of violence: religious riot in sixteenth century France', *Past and Present*, LIX (May 1973), pp. 51-91.

Duggal, K. S., *Twice Born Twice Dead*, (New Delhi, 1979), (J. Ara, trans.).

Durkheim, E., *The Elementary Forms of The Religious Life*, (London, 1961).

Estebe, J., *Tocsin Pour un Massacre. La Saison des Barthelemy*, (Paris, 1968).

Faruqi, M. A., *Sangam* (Karachi, 1971).

Flemming, L. A., *Another Lonely Voice: The Urdu Short Stories of Saadat Hasan Manto*, (Berkeley, 1979).

Flemming, L. A., 'Muslim self-identity in Quratulain Hyder's, *Aag ka Darya*', in, M. U. Memon (ed.), *Studies in the Urdu ghazal and prose fiction*, (Madison, 1979), pp. 243-256.

Freitag, S. B., *Collective Action and Community. Public Arenas and the emergence of Communalism in North India*, (Berkeley, 1989).

Freitag, S. B., Sacred Symbol as Mobilizing Ideology: The North Indian Search for a "Hindu" Community', *Comparative Studies in Society and History*, 22, (1980), pp. 597-625.

Gill, H.S., *Ashes and Petals*, (New Delhi, 1978),

Gilmartin, D., *Empire and Islam. Punjab and the Making of Pakistan*, (Berkeley, 1988).

Golwalker, M. S., *We, or Our Nationhood Defined*, (Nagpur, 1939).

Guha, R., *Elementary Aspects of Peasant Insurgency in Colonial India*, (Delhi, 1983).

Haider, Qurat ul-Ain, *Aag ka Darya*, (Lahore, 1968).

Halliday, F. and Alavi, H. (eds.), *State and Ideology in the Middle East and Pakistan*, (Basingstoke, 1988).

Hamerow, T.S., *Reflections on History and Historians*, (Madison, 1987).

Handa, R.L., *History of Freedom Struggle in the Princely States*, (New Delhi, 1968).

Hanson, J.A., 'Historical Perspectives in the Urdu Novel', in, M.U. Memon (ed.), *Studies in the Urdu ghazal and prose fiction*, (Madison, 1979), pp. 257–284.

Harcourt, M., Kisan Populism and Revolution in Rural India: The 1942 Disturbances in Bihar and East United Provinces', in, D.A. Low (ed.), *Congress and the Raj: Facets of the Indian Struggle 1917-47*, (London, 1977), pp. 315–48

Hardiman, D., *The Coming of the Devi: Adivasi Assertion in Western India*, (Delhi, 1987).

Hardy, P., *The Muslims of British India*, (Cambridge, 1972).

Henningham, S., *Peasant Movements in Colonial India: North Bihar 1917-42*, (Canberra, 1982).

Hijazi, Nasim., *Khak aur Khoon*, (Lahore, 1987).

Hobsbawm, E., *Primitive Rebels. Studies in Archaic Forms of Social Movement in the Nineteenth and Twentieth Century*, (Manchester, 1959).

Hodson, H. V., *The Great Divide. Britain-India-Pakistan*, (London, 1969).

Holton, R. J., 'The Crowd in History: Some problems of theory and method', *Social History*, 3, 2 (May 1978), pp. 219-33.

SELECT BIBLIOGRAPHY   *237*

Hosain, A., *Sunlight on a Broken Column*, (London, 1961).
Husain, Abdullah, *Udas Naslen*, (Lahore, 1963).
Husain, Intizar, *Akhri Admi*, (Lahore, 1987).
Husain, Intizar, *Gali Kuche*, (Lahore, 1952).
Husain, Intizar, *Kankari*, (Lahore, 1987).
Husain, Intizar, *An Unwritten Epic*, L.A. Flemming & M.U. Memon (trans.), *Journal of South Asian Literature*, XVIII, 2 (1983), pp. 6-19.
Iftikhar, Khwaja, *Jab Amritsar Jal Raha Tha* (9th ed), (Lahore, 1991).
Ikramullah, Begum S., *From Purdah to Parliament*, (London, 1963).
Iqbal, Muhammad, *The Reconstruction of Religious Thought in Islam*, (Lahore, 1971).
Jalal, A., *The Sole Spokesman. Jinnah, The Muslim League and the Demand for Pakistan*, (Cambridge, 1985).
Jamal, A., *Samjhota Express*, (Lahore, 1989).
Jansson, E., *India, Pakistan or Pakhtunistan?* (Uppsala, 1981).
Khaliquzzaman, C., *Pathway to Pakistan*, (Lahore, 1961).
Khan, S. A., *Be Tegh Sipahi*, (Lahore, 1971).
Kiernan, V., (trans.), *Poems by Faiz*, (London, n.d.).
Kumar, K., *Peasants in Revolt: Oudh 1918-22*, (Delhi, 1984).
Low, D.A., *Congress and the Raj*, (London, 1977).
Malik, H., 'The Marxist Literary Movement in India and Pakistan', *Journal of Asian Studies* XXVI, 4 (August, 1967), pp. 649-665.
Malik, Iftikhar, *Sikander Hayat Khan. A Political Biography*, (Islamabad, 1985).
Mandal, T., *Women Revolutionaries of Bengal 1905–1939*, (Calcutta, 1991).
Manto, S., *Khuda ki qasm*, Mohammad Ali (trans.), *Pakistan Review*, 13 (April 1965), pp. 33-4.
Manto, S., *Siyah Hashiye*, (Lahore, 1948).
Manto, S., *Thanda gosht*, C.M. Naim & R.L. Schmidt (trans.), *Journal of South Asian Literature*, 1 (1965), pp. 14-19.
Manto, S., *Toba Tek Singh*, R.B. Haldane (trans.), *Journal of South Asian Literature*, 6 (1970), pp. 19-23.
Mashkur, Hassan Yad, *Azadi kay charagh* (3rd ed), (Lahore, 1986).
McCelland, J. S., *The Crowd and the Mob. From Plato to Canetti*, (London, 1989).
Mehta, A., and Patwardhan, A., *The Communal Triangle in India*, (Allahabad, 1941).
Memon, M.U., 'Partition Literature. A Study of Intizar Husain', *Modern Asian Studies* 14, 3 (1980), pp. 377-410.
Memon, M.U., (ed.), *Studies in the Urdu ghazal and prose fiction*, (Madison, 1979).
Minault, G., *The Khilafat Movement. Religious Symbolism and Political Mobilization in India*, (New York, 1982).

Mirza, M.M., & Bakht, S., (eds.), *Azadi kay Mujahid*, (Lahore, 1989).

Moon, P., *Divide and Quit*, (London, 1961).

Nahal, C., *Azadi*, (London, 1976).

Nanda, B.R., (ed.), *Indian Women: From Purdah to Modernity*, (Delhi, 1990).

Narang, G.C., 'Major Trends in the Urdu short story', *Indian Literature* 16, nos. 1–2 (1973).

Nawaz, Mumtaz Shah, *The Heart Divided*, (Lahore, 1990).

Page, D., *Prelude to Partition: The Indian Muslims and the Imperial System of Control, 1920–1932*, (Delhi, 1982).

Pandey, B.N., *The Break-up of British India*, (London, 1969).

Papenek, H., & Minault, G., (eds.), *Separate Worlds. Studies of Purdah in South Asia*, (Delhi, 1982).

Pirzada, S.S., *Foundations of Pakistan*, 2 vols. (Karachi, 1970).

Pritchett, F.W., 'Narrative Modes in Intizar Hussain's Short Stories', *Journal of South Asian Literature*, XVIII, 2 (1983), pp. 192–200.

Qureshi, I.H., *The Struggle for Pakistan*, (Karachi, 1965).

Rahman, M., 'Political Novels in Urdu', *Contributions to Asian Studies*, 6 (1975), pp. 140–53.

Randhawa, M.S., *Out of the Ashes*, (Jullundur, 1954).

Riaz, F., *Pakistan Literature and Society*, (New Delhi, 1986).

Ricklefs, M.C.A., *A History of Modern Indonesia c.1300 to the Present*, (Bloomington, 1981).

Robinson, F., 'Nation-Formation: The Brass Thesis and Muslim Separatism', *Journal of Commonwealth and Comparative Politics*, 15, 3 (1977), pp. 215-30. *Separatism Amongst Indian Muslims—The Politics of the United Provinces' Muslims 1860-1923*, (Cambridge, 1974).

Rokri, A.A.K., *Mayn aur Mera Pakistan*, (2nd ed), (Lahore 1989).

Rude, G., *The Crowd in History, 1730-1848*, (New York, 1964).

Russell, R., *The Pursuit of Urdu Literature. A Select History*, (London, 1992).

Sadiq, M., *A History of Urdu Literature* (2nd ed), (Delhi, 1984).

Saini, B., (J. Ratan, trans.), *Tamas*, (New Delhi, 1990). *We Have Arrived In Amritsar* (J. Ratan, trans.) and other stories, (London, 1992).

Sarkar, S., *Modern India.1885–1947* (London, 1989).

Sayeed, K.B., *Pakistan. The Formative Phase 1857-1948*, (London, 1968).

Schechtman, J.B., 'Evacuee Property in India and Pakistan', *Pacific Affairs*, 24 (1951), pp. 406–13.

Sen, Shila, *Muslim Politics in Bengal 1937-47*, (New Delhi, 1971).

Shahane, V.A., 'Theme, Title and Structure in Khushwant Singh's *Train to Pakistan*', *Literary Criterion*, 9, 111 (1970), pp. 68-76.

Shaikh, F., *Community and Consensus in Islam: Muslim Representation in Colonial India 1860–1947*, (Cambridge, 1989).

Sharma, M., 'Remembrances of Things Past. Partition experiences of Punjabi Villagers in Rajasthan', *Economic and Political Weekly*, 4 August 1990, pp. 1728–35.

Shirin, M., (ed.), *Zulmat-i-Neem Roze*, (Karachi, 1990).

Sidhwa, B., *Ice-Candy-Man*, (New Delhi, 1989).

Singh, K., *Train to Pakistan*, (New York, 1956).

Singh, N., *Khoon ke Sohile*, (Amritsar, 1984).

Stephens, I., *Pakistan*, (London, 1963).

Sukhochev, A. S., *Krishan Chander*, (Moscow, 1983).

Symonds, R., *Making of Pakistan*, (Karachi, 1966).

Talbot, I.A., *Provincial Politics and the Pakistan Movement. The Growth of the Muslim League in North-West and North-East India 1937-47*, (Karachi, 1988).

Taylor, D., and Yapp, M., (eds.), *Political Identity in South Asia*, (London, 1979).

Tilly, C., *La Vendee*, (Cambridge Mass., 1964).

Tuker, F., *While Memory Serves*, (London, 1950).

Wilcox, W.A., *Pakistan: The Consolidation of A Nation*, (New York, 1963).

Wolpert, S., *Jinnah of Pakistan*, (New York, 1984).

Wood, G.S., 'A Note on Mobs in the American Revolution', *William and Mary Quarterly*, XXIII, 4 (1966).

Wright. T.P., 'Indian Muslim Refugees in the Politics of Pakistan', *Journal of Commonwealth & Comparative Politics* XII, (1975), pp. 189–205.

Yang, A., 'Sacred Symbol and Sacred Space in Rural India. Community Mobilization in the "Anti-Cow Killing" Riot of 1893', *Comparative Studies in Society and History*, 22, (1980), pp. 579–96.

Glossary

Ahrar	'The Free'. Punjabi Muslim Party founded in 1931 by Mazhar Ali Khan and Maulana Ataullah Shah Bukhari
Akhharas	Groups of Wrestlers
Anjuman	Association
Ansars	Helpers, refers back to the inhabitants of Medina who assisted the Prophet and his followers after their flight from Mecca.
Badmashs	Bad characters
Biraderi	'Brotherhood', patrilineal kinship group
Ghee	Clarified butter
Goonda	Hired thug, hooligan
Gurdwara	Sikh Temple
Hartal	Strike
Hijrat	Flight, exodus of Muslims for religious purposes
Jagirdar	Landholder
Kafelas	Processions
Khaksar	Literally 'humble' member of para-military organization of Allama Mashriqi
Lambardar	Village headman
Lashkar	Tribal war party
Lathi	Wooden club
Malik	Tribal chief
Marakka	General tribal council
Maulana	Muslim scholar learned in the Koran
Mohalla	Ward or quarter of a town
Mullah	Preacher
Murid	A Sufi's disciple

Pandal	Tent
Pir	A Muslim Sufi Saint, spiritual guide
Quaid-i-Azam	'The Great Leader'. Title given to Mohammad Ali Jinnah
Salar	Chief
Sajjada Nashin	Literally, one who sits on the prayer rug; custodian of a Sufi shrine
Sufi	Muslim mystic
Tabaljung	Mounted drum
Tehsil	Revenue subdivision of a district
Yassawal	Mace-bearer in Mughal ceremonial
Zamindar	Loosely used to refer to any landholder; strictly speaking, a landowner responsible for paying land revenue to the government.

Index